TAX POLICY
AND THE ECONOMY 9

edited by **James M. Poterba**

National Bureau of Economic Research
The MIT Press, Cambridge, Massachusetts

Send orders and business correspondence to:
The MIT Press
55 Hayward Street
Cambridge, MA 02142

In the United Kingdom, continental Europe, and the Middle East and Africa, send orders and business correspondence to:
The MIT Press Ltd.
Fitzroy House, 11 Chenies Street
London WC1E 7ET
ENGLAND

ISSN: 9892-8649
ISBN: hardcover 0-262-16153-2
        paperback 0-262-66095-4

CONTENTS

INTRODUCTION

James M. Poterba
MIT and NBER

Tax policy debates inevitably involve controversy about the efficiency and distributional effects of alternative means of raising revenue. They involve political compromise as well as detailed economic analyses by both academics and policy makers. To encourage interaction between these groups, for the last nine years the NBER has sponsored an annual Tax Policy and the Economy conference in Washington, D.C. The conference facilitates communication between academic researchers studying questions involving tax policy, and those in industry and government who are directly involved in the tax policy-making process. The conference is devoted to the presentation of new research findings of relevance for tax policy.

The five papers in this volume represent a cross section of some of the best applied research that bears on tax policy deliberations. Each paper provides new data and new insights about an important question in tax or expenditure policy. In several cases, the research papers were motivated by suggestions or questions at previous Tax Policy and the Economy meetings.

The first paper, by J. Karl Scholz, Stacy Dickert, and Scott Houser, investigates the determinants of transfer program participation. One of the long-standing questions in analyzing voluntary transfer programs, such as the earned income tax credit, is why some eligible households fail to take advantage of these programs. In "The EITC and Transfer Programs: A Study of Labor Market and Program Participation," the authors develop a new household-level data base for analyzing program participation decisions. In particular, they model the net benefits that different households would receive from participating in their state's Aid to Families with Dependent Children (AFDC) program, as well as their after-tax income from labor market activity. They find a consistent negative effect of prospective benefit levels on labor market activity, and a consistent positive effect of these benefits on the level of AFDC program participation. They also find that higher after-tax wages raise labor force activity and lower participation rates on AFDC. These empirical results lead the authors to predict that the changes in the earned income tax credit that were enacted in 1993 will ultimately lead to a substantial increase in labor force participation among single-parent households.

In "Cigarette Taxation and the Social Consequences of Smoking," W. Kip Viscusi presents new evidence on the social externalities associated with cigarette consumption. His analysis begins with a summary of changing trends in the tar and nicotine content of cigarettes sold during the last three decades. Because the average tar content of cigarettes has declined over time, Viscusi argues that applying estimates of the health damages from cigarettes consumed in the 1950s and 1960s to current cigarette consumption may overstate actual effects. He then develops an estimate of the total private as well as social cost of cigarette consumption, and concludes that such costs are no greater, and probably less than, the current federal and state excise tax levied on cigarettes.

Martin Feldstein and Jonathan Gruber explore the potential for changes in the structure of health insurance to alter the demand for medical care in their paper, "A Major Risk Approach to Health Insurance Reform." Their paper uses previous estimates of the price elasticity of demand for health care, along with detailed data from the National Medical Expenditure Survey, to estimate how changing the current health insurance system would affect total health care outlays. They consider in particular an insurance system that would limit an individual's out-of-pocket medical care spending in any year to 10 percent of income, but impose a substantial coinsurance rate, such as 50 percent, on medical costs below this level. They did find that for plausible values of the demand elasticity, such a policy could reduce total health care spending by approximately 20 percent, while still providing households with full insurance for catastrophic medical expenses. The authors also consider the net cost to the federal government of providing major risk insurance to all households. They conclude that the increase in income and payroll taxes that would result from eliminating the current tax exemption for employer-provided health insurance and the deduction for health care outlays above 7.5 percent of adjusted gross income, and reduced spending that would be associated with lower Medicaid outlays under such a plan, would finance more than 80 percent of the total cost of major risk insurance.

The effect of the investment tax credit, and investment incentives more generally, on investment behavior is one of the perennial controversies in applied public finance. Jason Cummins, Kevin Hassett, and R. Glenn Hubbard present new evidence on this issue in their paper, "Have Tax Reforms Affected Investment?" The authors argue that comparisons of the level of aggregate investment in years with and without the investment tax credit provide tainted evidence of the credit's effect, because the credit is enacted precisely when investment is expected to be weak. Instead of such time series comparisons, the authors rely on comparisons of investment growth across different assets that receive different treatment under the ITC. They find that investment in assets that qualify for the ITC tends to increase relative to investment in other assets when the credit takes effect, and that a reverse pattern is observed when the credit is eliminated. Their results provide some of the strongest evidence to date that investment incentives affect investment patterns.

In the final paper, "Taxation and Mutual Funds: An Investor Perspective," Joel Dickson and John Shoven explore how trading and capital gain realization decisions by mutual fund managers affect the after-tax returns to fund investors. If an individual purchases shares of common stock, he or she can decide when to sell these shares and realize any resulting capital gains or losses. If the individual invests in a mutual fund, however, decisions about when to sell the fund's underlying shares are made by the mutual fund manager, while investors pay taxes on capital gains or losses, and dividends, that are passed through the mutual fund. Dixon and Shoven demonstrate that mutual funds vary widely in the degree to which they realize capital gains, with corresponding differences in the tax liabilities of their investors. The authors estimate that taxes on mutual fund distributions currently amount to between $1.5 and $3 billion and observe that these revenues are highly dependent on what may be tax-inefficient behavior on the part of mutual fund managers. A number of new mutual funds have recently been established with the explicit intention of reducing investor tax liabilities associated with portfolio management decisions.

The need for interaction between academics and policy makers in the field of taxation is self-evident. Academic researchers often find research topics in the ongoing debates that take place in Washington, D.C., and state capitals. The recent expansion of academic research on health economics and insurance markets testifies to this link. In turn, many of the estimates of key parameters in tax policy debates, and to some degree even the vocabulary that guides policy debates, are derived from academic research. The papers in this volume represent a contribution to continuing, and improving, interaction between academics and policy makers concerned with tax policy.

ACKNOWLEDGMENTS

Many individuals played a key role in planning and organizing this year's Tax Policy and the Economy meeting. Martin Feldstein, president of the NBER, and Geoffrey Carliner, executive director, have been active supporters of this annual conference for the last nine years. Deborah Mankiw, the NBER's director of Corporate and Foundation Relations, and Liz Cary helped throughout the conference planning process. Candace Morrissey managed the daunting task of ensuring that the five conference papers were prepared on time and in a format that was acceptable for publication. The tireless efforts of the NBER Conference Department, particularly Conference Director Kirsten Davis, and Lauren Lariviere, ensured an outstanding level of efficiency at the Washington conference at which the papers were presented.

I am also grateful to each of the conference paper authors for striving to communicate their important research findings to a largely nonacademic audience. I appreciate their efforts and willingness to participate in this very important opportunity for interchange between academics and policy makers.

THE EARNED INCOME TAX CREDIT AND TRANSFER PROGRAMS: A STUDY OF LABOR MARKET AND PROGRAM PARTICIPATION

Stacy Dickert, Scott Houser
University of Wisconsin–Madison

John Karl Scholz
University of Wisconsin–Madison and NBER

EXECUTIVE SUMMARY

The cornerstone of the Clinton administration's welfare reform agenda is a large expansion of the earned income tax credit (EITC), a refundable tax credit directed primarily toward low-income taxpayers with children. This paper reviews existing studies and provides new evidence on the degree to which policies, like the EITC, that alter after-tax wages affect hours of work, labor market participation, and transfer program partici-

This paper was prepared for the November 1994 conference on Tax Policy and the Economy, sponsored by the National Bureau of Economic Research. Karen Bachrach, Paul Dudenhefer, Bill Gale, Robert Moffitt, and Jim Poterba provided helpful comments. This project was funded in part through grant number 59-3198-3-073 from the Food and Nutrition Service, U.S. Department of Agriculture. We also gratefully acknowledge support from the U.S. Bureau of the Census and the Department of Health and Human Services, Office of the Assistant Secretary for Planning and Evaluation. The opinions and conclusions expressed in this paper do not necessarily reflect the views of any of the sponsoring organizations.

pation. Simulations based on recent labor supply estimates suggest that the overall effect of the EITC expansion on hours of work from those in the labor market will be negative but fairly small. We then examine the effect of the EITC on labor market participation. We use a detailed SIPP-based microsimulation model of the tax and transfer system to accurately characterize families' budget constraints. Our empirical model relates labor market and program participation decisions to budget constraint variables and other characteristics. We find that the positive effect of the EITC on labor market participation offsets and, depending on the hours and weeks worked by new labor market participants, can exceed the negative effect of the EITC on hours worked by those already in the labor force. We also show that transfer program participation is negatively correlated with after-tax wages, which should, over time, lower the cost of the EITC.

1. INTRODUCTION

The cornerstone of the Clinton administration's welfare reform agenda is a large expansion of the earned income tax credit (EITC), a refundable tax credit directed primarily toward low-income taxpayers with children. In fiscal year 1998 the EITC is expected to cost the federal government $24.5 billion, $7 billion of which will result from expansions incorporated in the 1993 Omnibus Budget Reconciliation Act (OBRA93). In contrast, the federal share of the Aid to Families with Dependent Children (AFDC) program is expected to be $16 billion in 1998. Even though the EITC has been in the tax code since 1975 and now takes a central role in the nation's antipoverty policy, relatively little has been written about it.

Like the federal government, many states also have embarked on ambitious plans to reform welfare. From January 1, 1992, to June 14, 1994, 20 states received waivers from the Department of Health and Human Services to alter aspects of the AFDC program (Wiseman, 1993, 1994). Although the range of experiments is very broad, one of the most popular changes, adopted by California, Colorado, Florida, Illinois, Iowa, Michigan, Utah, Vermont, and Wisconsin, reduces the rate at which recipients lose AFDC benefits as they earn income.

The EITC and many of the state welfare waivers are part of a "make work pay" strategy of welfare reform. These policies attempt to reduce families' reliance on AFDC and other transfers by increasing the after-tax return to work, which in turn is expected to increase labor market participation and hours of work. The effectiveness of these policies depends, in part, on the degree to which people respond to change in incentives. This paper reviews existing studies and provides new evidence on the degree to which after-tax wages and other factors affect labor market participation, hours of work, and transfer program participation.

Many papers have been written on various aspects of these issues. In the following section, we survey portions of the literature, paying special attention to the studies' implications for the OBRA93 EITC expansions. Estimates from the literature imply that the 1993 EITC expansion will reduce hours of work by taxpayers already in the labor force because most EITC recipients have incomes in the phaseout range of the credit, where additional earnings reduce credit payments. Nevertheless, most labor supply estimates imply that the elasticity of hours of work with respect to the after-tax wage is small for both men and women, so the overall effect of the EITC expansion on hours is expected to be fairly small.

Less attention has been paid in the labor supply literature to the effects of wage rates, taxes, and transfers on labor market participation, particularly for women. Heckman (1993), for example, notes the lack of attention paid to participation decisions in the literature and then writes, "Participation (or employment) decisions generally manifest greater responsiveness to wage and income variation than do hours-of-work equations for workers." The participation margin is particularly important for the EITC, because the structure of the credit ensures that it will have its most beneficial labor market effects through participation. Consequently, we concentrate on participation rates in our empirical analysis. Because studies have also found that transfer programs affect the behavior of single-parent families differently than their two-parent counterparts, we also focus on differences between family types.

We examine the determinants of labor market and transfer program participation by first carefully modeling the budget constraints that families face. State income tax and AFDC rules vary across states, and all transfer programs have asset tests, income restrictions, rules on household composition, and complex interactions with other programs. These features, together with the intricacies of the federal income tax, make modeling these programs and their interactions a major undertaking. We develop a detailed microsimulation model, described in Section 3, that uses monthly data for the 1990 calendar year drawn from the Survey of Income and Program Participation (SIPP) to calculate benefits and taxes. The model is coded in the computer language C, runs on a personal computer, and contains detailed modules for SSI, AFDC, food stamps, the federal income tax, state income taxes, and payroll taxes. The current version of the model contains more than 10,000 lines of executable code, fully reflects tax and program interactions, and provides accurate estimates of program benefits and taxes. Section 3 also describes the policy variables (wage rates, taxes, and transfers) and out-come variables (transfer program participation, labor market participation, and hours) that are the focus of our research.

In Section 4 we describe a simple empirical model of labor market and program participation based on work by Moffitt and Wolfe (1992). The empirical model relates participation decisions to budget constraint variables and other characteristics. Estimates from the model suggest that wage rates are positively correlated and benefit guarantees are negatively correlated with labor market participation. In Section 5 we use our estimates to simulate the effect of the EITC on labor supply across family types. Our results imply that the OBRA93 EITC changes will increase the labor force participation of single-parent families in our sample by 3.3 percentage points, evaluated at the mean characteristics of the sample. The response of other family types is smaller. We find that the positive effect of the EITC on labor market participation offsets and, depending on the hours and weeks worked by new labor market participants, can exceed the negative effect of the EITC on hours worked by those already in the labor force. We also show that transfer program participation is negatively correlated with after-tax wages, which should, over time, lower the cost of the EITC.

2. THE LABOR SUPPLY LITERATURE AND THE EITC

The EITC is a credit on the federal income tax available to working poor families with children. Unlike most credits and deductions in the federal individual income tax system, the EITC is refundable—that is, if the amount of the credit exceeds what the taxpayer owes, he or she receives a payment from the U.S. Treasury for the difference.[1]

The EITC schedule can be divided into three ranges. In the subsidy range, the amount of the credit increases with every dollar of earned income. In 1994, for example, the credit equals 26.3 percent of earned income (wages, salaries, self-employment income, and farm income) for taxpayers with one child, up to an earned income of $7,750; hence, their maximum benefit is $2,038 (26.3 percent of $7,750). In the flat range—which, in 1994, is between $7,751 and $11,000 for taxpayers with one child—taxpayers receive the maximum credit. In the phaseout range, EITC benefits are reduced with every dollar of earned income. In 1994,

---

[1] Scholz (1994) discusses the EITC and shows that the participation rate—the percentage of eligible taxpayers who actually receive the credit—was 80 to 86 percent in 1990. Holtzblatt, McCubbin, and Gillette (1994) discuss the labor market incentives of the EITC. Alstott (1995) discusses the design of and policy checks surrounding the EITC in the context of the broader tax and transfer system.

taxpayers with one child and incomes exceeding $11,000 have their $2,038 credit reduced by 15.98 cents for every dollar of income until the credit is eliminated at an income of $23,760.[2] For the first time, the EITC is also available to childless taxpayers in 1994, though the maximum credit ($306, or 7.65 percent of $4,000) is considerably smaller than that available to other taxpayers.

The EITC, which was adopted in 1975, was originally promoted as a way to relieve the burden of the social security payroll tax on low-wage working parents.[3] The credit has grown dramatically in the last 20 years. The original EITC equaled 10 percent of earnings up to a maximum credit of $400 for taxpayers with children and was phased out at a rate of 10 cents per dollar of earnings (or adjusted gross income, whichever was higher) for incomes between $4,000 and $8,000. In 1996 when the OBRA93 changes are fully phased in, the credit rate will be 40 percent of earnings for families with two or more children and 34 percent for families with one child. The maximum credit (in 1994 dollars) for taxpayers with two or more children will be $3,370; for taxpayers with one child, $2,040; and for taxpayers with no children, $306. Table 1 summarizes EITC parameters for several years discussed in this paper.

The EITC has different labor supply incentives depending on the taxpayer's income relative to the subsidy, flat, or phaseout range of the credit. For taxpayers with no earned income, the substitution effect associated with higher wages will provide an unambiguous incentive to enter the labor market.[4] For taxpayers with incomes in the subsidy range, the substitution effect provides an incentive to increase hours of work, whereas the income effect provides an incentive to decrease hours of work. The net effect is ambiguous. There is only an income effect in

[2] Taxpayers with two or more children in 1994 are entitled to a larger credit ($2,528, or 30.0 percent of income up to $8,425). This credit is phased out at a 20.22-percent rate for taxpayers with incomes between $11,000 and $26,000.

[3] The credit also has been defended as an income security program for low-income families, a work incentive for welfare recipients, a subsidy to take into account the child care and health care needs of children in low-income families, and an efficient mechanism for offsetting the effects of regressive federal tax proposals. See Yin et al. (1994) for further discussion of the credit.

[4] Price changes can be decomposed into two effects. A wage subsidy increases the return to labor, making leisure more expensive. The substitution effect suggests that as leisure becomes more costly, people take less (work more) holding utility constant. The income effect suggests that with a higher wage rate, people have more income for given hours of work. With higher income, people buy more of everything they like, including leisure, which implies they will work less. For people just entering the labor market, there is no income effect. Hence, the EITC, by offering a higher wage, provides an unambiguous incentive to enter the labor market.

TABLE 1.
EITC Parameters under Law Prior to OBRA93 and under OBRA93, Selected Years

	Credit rate (percent)	Flat region Beginning income	Flat region Ending income	Maximum credit	Phaseout region Phaseout rate (percent)	Phaseout region Income cutoff
Pre-OBRA93 Law						
1990						
1+ Children	14	$6,800	$10,750	$953	10.00	$20,264
1993						
1 Child	18.5	7,750	12,200	1,434	13.21	23,050
2+ Children	19.5	7,750	12,200	1,511	13.93	23,050
Young child[a]	5	7,750	12,200	388	3.57	23,050
Health credit[b]	6	7,750	12,200	465	4.285	23,050
Omnibus Budget Reconciliation Act of 1993 (OBRA93)						
1994						
1 Child	26.3	7,750	11,000	2,038	15.98	23,760
2+ Children	30.0	8,425	11,000	2,528	17.68	25,300
No child[c]	7.65	4,000	5,000	306	7.65	9,000
1996 and beyond						
1 Child	34.0	6,000	11,000	2,040	15.98	23,760
2+ Children	40.0	8,425	11,000	3,370	21.06	27,000
No child[c]	7.65	4,000	5,000	306	7.65	9,000

Source: Figures for the August 1993 budget agreement (OBRA93) were kindly provided by Janet Holtzblatt at the Office of Tax Analysis, U.S. Department of Treasury. The other figures are from U.S. Congress (1993).

Note: Figures for 1994 and beyond are in 1994 dollars.

[a] The young child (or "wee tots") credit was for taxpayers who had a child under the age of one in the tax year and incomes in the ranges designated in the table.

[b] The supplemental health insurance credit goes to taxpayers with incomes in the ranges designated in the table who paid health insurance premiums that included coverage for one or more qualifying children. The taxpayer cannot take advantage of the supplemental health insurance credit on expenses used for the medical expense deduction or health insurance deduction for the self-employed (and vice versa).

[c] The taxpayer must be between the ages of 25 and 65.

the flat range of the credit, which provides an incentive to decrease hours of work. In the phaseout range, the substitution and income effects work in the same direction and both provide an incentive to decrease hours of work.

The labor market effects of the credit depend on the distribution of taxpayers within the credit's ranges and the degree to which people in and out of the labor market respond to incentives. Scholz (1994) estimates that in 1996, 77 percent of EITC recipients will have incomes that fall in the flat or phaseout range of the credit, which raises the concern that the EITC may lead to a net reduction in the labor supplied by low-income workers. The large literature on the determinants of hours of work yields labor supply elasticities that enable us to estimate the effects of the EITC on hours of work. We discuss the literature—conventional labor supply models, models that incorporate kinked budget constraints, evidence from the income maintenance experiments, and other studies of transfer programs—in the following subsections. Fewer papers provide guidance for thinking about the effects of the EITC on labor market participation. Consequently, the primary focus of our empirical work is on the determinants of labor market and transfer program participation.

2.1 Empirical Models of Men's and Women's Hours of Work

A common empirical model of labor supply (see Pencavel, 1986, p. 52) is

$$H_i = \alpha_0 + \alpha_1 W_i + \alpha_2 Y_i + \alpha_3 A_i + \epsilon_i, \tag{1}$$

where H_i is the hours of work, W_i is the market after-tax wage rate, Y_i is nonlabor income, A_i is a vector of exogenous household characteristics, α_i's are parameters to be estimated, and ϵ_i is a normally distributed error term. This specification, along with the assumption that a worker with a specific set of characteristics faces a horizontal demand curve for his or her services, is sufficient to identify a labor supply function consistent with utility maximizing behavior. Because U.S. labor force participation rates for prime-age males are very high,[5] and, hence, wages and hours for virtually all prime-age males are observed, Equation (1) can be estimated to study the labor supply of men directly.

Models similar to equation (1) are also a common specification of female labor supply. Although women's labor force participation rates have risen sharply over the last 100 years, labor force participation rates for women are still not nearly as high as they are for men.[6] For familiar reasons of sample selection, estimating equation (1) with a sample of working women can lead to biased estimates of all the parameters of interest. Consequently, empirical models of female labor supply frequently adopt a two-stage estimation approach (Heckman, 1976, 1979).

---

[5] In data from the Survey of Income and Program Participation (described below), 93.0 percent of males age 25 to 64 work.

[6] The labor force participation rate for women age 25 to 64 is 59.3 percent in our data from the Survey of Income and Program Participation.

In the first stage, parameters governing the decision to work or not to work are estimated, generally through probit regression. In the second stage, an equation similar to equation (1) is estimated, augmented with a term reflecting the conditional mean of ϵ_i (and often using instrumental variables for the wage rate).

Labor supply models derived from equation (1) have considerable appeal.[7] Models for both men and women are easily estimated using common statistical software, the linear labor supply equation results from a somewhat unusual but nevertheless well-defined utility function,[8] and the parameter estimates are easily interpreted as income and substitution effects (see footnote 4). Specifically, the income effect is equal to $H\alpha_2$, while the substitution effect is $\alpha_1 - H\alpha_2$.

Estimated elasticities from equation (1) for the labor supply of men show a fairly consistent pattern. Pencavel (1986) surveys a number of studies of male labor supply up to 1982; he reports that estimates of the elasticity of hours worked with respect to wages (derived from α_1) cluster between -0.17 and -0.08. Estimates of the income effect, again in elasticity form, range from -0.63 to 0.08. In only 7 of the 12 studies, however, is the substitution effect positive as the conventional labor supply model suggests it should be, which leads Pencavel to question the empirical relevance of the conventional model.

Estimated elasticities of the labor supply of women are considerably more varied than those for men. Killingsworth and Heckman (1986, p. 179) write, "There has been a consensus of relatively long standing that compensated and uncompensated female labor supply wage elasticities are positive and larger in absolute value than those of men." They then summarize 31 studies with 93 sets of estimates, where uncompensated wage elasticities of annual hours (α_1 in elasticity form) range from -0.3 to more than 14.0. Estimates of the income effect appear to be more precisely estimated than the uncompensated wage elasticities and range (with a few exceptions) from -0.02 to -0.48. The view that women's labor force behavior differs significantly from that of men has shifted

---

[7] A number of complications that arise with empirical implementation of this model are described below. We do not discuss dynamic models of labor supply (MaCurdy, 1981; Blundell and Walker, 1986) or household bargaining models of family labor supply (McElroy, 1990).

[8] The utility function consistent with equation (1) is

$$U(X,H;A,\epsilon) = \left(\frac{\alpha_2 H - \alpha_1}{\alpha_2^2} \right) \exp \left\{ \frac{\alpha_2(\alpha_0 + \alpha_2 X + \alpha_3 A + \epsilon) - \alpha_1}{\alpha_2 H - \alpha_1} \right\}$$

(Deaton and Muellbauer, 1981; Hausman, 1981; Pencavel, 1986).

over the last 10 years, however, driven in part by an influential paper by Mroz (1987). In that study, Mroz presents a detailed sensitivity analysis of the economic and statistical assumptions used to estimate the conventional model of female labor supply. Unlike much of the previous literature, Mroz's paper finds in his most reliable specifications that the compensated and uncompensated wage elasticities of women workers are similar to those of men.

Studies based on equation (1) are poorly suited for estimating the labor supply effects of the EITC. For taxpayers in the subsidy range of the credit, the coefficient on wages, α_1, can be used to assess the effects of the credit as long as nonlinearities caused by the tax and transfer system are ignored. The EITC's effect on labor supply for households in the flat range of the credit, however, cannot be determined from α_2 in equation (1), because Y in the canonical model is exogenous nonlabor income (such as dividends and other capital income), while the EITC depends on labor market choices. A similar problem arises in the phase-out range of the credit, where the EITC will reduce net wages by 15.98 percent for taxpayers with one child and 21.06 percent for taxpayers with two or more children in 1996. The general problem arises because the standard model of labor supply treats the tax system as being proportional, while the EITC creates nonlinearities in the budget constraint.

Nonlinearities that arise from the tax and transfer system are addressed in an alternative approach to the labor supply problem, popularized by Hausman (1981). Each (linear) segment of the kinked budget constraint faced by taxpayers can be fully characterized by two parameters: the slope (the after-tax wage rate) and the intercept (the "virtual income").[9] Optimal hours are found for each linearized segment of the budget constraint (replacing Y in equation [1] with virtual income), with hours being determined by the segment or kink point that yields the highest utility (see Hausman, 1981, or Moffitt, 1986, 1990 for details).

Applying the kinked budget set approach to the labor supply problem, Hausman (1981) estimated an uncompensated wage elasticity for males that was close to zero. However, he also estimated a large negative income elasticity. Because each segment of the nonlinear budget constraint is characterized by a virtual income term that generally exceeds zero, Hausman's results implied that progressive income taxation in the United States generates large reductions in male labor supply and large efficiency losses. Hausman's work was the first to incorporate

---

[9] Virtual income is the income a household would have if the given linear segment of the budget constraint were extended to the vertical axis at zero hours of work in the typical leisure-consumption diagram.

rigorously the effects of the tax system in the empirical model, which raised the possibility that the small behavioral effects found in the earlier literature resulted from ignoring nonlinearities caused by the tax system.

This possibility is examined by MaCurdy, Green, and Paarsch (1990) and Triest (1990), who estimate kinked budget set models of labor supply.[10] Both studies conclude that the hours decisions of prime-aged married men are relatively invariant to net wages and virtual incomes. Triest finds that the hours decisions of married women are only slightly more sensitive to changes in taxation than are the hours decisions of men, but he raises the possibility that their participation decisions may be quite sensitive to changes in the net wage.

Estimates from kinked budget set studies provide a natural way to discuss the EITC's effects on hours of work, given the nonlinearities caused by the credit. To simulate the effects of the OBRA93 EITC expansion, we use labor supply parameters from the kinked budget constraint literature and data from the 1990 Survey of Income and Program Participation. Specifically, we simulate the EITC that each family in our sample would receive in 1993 and in 1996. We then calculate the percentage change in real net wages (assuming that all tax rates stay the same except for the EITC rate) and estimate the change in virtual income for each family.[11] We then apply representative estimates of the wage and income elasticities from the kinked budget set literature to simulate the effect on hours worked.

The first three columns of Table 2 summarize the implications of the kinked budget set literature for the OBRA93 EITC expansions in 1996, relative to the law that was in effect in 1993. We use elasticities estimated by Triest (1990) as the central parameters. Triest finds uncompensated wage elasticities of around 0.05 for men and 0.25 for women, and his estimates of the virtual income elasticity are 0.0 for men and -0.15 for women. These parameters imply that the EITC increases hours of work by 3.9 percent in the credit's subsidy range and imply a modest negative effect on labor supply for taxpayers in the phaseout range of the credit. Given that EITC recipients are disproportionately in the phaseout range of the credit and these households work more than other EITC recipi-

---

[10] MaCurdy, Green, and Paarsch (1990) and MaCurdy (1992) show that the kinked budget set approach requires that the substitution effect, $\alpha_1 - H\alpha_2$, be nonnegative for all interior kink points on all individuals' budget constraints. In practice, they argue that this requirement rules out the possibility that labor supply is backward-bending.

[11] For secondary wage earners, the changes in net wages and virtual incomes that arise from the EITC are calculated if one assumes the hours of the primary earner fixed at their observed value.

TABLE 2.
Simulated Labor Supply Responses to Changes in EITC Law from 1993 to 1996

	Estimated percent change in annual hours worked[a]					
	Kinked budget set simulations[b]			Simulations using NIT parameters[c]		
	MaCurdy et al.	Triest	Hausman	Johnson and Pencavel	Mean Parameters	Robins and West
All recipients	−0.09	−0.54	−4.04	−1.16	−1.17	−1.63
By credit range						
Subsidy	1.88	3.92	13.46	6.88	2.44	2.25
Flat	−0.09	−0.19	−1.79	−0.60	−1.08	−1.64
Phaseout	−0.53	−1.11	−4.73	−1.46	−1.50	−1.63
By marital status						
Husbands	0.00	−0.34	−3.17	−1.44	−1.32	−1.47
Wives	−1.47	−3.03	−11.36	−1.43	−2.64	−4.09
Single female heads	−0.53	−1.11	−4.02	−0.79	−1.08	−1.63
Single male heads	0.00	−0.18	−1.56	—	—	—
By sex						
Male	0.00	−0.34	−3.15	−1.44	−1.32	−1.47
Female	−0.57	−1.17	−4.33	−0.93	−1.08	−1.63

Note: The estimates given for the kinked budget set simulations are median percentage changes. Medians are presented instead of means because a small number of very low-income single parents in the subsidy range have extremely high marginal tax rates and, therefore, extremely large simulated wage effects.

[a] The median monthly hours for the sample is 160. If one reads down the rows of the table, median monthly hours are 80 (for the subsidy range), 148, 160, 180, 140, 160, 160, 180, and 160.

[b] The wage and virtual income elasticities for the kinked budget set simulations are as reported in Triest (1994). The elasticities from Triest (1990) are presented as the central estimates; MaCurdy, Green, and Paarsch (1990), the low estimates; and Hausman (1981), the high estimates.

[c] Parameters from the NIT studies are as reported in GAO (1993). The estimates from Johnson and Pencavel (1984) imply the least negative labor supply. The parameters from Robins and West (1983) imply the largest negative effects. These parameters along with the arithmetic mean have been adjusted to 1994 dollars.

ents, the overall effect of the EITC on the labor supply of working recipients, based on Triest's estimates, is negative, but small (−0.54 percent).

Triest's estimated elasticities imply that the EITC will affect the hours worked by men and women differently. Men are relatively unresponsive to the EITC's incentives to alter hours. Only the small wage effect is important, since the estimated income effect is zero. Consequently, Triest's parameters imply that men will reduce their hours by only 0.34 percent due to the EITC expansion. For women in the subsidy range of the credit, the wage elasticity of 0.25 implies a larger positive effect of the EITC on hours than his estimate for men. In all three ranges of credit, women will reduce hours of work due to the negative virtual income effect of -0.15, and women in the phaseout range will further reduce hours due to the positive uncompensated wage elasticity. The specific amount of the reduction in hours depends on the size of the maximum EITC relative to virtual income in the absence of the EITC. Overall, the Triest parameters imply that the EITC will reduce the labor supplied by women workers by 1.2 percent.[12] Estimates of MaCurdy, Green, and Paarsch (1990) imply slightly lower responses of both men and women to increases in the EITC, while the estimates of Hausman (1981), imply much higher effects relative to those using the Triest parameters, particularly for women and taxpayers in the subsidy range of the credit.

Like the older literature on labor supply, the kinked budget set papers provide little guidance for the way the EITC might affect labor force participation, though the aggregate effect of the EITC on labor supply will depend, in part, on the credit's effect on labor market participation. In addition, the observed responses to taxes, benefits, and wages by low-income households may differ from those of other households in ways not reflected by the common empirical specifications. For example, the transfer system sharply alters the budget constraints faced by low-income households. Papers in the labor supply literature typically either ignore or incorporate only simplified representations of the transfer system in their analyses.

2.2 Income Maintenance Experiments

Between 1968 and 1982, the United States sponsored two rural income maintenance experiments in North Carolina and Iowa, and two urban income maintenance experiments, one in Gary, Indiana, and one split between Seattle, Washington, and Denver, Colorado. Robins (1985) reports that $225 million (in 1984 dollars) was spent on these experiments, of which $63 million represented direct payments to families. The main purpose of these experiments was to measure the work effort and earnings effects of higher transfers, including a negative income tax (NIT), on the low-income population. Pencavel (1986) surveys NIT labor supply estimates for men, and Robins (1985) does the same for all family types.

Hoffman and Seidman (1990, Chap. 3) and the U.S. General Account-

---

[12] Triest (1994) simulates the welfare effects of several policies that would increase the progressivity of the U.S. individual income tax using estimated labor supply elasticities from the literature. He concludes that expanding the EITC is a particularly efficient way of increasing progressivity.

ing Office (1993, Chap. 3) simulate the effects of the EITC on hours of work, using behavioral parameters estimated from studies of the income maintenance experiments. These studies' results are difficult to compare with our simulations based on the kinked budget set literature because the underlying data differ and because the OBRA93 EITC expansion is more generous than the policies examined by Hoffman and Seidman and the GAO. Therefore, we extend the GAO simulations using data from the 1990 SIPP to examine the OBRA93 EITC expansion. Following the GAO's approach, we apply estimates of the wage effects on hours from the NIT experiments to the changes in EITC subsidy and clawback rates, and estimates of the income effects on hours to the change in the level of the EITC between 1993 and 1996. We use an arithmetic mean of estimates from several NIT studies for the central behavioral parameters. For comparison, we also use estimates from Johnson and Pencavel (1984), since those imply the least negative labor supply effects, and estimates from Robins and West (1983), since those imply the largest negative labor supply effects.

The results are summarized in the last three columns of Table 2. The labor supply responses implied by the NIT are somewhat larger than those implied by the low and medium kinked budget set estimates (the first two columns of Table 2). The discrepancy between the two sets of estimates primarily arises from differences in the underlying behavioral parameters for female heads of households. The NIT experiments allowed wage and income elasticities for female family heads to be estimated separately from the elasticities for other women. In the kinked budget set simulations, we used elasticities for women that mix what appear to be disparate labor market responses of married and unmarried women. Though the estimates differ between the two sets of elasticity estimates, the labor market simulations show that the large change in the EITC between 1993 and 1996 is expected to have a fairly small negative overall effect on the hours worked by EITC recipients, under all but the Hausman (1981) parameter estimates.

Like the rest of the literature, the NIT experiments provide little evidence about the likely effects of the EITC on labor market participation. In addition, an important qualification to both sets of labor market simulations is that we assume that workers perceive the EITC as an increase in their after-tax wage. The design of the income maintenance experiments made clear the links between transfer payments, earned income, and the benefit reduction rate. In contrast, 99.5 percent of EITC recipients receive the credit in a lump sum after filing a tax return (U.S. General Accounting Office, 1992), so the links between earnings, benefits, and the phaseout may be less clear to recipients. To the extent that workers do not associate the EITC with higher net-of-tax wages, our simulations presumably overstate the effects of the credit on hours.[13]

2.3 Microeconometric Studies of Transfer Programs

Several papers estimate structural models of the effects of income transfers on the labor market behavior of female-headed households with children.[14] Blank (1985) estimates a labor supply model, similar to equation (1), jointly with a welfare participation model to examine how cross-state variation in wages, welfare benefits, demographic characteristics, and taxes affects labor market behavior. AFDC participants are given a state-specific implicit tax rate, which, as we discuss below, masks variation in taxes within a state that depends on family size and structure, unearned income, and "disregards."[15] Tax rates for nonparticipants include federal and state income taxes and payroll taxes. Blank finds that wages are positively correlated with hours of work and that other income and welfare benefits are negatively correlated with hours, but the economic effects of these variables are relatively small for her sample.[16] She emphasizes that factors other than income and taxes are very important in influencing welfare decisions.

Fraker and Moffitt (1988) examine the effects of food stamps and AFDC on the labor supply of female-headed households with children. Their empirical approach models AFDC participation, food stamp participation, and a discrete hours decision (0, 20, and 40 hours) and addresses a number of complications that arise in the empirical labor supply literature. Wages for women not in the labor force are calculated in a manner consistent with Heckman and MaCurdy (1981).[17] Wages are also allowed

---

[13] Because almost all recipients receive the EITC as a lump-sum payment, we simulated the effects of the 1993 expansion on hours worked if recipients perceive only income effects. Using the parameters from Triest (1990), we find that the overall median change in hours is −0.13 percent, which is clearly smaller than the combined wage and income effects described above.

[14] Danziger, Haveman, and Plotnick (1981) provide a detailed, wide-ranging discussion of the research on income transfer programs on labor supply and saving up to 1981. Moffitt (1992) provides a more recent comprehensive survey of the incentive effects of transfer programs.

[15] Disregards are deductions from earnings used to calculate transfer program benefits. These deductions generally apply to child care expenses, work expenses, and, in some cases, general expenses.

[16] For example, a $1 increase in wages in her sample (the mean wage was $2.91 an hour) would increase hours by one per week.

[17] Potential wages of those who do not work are not observed. Often, wage rates for nonworkers are imputed from auxiliary wage rate regressions, and actual wage rates are used for workers (Triest, 1990; Moffitt and Wolfe, 1992). This is appropriate only if the

to increase with hours of work, and a "stigma" term is included in the model so not all families eligible for benefits actually receive them (Moffitt, 1983). Fraker and Moffitt find no detectable effects of benefit reduction rates on program participation. Their estimated uncompensated wage elasticities vary from 0.26 to 0.35, and their income elasticities vary from −0.07 to −0.11. The wage and income elasticities are comparable with those reported in the earlier literature. The study by Fraker and Moffitt is one of only a few that examines the effect of net wages on program participation. They find that the difference in net income at 20 hours of work and at zero hours of work has a statistically significant positive effect on the labor market participation of female heads of households.

Keane and Moffitt (1991) consider the effects of the tax rates imposed by AFDC, food stamps, and housing programs on the hours and participation decisions of female heads of households using simulation estimation methods. Along with addressing the complications raised by Fraker and Moffitt (1988), they account for the expected value of Medicaid benefits and the expected value of private health insurance in the budget constraint using calculations from Moffitt and Wolfe (1992).[18] Keane and Moffitt estimate an uncompensated wage elasticity with respect to hours of 0.66 and a total income elasticity with respect to hours of −0.24 for single-parent households using data from the 1984 Survey of Income and Program Participation. Thus, relative to the literature described above, their results suggest that the EITC would have considerably larger positive effects on hours in the credit's subsidy range and larger negative effects on hours in its phaseout range.

When Keane and Moffitt simulate the labor market effect of raising the gross wage rate by $1, they find that hours increase by only 38 percent of what their estimates of the uncompensated wage elasticity of hours imply. This occurs for two primary reasons. First, a change in the gross wage has only a small effect on the net-of-tax wage because they calculate that low-income women face extremely high cumulative marginal tax rates, often exceeding 100 percent. Even reducing the AFDC tax rate to 50 percent from 100 percent leaves cumulative tax rates of 60 to 80

---

wage rates of nonworkers are predicted without error. An alternative is to use the predicted wage for both workers and nonworkers (Blank, 1985; Hoynes, 1993). When the estimated model is nonlinear, this is appropriate only if all families base their decisions on the econometrician's predictions instead of their actual wage rates. Fraker and Moffitt (1988) rigorously account for missing wages by using the predicted wage for nonworkers and then integrating out over the error distribution of the unobserved wage rate.

[18] Moffitt and Wolfe (1992) examine the effects of AFDC and Medicaid on the welfare and labor market participation of female heads of families. They find both Medicaid and private health insurance have substantial effects on labor market and welfare participation.

percent. They write, "Such tax rates, especially at the low gross wage rates faced by women participating in welfare programs, imply very small income gains from working." Second, many families not in the labor force are not on the margin of working. This seems to indicate that labor supply studies of low-income households that do not model the labor force participation decision may give a misleading impression of the effect of economic variables on labor market behavior.

Hoynes (1993) presents the only structural empirical model of two-parent families in the literature on labor supply and transfer program participation. She restricts her sample, taken from the 1984 SIPP (but applying to 1986), to two-parent families that in the absence of labor market participation would be eligible for AFDC-UP (the AFDC program for intact families with an unemployed parent). Hoynes finds that two-parent families are considerably more responsive to changes in AFDC-UP program parameters than would be expected from studies of single-parent households. For example, she estimates that eliminating AFDC-UP would increase men's labor supply by 46.9 hours and women's labor supply by 31.6 hours per month, while Moffitt (1983) estimates that eliminating AFDC would increase hours worked by female heads of household by roughly four hours per week. Hoynes also finds fairly large effects on program participation and hours of work from changes in benefit reduction rates, in contrast to much of the literature. She speculates that the more elastic behavior may reflect behavioral differences between one- and two-parent families, but reconciling the results is beyond the scope of her study.

2.4 Lessons from the Literature and Empirical Questions

The literature yields consistent evidence that the labor supply of prime-age males is fairly insensitive to changes in wages and incomes. In the standard literature and the income maintenance experiments, uncompensated wage elastics are often estimated to be small and negative (around -0.1), while income elasticities are small and positive (around 0.15). Using the kinked budget set approach, Triest (1990) estimates an income elasticity of 0.0 and an uncompensated wage elasticity of 0.05. As shown in Table 2, estimates in this range imply that the EITC will have only minor effects on the hours worked by prime-age males. Because the labor force participation rate for this group is very high, it is also clear that the EITC will not have an important effect on labor force participation.[19]

---

[19] Even if taxes do not affect hours of work or participation, they may affect other dimensions of labor market behavior such as commuting distances, stress on the job, and forms of compensation (Feldstein, 1993).

Labor supply estimates from the literature on married women show considerably more variability, but recent estimates from the traditional literature (Mroz, 1987), the NIT experiments (Robins, 1985), and the kinked budget set literature (Triest, 1990) suggest that the elasticities of women's hours of work to changes in wages and incomes are similar to those estimated for men. Triest's estimates of an uncompensated wage elasticity of 0.25 and an income elasticity of −0.15 are representative of recent studies. These estimates imply that substantial increases in the EITC are likely to have negative, but not particularly large, effects on hours worked. A sophisticated, careful study by Keane and Moffitt (1991) generates wage and income elasticities that are somewhat larger than those mentioned above, so additional work in this area could still be valuable.

Keane and Moffitt (1991) and Giannarelli and Steuerle (1994) use a microsimulation approach to calculate detailed tax rates on households caused by the tax and transfer system. Their results have pessimistic implications for the effect of the EITC on labor market behavior. Keane and Moffitt find the tax rates faced by a representative low-income, female-headed family range from 75 percent (in Ohio) to 124 percent (in California).[20] Even large increases in after-tax wages, such as those offered by the OBRA93 expansions of the EITC, are likely to have only modest effects on labor market participation given these tax rates. At the same time, the relatively large uncompensated wage and income elasticities they estimate imply that the EITC will have a larger, negative effect on the hours of taxpayers that work than suggested by much of the literature. Thus, Keane and Moffitt's results would imply a fairly substantial reduction in aggregate labor supply by those already in the labor market, which would not be offset by increases in labor market participation.

3. TAXES, TRANSFERS, AND LOW-INCOME FAMILIES

The central focus of our empirical work is on the determinants of labor force and transfer program participation. One difficulty with examining the effects of policies that may affect participation is that a broad range of programs exist that, in conjunction with state and federal tax systems, create a complex set of incentives that are difficult for analysts to characterize. In much of the previous literature, for example, research-

---

[20] The reported tax rates are calculated from changes in after-tax and after-transfer income associated with increasing hours of work from 0 to 20 hours, and from 20 to 40 hours.

ers use uniform tax rates for all transfer program recipients in a given state. Even within a state, however, taxes and benefits vary depending on sources of income, program participation, assets, demographic characteristics, and income exemptions. To characterize the budget sets facing households, we have developed a simulation model that accurately represents transfer program rules, tax systems, and their complex interactions.

3.1 The Simulation Model and Data

Detailed modules for AFDC, food stamps, Supplemental Security Income (SSI), the federal income tax, state income taxes, and the payroll tax are the building blocks for the microsimulation model. All modules have a common structure: Each defines the unit of analysis for tax and transfer programs, performs income and asset tests or determines adjusted gross income and taxable income, and determines benefits or taxes.[21]

The model uses monthly data from the 1990 SIPP for the period January to December 1990. Using SIPP allows us to make fewer imputations than would be required if we used annual data, such as the Current Population Survey (CPS).[22] In addition, SIPP provides a high level of detail on sources of income, particularly for low-income households. The main advantage of SIPP, however, is that it provides data that allow us to calculate program eligibility and benefits in every month. Over time frames longer than a month, variation in income, labor force participation, assets, and family composition leads to an ambiguous definition of program eligibility and participation. Thus, when we refer to labor market participation, transfer program participation, or other point-in-time concepts, we are referring to the last month in wave 3 of the 1990 SIPP panel, which was collected from September through December 1990.[23] State and federal taxes, which are calculated on an annual basis,

---

[21] The simulation model is described in more detail in Dickert, Houser, and Scholz (1994). The current version of the model also incorporates data on child care expenses from the SIPP topical modules. These data are used in all the transfer program modules, for federal tax credits, and, in some cases, for state tax credits or deductions. We also use asset information from the SIPP topical modules to implement asset tests associated with transfer programs. Data on alimony payments are also used to assess income eligibility in transfer programs (through "deeming" rules) and as an adjustment to income in the federal income tax module.

[22] SIPP's sample includes roughly one-third as many households as the CPS's sample. SIPP does not separately identify all 50 states because nine smaller states are combined into three groups for confidentiality reasons.

[23] There are four rotation groups in SIPP whose interviews are staggered across months. A "wave" is completed when each of the four groups has been interviewed once. Each SIPP panel generally consists of seven or eight waves.

are appropriately accounted for by adding incomes and benefits over the calendar year.

We restrict our sample in several ways that are common in the literature on transfer programs. We exclude families in which the head or spouse (1) is older than 65 or has a disability, (2) would not be eligible for program benefits even if he or she did not work, (3) does not have children under 18, or (4) is self-employed. The first restriction arises from our focus on labor market behavior.[24] The second restriction, which primarily excludes families with assets that exceed program asset tests, arises from our focus on transfer program participation. The third restriction arises from our focus on the EITC. In 1990 a taxpayer had to support a child to be eligible for the EITC.[25] The fourth restriction arises from the difficulty of calculating wage rates for the self-employed.

The simulation model allows us to identify families eligible for benefits, which is necessary for participation rate analyses. In the following subsection we use the model to describe patterns of eligibility and participation in the food stamp and AFDC programs, focusing on three different groups: single-parent families, primary earners in married couples, and secondary earners in married couples. The data described in the remaining parts of Section 3 are summarized in Table 3.

3.2 Program Eligibility and Participation

AFDC eligibility rules and benefits vary sharply by family structure and across states. Roughly 15 percent of the individuals in the sample are eligible for AFDC. Almost all of these are single parents, of whom 43.8 percent are eligible. Average AFDC benefits, conditional on eligibility, are $372 per month for single-parent families and are somewhat larger for two-parent families. In 1990, the maximum AFDC benefit for a three-person household in the continental U.S. ranged from $120 in Mississippi to $694 in California (U.S. Congress, 1990). The model shows similar variation in AFDC benefits across large states, ranging from an average of $115.53 per month in Mississippi to an average of $652.06 per month in

---

[24] The labor market behavior of the disabled population is clearly an interesting topic of research (see, e.g., Haveman, de Jong, and Wolfe, 1991), but SIPP does not have information on the severity of the disability. Because the type of disability may inordinately influence labor market behavior, we have chosen to drop the disabled from our sample.

[25] The second and third restrictions imply that we treat asset accumulation and fertility decisions as exogenous to transfer programs. Hubbard, Skinner, and Zeldes (1993) discuss a dynamic, stochastic, life-cycle simulation model where the transfer system has a large effect on asset accumulation. Moffitt (1992) surveys the literature on transfer programs and fertility decisions.

TABLE 3.

Means of Selected Sample Characteristics for Single Parents and Primary and Secondary Earners in Two-Parent Families (standard deviations in parentheses)

	Total sample	Single parents	Primary wage earner	Secondary wage earner
% Eligible AFDC	14.87	43.80	1.74	1.85
Conditional AFDC benefit	372.26	367.88	442.00	408.58
	(214.20)	(206.86)	(313.55)	(272.25)
AFDC participation rate (%)	71.79	76.10	25.00	23.53
% Eligible food stamps	39.94	70.04	26.33	26.33
Conditional food stamp benefit	207.64	204.12	221.58	222.09
	(96.64)	(96.29)	(110.08)	(90.84)
Food stamp participation (%)	51.59	66.67	32.23	34.71
Wage ($ per hour)	7.52	6.55	8.62	7.30
	(4.16)	(3.19)	(3.75)	(4.99)
Tax rate (0 to 20 hours)	40.93	49.62	31.92	42.07
	(25.57)	(28.69)	(24.43)	(16.22)
% Working	70.10	56.44	91.62	60.94
Usual hours worked/week	27.91	20.49	39.19	23.33
	(20.68)	(19.66)	(15.70)	(21.18)
Family size	3.89	3.01	4.28	4.28
	(1.30)	(1.16)	(1.16)	(1.16)
Number of dependents	2.08	1.91	2.15	2.15
	(1.11)	(1.10)	(1.10)	(1.10)
% with children < 6	52.72	46.81	55.39	55.39
% w/ poor or fair health	10.94	17.45	7.07	8.92
% Women	63.84	94.46	26.00	73.99
% Nonwhite	27.84	44.52	20.57	20.02
% Urban	74.19	78.22	72.36	72.36
Region—East	17.57	21.30	15.89	15.89
Region—Midwest	20.91	23.10	19.91	19.91
Region—South	46.50	39.83	49.51	49.51
Region—West	15.40	15.76	15.23	15.23
Number of observations	2669	831	919	919
% of Total sample		31.14	34.43	34.43

Notes: Data are from the 1990 Survey of Income and Program Participation. The mean age is 33.7 years, and this does not vary greatly among the types. The mean level of education is 11.67 grades, and this also does not vary greatly among the types.

California.[26] The variation in AFDC benefits across states dwarfs the variation required to adjust for cost-of-living differences.[27]

Not every family eligible for program benefits actually receives them. (Moffitt [1983] presents a well-known discussion of this issue.) With our model simulations of eligibility and SIPP data on participation, we can examine the participation rate—the fraction of eligible families that report receiving program benefits. In our sample, the ADFC participation rate is 71.8 percent, and 76.1 percent for single-parent families. These rates are comparable to the 62- to 72-percent rates reported by Blank and Ruggles (1993) in their study of participation rates using the 1986 and 1987 SIPP panels, but somewhat higher than earlier results in the literature (Moffitt, 1983). The empirical model estimated in Section 4 examines factors correlated with transfer program participation.[28]

Uniform national rules govern food stamp eligibility and benefits. In our sample, 39.9 percent of families are eligible for food stamps. By family type, 70.0 percent of single-parent families and 26.3 percent of two-parent families are eligible. Average food stamp benefits, conditional on eligibility, are $208 per month, and there is little difference across family types. Because of uniform national standards, there is little cross-state variation in food stamp benefits. The average benefit of $140.62 per month in California, however, is considerably below the sample mean of $207.64. This occurs because California's generous AFDC system reduces the amount of food stamps a family is eligible to receive as AFDC is included in food stamp "countable income."

Studies typically find the food stamp participation rate to be lower than the AFDC rate. We find the participation rate in the food stamps program is 51.6 percent, which is higher than an older estimate of 38 percent by MacDonald (1977) but similar to recent estimates of 54 to 66 percent by Blank and Ruggles (1993). The average participation rate masks sharp variation across family types. The participation rate is 66.7

---

[26] We define a large state as one with at least 50 observations in the sample, which includes 22 states.

[27] For example, cost-of-living indices reported in the *New York Times* (8/5/94, A.1) give Mississippi an index value of 86.7 and California a value of 112.3; Los Angeles had a value of 127.9, while Dothan, Alabama, had a value of 87.4. (In both the state and urban indices, 100 denotes an average value.) If cross-state AFDC differences solely reflected cost-of-living differences, maximum benefits in Mississippi would exceed $500, given California's benefit.

[28] Both primary earners and secondary earners in two-parent families respond to questions about program participation and benefits, which may account for the slight difference in reported participation and conditional benefits between primary and secondary earners in Table 3. In addition, stepparents may not be eligible for benefits in some states.

percent for single-parent families and around 33 percent for two-parent families.

3.3 Taxes

The simulation model also allows us to calculate families' marginal and average tax rates corresponding to actual or counterfactual situations. In our empirical work, for example, we need a tax rate measure that is exogenous to labor market and transfer program participation decisions. Like Keane and Moffitt (1991), we calculate an exogenous tax rate that is based on the change in after-tax and transfer income that would result from increasing hours of work from 0 to 20 (or 40) hours per week. An inevitable problem in labor market studies, however, is that wages are only observed for people who work.

We follow Triest (1990) and Moffitt and Wolfe (1992) and use predicted wages for adults that are not in the labor market.[29] Predictions are based on log wage regressions estimated separately for men and women, dropping the self-employed and adjusting for selection. Covariates include quadratics in age and education, an interaction of age and education, the state unemployment rate for women (in the male wage regressions we use the general state unemployment rate), and dummy variables for Hispanic, African-American, married, and residence in a metropolitan area. We use number of children and a dummy variable for the presence of children younger than six as exclusion restrictions in the probit regression for being in the labor force. Like Hoynes (1993), we calculate median wages from our empirical model because of the skewness of the wage distribution. For both men and women, the regression estimates are similar to other studies in the literature, and predicted wages closely match actual wages. Descriptive statistics for the samples used to estimate wages and the regression results for men and women are available from the authors on request.

Taxes in the model arise from benefit reduction rates associated with income transfer programs (often called implicit taxes) and from payroll, state income, and federal income taxes (often called explicit taxes). When the combined effect of the tax and transfer system is considered, it is clear that tax burdens on low-income families can be very high.

A family receiving AFDC that has earned income is entitled to a number of disregards before AFDC benefits are reduced. A recipient with earnings can subtract $90 per month for work expenses, as much as $175

---

[29] See footnote 17 for a more detailed discussion of unobserved wages. In every empirical model that we estimate, we examine the sensitivity of our results to using predicted wage for each adult in the sample.

per child per month for child care expenses, and, for the first four months of work, $30 plus an additional one-third of remaining earnings. For earned income exceeding these disregards, AFDC benefits are reduced by $66\frac{2}{3}$ cents for every dollar of income for the first four months of work. After four consecutive months, the tax rate increases to 100 percent after deducting work and child care expenses (and $30 for eight additional months).[30]

Food stamp recipients who have earned income are also entitled to a number of disregards before food stamp benefits are reduced. A recipient with earnings receives a standard deduction of $127, a deduction for dependent-care expenses up to $160, and an additional deduction of 20 percent of earned income.[31] Participating households are expected to contribute 30 percent of their income exceeding deductions toward food purchases. Thus, the implicit marginal tax rate on income exceeding deductions (including AFDC and SSI benefits) is 30 percent.

The layering of programs is complicated and may lead to even higher benefit reductions than would occur when programs are examined in isolation. The model captures these program interactions. For example, a person receiving benefits from both AFDC and food stamps and who has earned income exceeding the AFDC disregards would face a $66\frac{2}{3}$-percent marginal tax rate on AFDC. From the perspective of the food stamps program, earned income increases by 80 cents for every dollar of earnings (due to the 20-percent disregard for earnings), but unearned income falls by $66\frac{2}{3}$ cents for every dollar of earnings (the reduction in AFDC benefits). The net of these amounts, $13\frac{1}{3}$ cents, is the increase in food stamp "countable income" for every dollar of earnings, and is taxed at a 30-percent rate, which adds 4 percentage points to the AFDC marginal tax rate. Thus, the implicit tax rate on earnings (beyond the disregards) in the first four months of employment for a person receiving AFDC and food stamps is $70\frac{2}{3}$ percent; after four months it is 94 percent.[32]

---

[30] In the calculations below, we do not account for the additional one-third earned income deduction because we cannot assess the duration of AFDC receipt in our data. Thus, our AFDC tax rate is akin to a "long-run" tax. Of AFDC households with earned income, 50.6 percent have the $30 plus one-third disregard, while roughly 13 percent of all AFDC households have earned income (U.S. Congress, 1993).

[31] There are additional deductions for shelter expenses that exceed 50 percent of countable income after the other deductions and for medical expenses for households that include an elderly or disabled member. SIPP does not have data on shelter and medical expenses, so we do not account for these deductions in the model.

[32] After four months of earnings, the AFDC tax rate on earnings increases to 100 percent so AFDC benefits fall dollar for dollar. This 100-percent marginal tax is slightly offset by the food stamps program because, although food stamp earned income still increases by 80 cents for every dollar of earnings, unearned income would have fallen by $1. Food stamp

Explicit taxes also affect low-income families. We assume that the combined 15.3-percent employee and employer shares of the payroll tax are borne by employees. The federal income tax is modeled as precisely as possible given available information in SIPP, except that we assume all taxpayers use the standard deduction. Special attention is paid to accurately modeling the EITC (see Scholz, 1994, for details). Average effective tax rates from the model closely match data from the Internal Revenue Service (1993), though average tax rates on low-income households in our model are somewhat lower than those shown in income tax data. Relative to the IRS data, our low-income tax-reporting units are more likely to be families as opposed to children working part-time jobs and, thus, are more likely to receive the EITC, which leads to lower average effective rates in our model.

We calculate state income taxes using tax forms collected from the 41 states (including the District of Columbia) with state income taxes in 1990. Nine states have credits for low-income filers (including state EITC's in Iowa, Maryland, Rhode Island, Vermont, and Wisconsin); eight states have credits for the elderly and disabled. In addition, we incorporate many other special provisions for dependents and exemptions. Credits vary among states with regard to eligibility, generosity, and whether the credits are refundable. New Mexico, for example, has a low-income credit that uses "modified Adjusted Gross Income (AGI)." Modified AGI includes AFDC, SSI, and food stamp benefits that are calculated in our simulations. Average effective state income tax rates vary in the model from 0.0 percent (several states) to 5.5 percent in the District of Columbia and are strikingly similar to those reported in the Bureau of the Census (1992, Tables 463 and 687).[33]

3.3.1 Cumulative Average and Marginal Tax Rates

The layering of implicit and explicit taxes can lead to high average and marginal tax rates on low-income households. To illustrate these tax rates, we present a series of figures showing marginal and average tax rates along several dimensions: a median- versus high-tax family, a low- versus high-benefit state, and single-parents versus primary earners in two-parent families.

Figure 1 shows marginal tax rates for four single-parent families in Texas (a low-benefit state) and New York (a high-benefit state). The families shown are the median and 90th percentile families in each state

---

countable income, therefore, falls by 20 cents and food stamp benefits would increase by six cents for every dollar of earnings, leading to a cumulative tax rate of 94 percent.

[33] Dickert, Houser, and Scholz (1994) provide comparisons of the simulation model's output with administrative sources.

when ranked according to the cumulative tax rate distribution (going from 0 to 20 hours of work). We calculate marginal tax rates for these representative families from the incremental change in after-tax and after-transfer income resulting from an increase in one hour of work at the earner's market wage. The marginal tax rate is relevant for incremental labor supply decisions.

Each graph has several shaded bars. The dark gray bottom bar in each figure (at low hours of work) shows the marginal federal income tax rate for each family. It is −14 percent at low hours because each family is eligible for the EITC subsidy, which was 14 percent in 1990 (see Table 1). The large, unshaded portion of each bar reflects the marginal tax rate from AFDC. The marginal rate on AFDC is initially zero because of disregards. As hours increase, the AFDC marginal rate is 100 percent until benefits are fully "clawed back." The light gray bars reflect the food stamp marginal tax rate, which is 24 percent when AFDC is untaxed. When AFDC is taxed, the food stamp marginal tax rate is actually negative (see footnote 32). There is a uniform 15.3-percent payroll tax on all families. Low-income families in New York also pay a modest state income tax, shown in black.

Several features are apparent in Figure 1. First, until benefits are fully clawed back, AFDC is the primary source of high tax rates on low-income families. Second, Figure 1 illustrates the progression of federal marginal tax rates for each family. The tax rate is −14 percent when families are in the EITC subsidy range, zero when families are in the flat part of the credit, and 10 percent in the phaseout range. The two New York families reach the 15-percent federal tax bracket (along with the EITC phaseout) at 38 or more hours of work. Third, Figure 1 shows the effect of a "notch" for the median Texas family. Moving from 36 to 37 hours of work, this family would lose $1.50 of food stamp benefits for every $1 of earned income. Families eligible for food stamps must have "gross" income less than 130 percent of the poverty line and must also meet a "net" income test. Our median Texas family, while still meeting the net income test at 37 hours, fails the gross income test and, hence, loses all remaining benefits. Notches are common in the income transfer system due to various asset and income tests.[34] Fourth, cumulative marginal tax rates in the figures are equal to the sum of the positive and negative rates, and they can be very high. Thus, for example, the cumulative marginal tax rate for the median family in Texas working two hours per week is 95.3 percent (the 100-percent AFDC rate + the 15.3-percent

---

[34] Lyon (1994) and Giannarelli and Steuerle (1994) also discuss notches in income transfer programs.

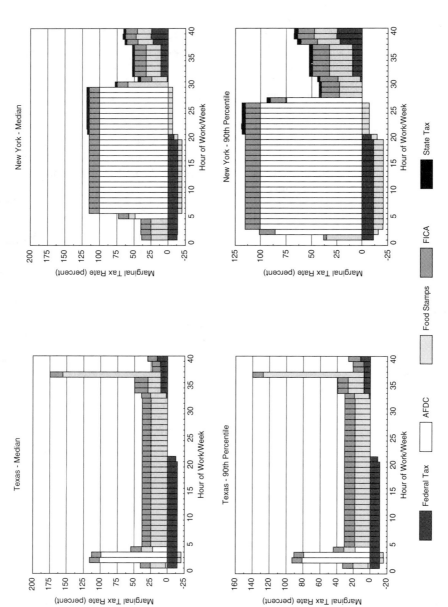

FIGURE 1. *Marginal Tax Rates for Low-(TX) and High-(NY) Benefit States—Single-Parent Families.*

FICA rate + the −14-percent EITC rate + the −6-percent food stamp rate).

The marginal tax rates for the four families lead to the average tax rates shown in Figure 2. Average tax rates are defined from the change in after-tax and after-transfer incomes when weekly hours of work increase from zero to the number of hours shown on the horizontal axis. We view these average tax rates as being most relevant when families are making labor force participation decisions. The average tax figures tend to have a concave shape that is driven by AFDC. The AFDC average tax rate increases at low hours of work as disregards dissipate. Once disregards are exhausted, average AFDC rates are pulled up by the high marginal rates on AFDC. After benefits are fully clawed back, average AFDC rates again fall. Because the AFDC guarantee in Texas is low, cumulative tax rates in Texas tend to be considerably lower than in New York, particularly when one is looking at the rates from 0 to 20, or 0 to 40 hours of work, which are the relevant participation margins for most families.[35]

Cumulative average tax rates, which again are the sum of the positive and negative bars, can also be extremely high. For example, the average tax rate exceeds 85 percent for the high-tax New York family that enters the labor market and works anywhere from 8 to 35 hours per week. This implies that this family, when making labor market participation decisions, will receive no more than 15 cents for every dollar earned in the labor market over a broad range of hours. Tax rates like these undoubtedly discourage labor market participation. Average tax rates tend to be somewhat lower in low-benefit states and are much lower for families that do not receive transfers, particularly AFDC.

Appendix Figures 1 and 2 show similar figures for the median and 90th percentile two-parent families in Texas and New York. Tax rates apply to the earnings of the primary earner and assume the secondary earner is not in the labor market. The marginal tax rate figure shows several food stamp notches and marginal tax rates that tend to be considerably lower than those faced by one-parent families. This occurs because very few two-parent families are eligible for AFDC-UP in our data. The 90th percentile two-parent family in New York received AFDC-UP and, hence, faced marginal and average tax rates that are similar to those shown in Figures 1 and 2. Otherwise, marginal rates rarely exceed 50 percent, and average rates rarely exceed 40 percent for two-parent families.

The tax rates presented in the top panel of Figure 2 are lower—in

---

[35] We have made similar graphs for families in Illinois, a medium benefit state, that are available on request. For the median single-parent family the figures show patterns similar to those in Texas, while tax rates on the high-tax family are similar to those in New York.

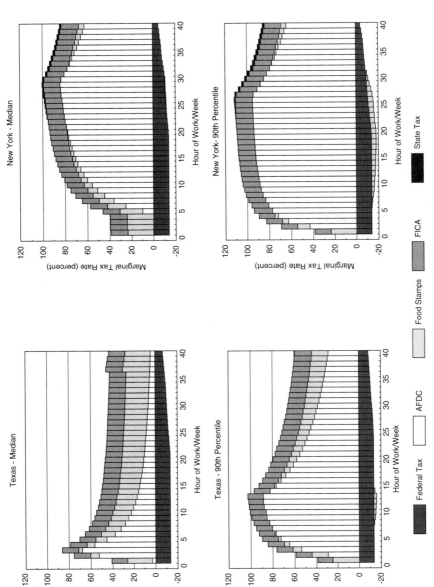

FIGURE 2. *Average Tax Rates for Low-(TX) and High-(NY) Benefit States—Single-Parent Families.*

some cases significantly lower—than those described in Keane and Moffitt's (1991) Table B-1.[36] Their 20-hour average rates, for example, are 95 percent in Texas, 112 percent in Ohio (a medium-benefit state), and 124 percent in California (a high-benefit state). Several factors make our estimated rates lower. The EITC was considerably more generous in 1990 than it was in 1984, the year of their calculations. The wage rate for the representative family in the Keane and Moffitt simulations is lower than the wage rates received by our families, which means AFDC benefits tend to be clawed back over a longer hours interval leading to higher average rates. Keane and Moffitt also assume all families receive housing benefits, which we do not model. Benefit reductions associated with housing increase cumulative rates by 4 to 33 percentage points in their calculations, depending on the state.[37] Finally, Keane and Moffitt include a fixed cost of working that adds 20 percentage points to all families' tax rates. We have no way of assessing the size of work-related expenses, but their existence means our calculations underestimate the change in net disposable income that would result from working. Two modeling differences make our rates higher than Keane and Moffitt's. We incorporate state taxes and treat the combined employer and employee share of payroll taxes as falling completely on workers. (Keane and Moffitt include only the employee share.)

3.4 Labor Force Participation and Hours of Work

Labor force participation rates in our sample vary from 56.4 percent among single parents to 91.6 percent for primary wage earners in two-parent families. In two-parent families in our sample, 61.0 percent of spouses work outside the home. In Section 4 we examine factors correlated with labor market and transfer program participation.

Figure 3 shows the distribution of the usual hours worked per week for single-parent families, primary earners in two-parent families, and secondary earners in two-parent families. Part-time work is uncommon

---

[36] Table B-1 in Keane and Moffitt (1991) shows implicit and explicit tax rates faced by representative single-parent families; if one assumes wages are $5.20 an hour, nonlabor income is $4 per month, child care expenses are zero, and all families participate in programs for which they are eligible. In contrast, we use data for each family in our sample to make our calculations. We calculate tax rates for all families in the data using their reported characteristics and present rates applying to the median and 90th-percentile families in a low- and high-benefit state.

[37] Housing benefits are clearly important for those who receive them; however, housing programs are not operated as entitlements (i.e., not everyone who meets eligibility criteria is entitled to benefits), and only around 30 percent of eligible families receive housing benefits (see, e.g., Casey, 1992). Thus, the Keane and Moffitt convention for housing overstates tax rates for the typical family.

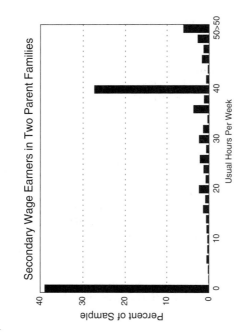

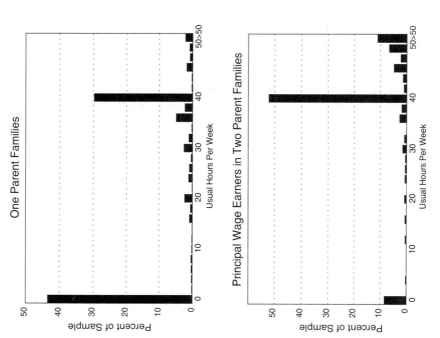

FIGURE 3. *Distribution of Usual Hours Worked per Week by Person Type.*

for families in our sample. Among single parents who work in the paid labor market, 76.1 percent work 35 or more hours in the typical week. Similarly, of the secondary earners in two-parent families who work in the paid labor market, 74.5 percent work 35 or more hours in the typical week. Part-time work is even less common for employed primary earners, 92.6 percent of whom work 35 or more hours a week. As is also clear from the figures, hours in part-time jobs are distributed fairly uniformly between 20 and 35 hours.

Our data showing few families working part-time are consistent with other data. Commonly cited explanations for the paucity of part-time jobs focus on fixed labor-hiring costs to the employer. Because of these fixed costs, empirical models that treat the wage rate as being exogenous generally overpredict the number of people working part-time. One approach to addressing this problem is to model wages as increasing with hours of work (Moffitt, 1984; Rosen, 1976) or to model some process of rationing part-time jobs (Dickens and Lundberg, 1993). As a practical matter, the empirical distribution of hours leads us to follow most others in the literature (Moffitt, 1984; Fraker and Moffitt, 1988; Keane and Moffitt, 1991; Moffitt and Wolfe, 1992; Hoynes, 1993) who treat families as having three choices in the number of hours they can work: 0, 20, and 40. Thus, in our empirical work, the taxes and benefits families pay and receive generally will be based on the difference between working 0 and 20 hours.

4. THE EFFECTS OF WAGES, TAXES, AND TRANSFERS ON LABOR MARKET AND PROGRAM PARTICIPATION

The literature on taxes and labor supply focuses primarily on the intensive margin—the effect of taxes on hours of work for those in the labor market. In Table 2 we showed that estimates from this literature imply that the 1993 EITC expansion, when fully phased in, will have a modest negative overall effect on the hours of work among families already working, relative to the EITC in 1993. The negative effect occurs because nearly 80 percent of working families that receive the credit are in its flat or phaseout range, where the incentives are to reduce hours. The EITC is expected to have a beneficial effect on the extensive margin—the decision to work for those not in the labor market. Existing studies of the EITC's effect on labor market behavior ignore labor market participation. The broader literature on the effects of taxes and transfers on labor market behavior also provides little guidance for understanding the EITC's likely effects on labor market participation.

In this section we examine the responsiveness of labor market and transfer program participation to changes in after-tax wages, controlling for transfer benefits, demographic characteristics, and other factors likely to affect labor market and transfer program participation.

4.1 *Empirical Model*

To study the effect of wages, taxes, and program benefits on labor market and program participation, we follow Moffitt and Wolfe (1992) and estimate bivariate probit models of labor market and transfer program participation.[38] We include variables for incomes, transfers, and demographic characteristics in both participation equations. The models are estimated separately for one-parent families and primary earners in two-parent families. We also estimate a single-equation probit model for the labor market participation decisions of secondary earners in two-parent families.

Income, tax rates, and benefits depend on labor market and transfer program participation decisions, which leads to a potential endogeneity problem with these policy variables. To circumvent this problem we simulate families' taxes and benefits if they work 0 hours and if they work 20 hours at their market wage rates. Explicit tax rates are then defined as one minus the change in after-tax income divided by gross earnings.

The main effect of the EITC on participation will be through its influence on net wages. We include net wages in the empirical model, defined as gross wages (predicted wages for those not in the labor market) multiplied by one minus the explicit tax rate. We expect that net wages are positively correlated with labor market participation and negatively correlated with transfer program participation. In sensitivity analyses we examine the robustness of our results to (1) using the tax rate that would arise from moving from 0 to 40 hours of work, and (2) using predicted wages for all observations in the sample rather than for only those people not in the labor force.

We examine the effects of program benefits by including the AFDC and food stamp benefits available to a family if members work 0 hours. We expect benefit guarantees to show a negative relationship to labor market participation and a positive relationship to program participa-

---

[38] To make inferences about behavioral effects from cross-state variation in benefit and tax rules, it is important that households do not make location decisions based on these benefits and taxes. If households with unobserved "tastes" for work systematically locate in low-benefit, low-tax states, we would observe a spurious negative correlation between taxes and benefits on one hand and hours (or labor market participation) on the other. In a careful study using the 1980 Census, Walker (1994) finds little evidence of welfare-induced migration.

tion. We include family income at 0 hours of work, which is primarily capital income. Income at 0 hours is expected to have a negative effect on both labor market and transfer program participation.

We also include a number of other variables that are common to studies of labor market and transfer program participation. Age and age squared are included to capture life-cycle effects that might affect labor market or program participation. We include years of education, family size, and dummy variables for nonwhite, female, a self-reported measure of being in poor or fair health, presence of children under 6 years old, presence of children aged 6–12, and region of the country. The dependent variable in the labor force participation model takes the value 1 if the person is usually employed during the sample month. The dependent variable in the transfer program model takes the value 1 if the family reports participating in either the AFDC or the food stamps program during the sample month.

4.2 Empirical Results

Empirical results for our primary specifications are given in Table 4. The primary variable of interest for this study is the effect of the net wage rate on labor market and program participation. For single parents (the first two columns of Table 4), we find that net wages positively affect labor market participation and negatively affect transfer program participation. Both coefficients are significant at typical levels of confidence. As shown in the following section, where we summarize the results through policy simulations, the economic significance of both estimates is fairly large. In particular, a 10-percent increase in the after-tax wage (a $0.61 increase) raises the single parent's probability of working by two percentage points and lowers the probability of transfer program participation by more than four percentage points, holding other variables in Table 3 at their means (and dummy variables at 0, except for female). Net wage takes the expected signs in the specifications for two-parent families, but it is not significant in the labor market decisions of primary earners. It is strongly significant in the transfer program participation regressions where a 10-percent increase in the net wage implies a reduction of 0.7 percentage points in the probability of participating (recall that relatively few two-parent families receive transfers). These results imply that policies, like the EITC, that alter the after-tax wage rate can substantially increase labor market participation and reduce transfer program participation.

The regression evidence showing strong effects of net wages is not an artifact of our particular empirical specification, but it clearly emerges in the underlying data even when we do not condition on other factors. In

TABLE 4.
Bivariate Probit Estimates of Labor Market and Program Participation

Variable	Single parents		Principal wage earners		Spouses
	Labor market	Transfers	Labor market	Transfers	Labor market
Constant	−0.833	−0.646	3.941	0.658	−1.871
	(0.863)	(0.937)	(1.805)	(1.461)	(0.747)
Net income at 0 hours	−0.982	−0.241	−3.232	0.102	−1.042
(1,000s)	(0.497)	(0.443)	(0.751)	(0.535)	(0.385)
Net wages (in 1,000s)	89.95	−195.3	78.23	−219.49	57.83
	(34.56)	(31.47)	(57.46)	(43.74)	(23.61)
AFDC at 0 hours (in 1,000s)	−1.986	1.739	−1.812	1.086	−1.394
	(0.435)	(0.406)	(0.675)	(0.409)	(0.538)
Food stamps at 0 hours	0.423	−1.064	−2.904	0.895	−0.206
(1,000s)	(1.326)	(1.291)	(1.936)	(1.06)	(0.637)
Female	−0.600	1.039	−1.551	0.159	−0.757
	(0.258)	(0.239)	(0.238)	(0.189)	(0.143)
Age	0.055	0.029	−0.093	−0.078	0.130
	(0.047)	(0.048)	(0.094)	(0.075)	(0.040)
Age squared	−0.00076	−0.00026	0.00076	0.00106	−0.00182
	(0.00065)	(0.00066)	(0.00119)	(0.00099)	(0.00053)

Education	0.061	-0.054	-0.020	-0.052	0.057
	(0.025)	(0.028)	(0.039)	(0.030)	(0.019)
Nonwhite	-0.066	0.229	-0.175	0.297	-0.124
	(0.116)	(0.125)	(0.23)	(0.175)	(0.115)
Bad or poor health	-0.592	0.572	-0.246	0.453	-0.533
	(0.141)	(0.154)	(0.290)	(0.228)	(0.159)
Kids under 6	-0.413	0.598	-0.255	0.247	-0.321
	(0.096)	(0.114)	(0.149)	(0.109)	(0.079)
Kids from 6 to 12	-0.122	0.258	-0.313	0.076	-0.035
	(0.088)	(0.097)	(0.136)	(0.106)	(0.072)
Family size	0.050	0.059	0.339	0.141	-0.049
	(0.105)	(0.102)	(0.175)	(0.091)	(0.061)
South	0.252	-0.227	0.702	-0.059	0.204
	(0.171)	(0.170)	(0.240)	(0.247)	(0.135)
Midwest	0.217	-0.382	0.183	0.138	0.144
	(0.177)	(0.185)	(0.283)	(0.260)	(0.159)
West	0.423	-0.511	0.613	-0.695	0.201
	(0.191)	(0.205)	(0.283)	(0.286)	(0.167)
Correlation of errors	-0.324			-0.083	
	(0.072)			(0.125)	

Note: The spouse's equation includes primary earner's income, which equals 0.101 (standard error of 0.120).

the top panel of Figure 4, we classify one-parent families by their predicted wage rate and then plot their probability of working. Within each wage group, we allocate families based on their quartile of the cumulative tax rate distribution when increasing hours from 0 to 20. If one looks across wage groups, it appears that the probability of working generally rises with wage rates, though the relationship is not monotonic. Within wage groups, the probability of working falls sharply with our exogenous measure of tax rates. Even after crudely controlling for human capital by looking within predicted wage categories, tax rates appear to exert a strong negative effect on the probability of labor force participation.

The labor force participation rate of primary earners in two-parent families is very high. In the bottom panel of Figure 4, therefore, we graph the effects of wages and taxes on the labor force participation of secondary earners in two-parent families. As with single parents, the probability of working generally increases with predicted wage rates. There is a weaker negative relationship between tax rates and labor market participation for secondary earners than there is for single parents. This result is somewhat surprising given that the literature suggests two-parent families are more responsive to economic variables than are single-parent families. However, the figures do not take into account many factors that are likely to affect labor market behavior.

The AFDC benefit guarantee appears to exert an economical and statistically significant effect in our regression specification of labor market and transfer program participation decisions. The influence of the AFDC variable presumably arises both from its size and from its influence on the benefit reduction rate. As is clear when one examines tax rates in Texas (a low-benefit state) and New York (a high-benefit state), there is a close positive relationship between the guarantee and the benefit reduction rate. The empirical estimates show a consistent negative relationship between the AFDC benefit guarantee and labor force participation, and a consistent positive relationship between the guarantee and program participation. For single-parent families, a 10-percent increase in the benefit guarantee implies a 1.65-percentage-point reduction in the probability of working and a 1.45-percentage-point increase in the probability of receiving program benefits. The economic significance of the effects is much smaller for two-parent families. As with wage rates, the estimated effects of benefits from the empirical model are also clearly present when we graph program or labor force participation against benefits, holding wages constant. (The figure is not shown.)

Several other coefficients generally have consistent patterns across family types and are economically and statistically significant influences

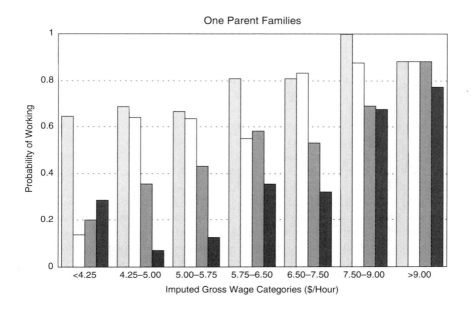

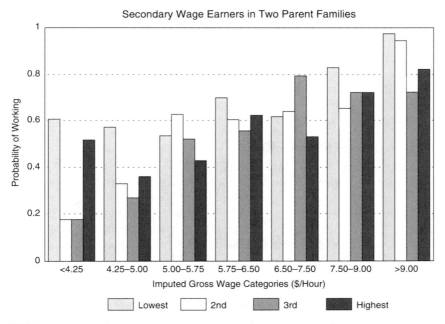

FIGURE 4. *Labor Force Participation by Wages and Tax Rates.*

on labor force and transfer program participation. The coefficient on net private income at 0 hours is negatively related to labor market and transfer program participation for single parents, but it is statistically significant only in the labor market participation equations. The economic significance of the other income variable is small. A 10-percent increase in other income, for example, reduces the probability of work by 0.13 percentage point for secondary earners in two-parent families. Labor force participation is generally negatively correlated with being female, in poor or fair health, and with the number of children in the family under six years of age, while these characteristics are positively correlated with transfer program participation (conditioning on other characteristics). Being in poor or fair health has an economically large effect, lowering the probability of working by 23 percentage points for single parents and 21 percentage points for secondary earners. It raises the probability of participation in transfer programs by 22 percentage points for single parents holding other variables at their means (and other dummy variables at 0 except for female). Whites, more highly educated persons, and individuals living in the South and West tend to have higher labor force participation rates and have lower rates of transfer program participation than others.

In the bivariate probit model for single-parent families, we estimate a highly significant negative correlation between the labor market and transfer program participation equations. The negative correlation implies that unobserved factors, such as parental background variables, that affect the probability of working are negatively correlated with the probability of participating in transfer programs. The correlation of the error terms in the two-parent primary earner specification is also negative but is much smaller and not significantly different from zero.

4.3 Alternative Specifications

In all the specifications reported in Table 4, we use the observed market wage rate for people in the labor force. A common alternative is to use predicted wages for all people in the sample (Blank, 1985; Hoynes, 1993). Using the predicted rather than observed wage nearly doubles the estimated effect of net wages on labor market participation for one-parent families, and the coefficient remains statistically significant at the 5-percent level. The wage effect more than doubles for secondary earners in two-parent families, and it is also significant at usual levels of confidence. The wage effect flips sign for primary earners, but the coefficient is imprecisely estimated. We conclude that using predicted wages would make the effects of the EITC on labor market participation considerably larger than those based on estimates from Table 4.

The net wage effect is again larger when we calculate the exogenous tax rate measures assuming people increase hours to 40 from 0, in this case by roughly 35 percent. The 40-hour tax rates are higher than the 20-hour rates for 60 percent of the sample, who generally live in high-benefit states. It is not clear which measure of tax burdens is preferable, but, like our treatment of wages, the net wage effects in Table 3 are lower than they would be in alternative, plausible specifications.

We also estimated the bivariate probit equations including benefit reduction rates in the specification, along with all other covariates. The benefit reduction rates are defined as the ratio of changes in AFDC or food stamps benefits to the change in earnings between 0 and 20 hours of work. Since families living in high-benefit states have more AFDC at 0 hours and, thus, a longer clawback range, our definition of benefit reduction rates is highly correlated with the benefit at 0 hours of work. The addition of the benefit reduction rate causes the coefficient on AFDC benefits at 0 hours to flip signs and lose significance. In this case, the net wage effects are lower than those in Table 4 for single parents but higher for both principal and secondary earners in two-parent families. We have little confidence that this specification adequately disentangles the independent effects of benefit guarantees and benefit reduction rates.

The labor market effects of the EITC depend on changes at the intensive and extensive margin. When we estimate hours equations like equation (1), adjusting for selection, we get small wage and income elasticities, though the parameters are estimated imprecisely. Our hours estimates are similar to others in the existing literature, which suggests that our data are consistent with data used in other studies of labor market behavior.

5. POLICY IMPLICATIONS

To help interpret the economic significance of the coefficient estimates, we use our regression results and labor market simulations to estimate the effects of the OBRA93 EITC expansion on labor force participation. As with Table 2, we simulate the effect of the 1996 EITC, when the increase is fully phased in, relative to the law that applied in 1993. We first model the effect of the expanded EITC on net-of-tax wages and calculate the implied change in the probability that individuals work. For people not in the labor force, we calculate the effect of the EITC on their after-tax and after-transfer wage in both 1993 and 1996, assuming that if they enter the labor force, they would work 20 hours per week.[39]

---

[39] As with our earlier simulations, we calculate the changes in net wages and virtual incomes that arise from the EITC for secondary wage earners, holding the hours of the primary earner fixed at their observed value.

The simulations show that the EITC increases the net wage of single parents by 15 percent. The higher net wage increases their probability of working by 3.3 percentage points.[40] If each of these single parents works an average of 20 hours per week for 20 weeks per year, our simulation implies that the hours of single-parent families would increase by roughly 72.8 million hours per year. The EITC expansion increases the mean net-of-tax wage of primary earners in two-parent families by 19.6 percent. This leads to a much smaller 0.7-percentage-point increase in labor force participation because most primary earners in two-parent families are already working. Our simulation implies that primary wage earners entering the labor force because of the EITC expansion will work about 12.1 million hours, again at an average of 20 hours per week for 20 weeks per year.

A feature of the EITC that has received little attention is that the average net wage of secondary wage earners decreases by 5.0 percent because the earnings of the second worker frequently either moves the family into the clawback range of the credit or makes the family ineligible for the EITC. Therefore, we expect secondary workers to reduce their hours of work by roughly 10.4 million because of their lower mean net wages. Overall, our simulation results imply that greater labor market participation will lead to an increase of 74.4 million hours, given our assumptions that new labor market participants will work 400 hours per year.

The increased hours resulting from higher rates of labor force participation can be compared with the reduction in hours caused by the credit shown in Table 2. We use Triest's (1990) labor supply parameters for the simulation. As is evident from Table 2, most EITC recipients in our sample are concentrated in the flat and clawback ranges of the credit and their reduction in hours is larger than the increase for those in the subsidy range. The results from Table 2 imply that single parents will reduce their hours of work by 26.4 million, primary earners in two-parent families by 13.6 million, and secondary earners by 14.5 million.

Together, the simulations suggest that the aggregate reduction in hours supplied by working households, 54.5 million, would be more than offset by the hours of new entrants, 74.4 million, if new labor force participants work an average of 20 hours per week for 20 weeks per year. If new labor market entrants work less, the "participation effect" will be smaller. If they work more, the participation effect will be larger. If

---

[40] We have not explicitly modeled Medicaid. Over time, a new labor force participant could, depending on income and family characteristics, lose Medicaid benefits, which presumably will inhibit labor market participation. Further work examining the degree to which incorporating Medicaid would alter our results would be worthwhile.

estimates of participation elasticities with respect to wages from the alternative specifications described in Section 4.3 were used, our estimated offset would also be somewhat higher. For example, using imputed wages for all persons implies that new labor market participants will increase hours of work by 108.4 million. Replacing the 20-hour average tax rate with the tax rate from 0 to 40 hours implies that the new workers will work 91.8 million hours.

We also use our empirical model to simulate the effects of the 1993 EITC expansion on participation in transfer programs. The results are summarized in the lower panel of Table 5. The 15-percent increase in net-of-tax wages for single parents implies that transfer program participation among this group will decrease by 7.2 percentage points or that almost 400,000 families will no longer participate either in AFDC or in the food stamps program. The increased net wages of primary wage

TABLE 5.
Labor Market and Transfer Program Effects of the OBRA93 EITC Expansion, 1993 to 1996

| | Labor market effects | | | |
| | New labor force participants | | Families in the labor market | |
	Percent change in net wage	*Annual hours change due to labor force participation (million)[a]*	*Annual hours reductions of workers (million)[b]*	*Average annual reduction in hours*
Single parents	15.0	72.8	26.4	10.1
Primary wage earners	19.6	12.1	13.6	7.7
Secondary wage earners	−5.0	−10.4	14.5	30.3
Total		74.4	54.5	11.2

| | Transfer program participation effects | | |
	Number leaving program	*Mean annual benefit*	*Mean EITC payment*
Single-parent families	398,384	$6,844	$2,040
Two-parent families	117,757	$4,702	$2,842

[a] The estimation of the change in hours from new labor force participation assumes that, on average, these persons work 20 hours per week for 20 weeks per year.

[b] The reductions in hours for workers are simulated using the kinked budget set approach described in Section 2.1 and in Table 2. We use the estimated net wage and virtual income elasticities from Triest (1990).

earners imply a reduction in transfer program participation of roughly 117,000 families. The mean annual benefits (in 1994 dollars) for single-parent families are $6,844 and $4,702 for two-parent families, and the mean EITC payments for these family types are $2,040 and $2,842, respectively. Therefore, our simulations imply that a potentially substantial savings in transfer payments could result from the EITC expansion.

6. CONCLUSION

Over the past 20 years the EITC has been a favored policy tool for assisting low-income families with children. Between 1978 and 1996 the maximum credit available to families with children will have increased nearly 800 percent in nominal dollars. No other major program directed toward low-income families has grown at a comparable rate. The EITC is now the cornerstone of the Clinton administration's welfare reform agenda.

The effectiveness of the EITC will depend, in part, on its effect on labor market behavior. Most workers that will receive the credit have incomes in the flat or phaseout range of the credit, where the credit provides an unambiguous incentive for people to work fewer hours. Using recent estimates from the empirical literature on taxes and labor supply, we find that the change in incentives caused by the 1993 expansion of the credit is expected to lead to a modest reduction in hours of work by those in the phaseout range of the credit. When evaluated over all workers that could receive the credit, our central estimate predicts an overall reduction of 0.54 percent in hours of work.

No EITC labor market study examines the effect of the credit on labor market participation, though it is through this dimension—"making work pay"—that the EITC appears to attract its favored status. The effect of the credit on labor market participation may be large. As Heckman (1993, p. 118) writes, "A major lesson of the past 20 years is that the strongest empirical effects of wages and nonlabor income on labor supply are to be found at the extensive margin—the margin of entry and exit—where the elasticities are definitely not zero."

Before estimating participation rates, one needs to characterize the tax environment families face. If the cumulative tax burdens faced by the poor are very high, even the 40-percent wage subsidy that the EITC will offer to low-income taxpayers with two or more children may not be enough to make work an economically attractive option relative to welfare. We use a detailed microsimulation model to characterize the tax rates associated with labor market decisions for each family in our sample. Using data from the Survey of Income and Program Participation, we calculate tax rates faced by low-income families. We show that both marginal and average tax rates can be very high (over 90 percent) for high-tax households in both high- and low-benefit states. At the same time, because of earnings disregards and other features of the tax transfer system, tax rates on families in both high- and low-benefit states are often considerably lower than this high-tax case.

We find, both in descriptive and empirical models, that the after-tax wage has an economically and statistically positive effect on labor market participation and a negative effect on transfer program participation. Our results imply that when fully phased in, the 1993 EITC expansion will increase labor force participation rates by 3.3 percentage points for single parents in our sample, increase participation of primary earners in two-parent families by 0.7 percentage point, and decrease participation of secondary earners in two-parent families. When we simulate the overall effect on hours, assuming new participants work 20 hours per week for 20 weeks, the increase in labor force participation more than offsets the adverse effects of the EITC on hours supplied by low-income individuals. If new labor market participants work fewer total hours, the beneficial labor market effects of the credit will be smaller. Regardless of the precise estimates that are favored, it is clear that the participation effects of the credit can substantially offset, in aggregate, the negative effect of the credit on the labor supplied by people already in the labor market. Future work on the effect of the EITC on labor supply should incorporate the credit's effect on participation.

APPENDIX TABLE 1.

Means and Standard Deviations for Variables Used in Table 4

Variable	Single parents		Principal wage earners		Spouses
	Labor market	Transfers	Labor market	Transfers	Labor market
Dependent variable	.564	.505	.916	.094	.609
	(.496)	(.500)	(.277)	(.291)	(.488)
Net income at 0 hours	0.092	0.092	0.018	0.018	0.033
(1000s)	(0.189)	(0.189)	(0.103)	(0.103)	(0.124)
Net wages (in 1000s)	0.006	0.006	0.008	0.008	0.005
	(0.002)	(0.002)	(0.003)	(0.003)	(0.004)
AFDC at 0 hours (in 1000s)	0.228	0.228	0.088	0.088	0.014
	(0.240)	(0.240)	(0.237)	(0.237)	(0.096)
Food stamps at 0 hours	0.192	0.192	0.314	0.314	0.099
(1000s)	(0.084)	(0.084)	(0.102)	(0.102)	(0.135)
Female	0.945	0.945	0.260	0.260	0.740
	(0.229)	(0.229)	(0.439)	(0.439)	(0.439)
Age	32.832	32.832	34.654	34.654	33.541
	(8.081)	(8.081)	(7.444)	(7.444)	(7.628)
Age squared	1143.100	1143.100	1256.300	1256.300	1183.100
	(578.980)	(578.980)	(563.600)	(563.600)	(561.920)

Education	11.528	11.528	11.749	11.749	11.730
	(2.396)	(2.396)	(2.847)	(2.847)	(2.865)
Nonwhite	0.445	0.445	0.206	0.206	0.200
	(0.497)	(0.497)	(0.404)	(0.404)	(0.400)
Bad or poor health	0.174	0.174	0.071	0.071	0.089
	(0.380)	(0.380)	(0.257)	(0.257)	(0.285)
Kids under 6	0.635	0.635	0.775	0.775	0.775
	(0.813)	(0.813)	(0.830)	(0.830)	(0.830)
Kids from 6 to 12	0.709	0.709	0.814	0.814	0.814
	(0.800)	(0.800)	(0.846)	(0.846)	(0.846)
Family size	3.008	3.008	4.283	4.283	4.283
	(1.164)	(1.164)	(1.159)	(1.159)	(1.159)
South	0.398	0.398	0.495	0.495	0.495
	(0.490)	(0.490)	(0.500)	(0.500)	(0.500)
Midwest	0.231	0.231	0.194	0.194	0.194
	(0.422)	(0.422)	(0.395)	(0.395)	(0.395)
West	0.158	0.158	0.152	0.152	0.152
	(0.365)	(0.365)	(0.360)	(0.360)	(0.360)

Note: The spouse's equation includes primary earner's income divided by 1000. The mean is 1.114, and the standard deviation is 0.645.

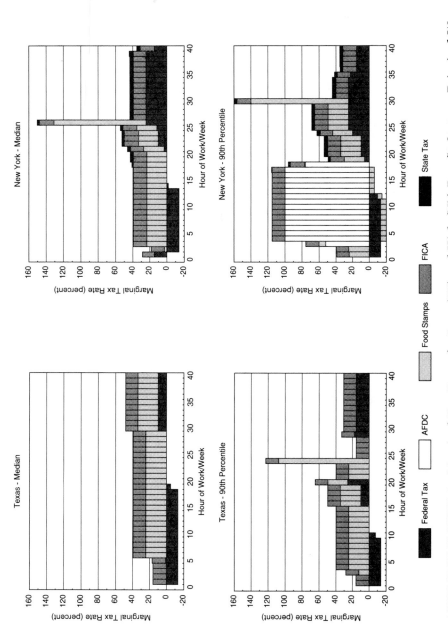

APPENDIX FIGURE 1. *Marginal Tax Rates for Low-(TX) and High-(NY) Benefit States—Principal Wage Earners in Two-Parent Families.*

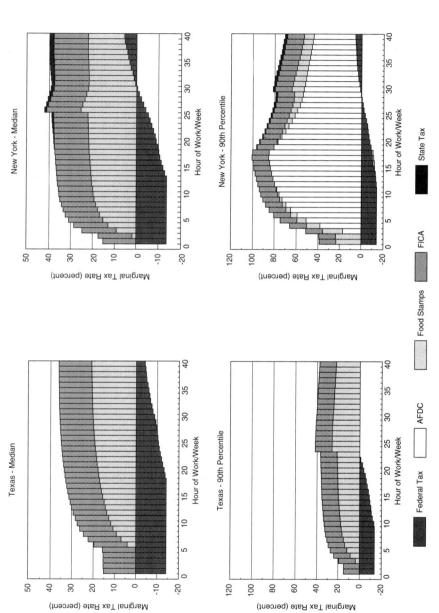

APPENDIX FIGURE 2. *Average Tax Rates for Low-(TX) and High-(NY) Benefit States—Principal Wage Earner in Two-Parent Families.*

REFERENCES

Alstott, Anne L. (1995). "The Earned Income Tax Credit and the Oversimplified Case for Tax-Based Welfare Reform." *Harvard Law Review*, 108:533–592.

Blank, Rebecca M. (1985). "The Impact of State Economic Differentials on Household Welfare and Labor Force Behavior." *Journal of Public Economics* 28:25–58.

———, and Patricia Ruggles. (1993). "When Do Women Use AFDC and Food Stamps? The Dynamics of Eligibility vs. Participation." National Bureau of Economic Research Working Paper no. 4429, August.

Blundell, Richard W., and Ian Walker. (1986). "A Life Cycle Consistent Empirical Model of Labor Supply using Cross Section Data." *Review of Economic Studies* 53:539–558.

Casey, Connie H. (1992). *Characteristics of HUD-Assisted Renters and Their Units in 1989.* U.S. Department of Housing and Urban Development, March.

Danziger, Sheldon, Robert Haveman, and Robert Plotnick. (1981). "How Income Transfer Programs Affect Work, Savings, and the Income Distribution: A Critical Review." *Journal of Economic Literature* 19:975–1028.

Deaton, Angus, and John Muellbauer. (1981). "Functional Forms for Labour Supply and Commodity Demands With and Without Quantity Restrictions." *Econometrica* 49:1521–1532.

Dickens, William T., and Shelly J. Lundberg. (1993). "Hours Restrictions and Labor Supply." *International Economic Review* 34:169–192.

Dickert, Stacy, Scott Houser, and John Karl Scholz. (1994). "Taxes and the Poor: A Microsimulation Study of Implicit and Explicit Taxes." *National Tax Journal* September: 621–638.

Feldstein, Martin. (1993). "The Effect of Marginal Tax Rates on Taxable Income: A Panel Study of the 1986 Tax Reform." National Bureau of Economic Research Working Paper no. 4496, October.

Fraker, Thomas, and Robert Moffitt. (1988). "The Effect of Food Stamps on Labor Supply." *Journal of Public Economics* 35:25–56.

Giannarelli, Linda, and Eugene Steuerle. (1994). "It's Not What You Make, It's What You Keep: Tax Rates Faced by AFDC Recipients." The Urban Institute, October 25. Mimeo.

Hausman, Jerry A. (1981). "Labor Supply." In *How Taxes Affect Economic Behavior,* Aaron and Pechman (eds.), pp. 27–72. Washington, DC: The Brookings Institution.

———. (1985). "Taxes and Labor Supply." In *Handbook of Public Economics,* Auerbach and Feldstein (eds.), pp. 213–263. Amsterdam: North Holland.

Haveman, Robert, Philip de Jong, and Barbara Wolfe. (1991). "Disability Transfers and the Work Decision of Older Men." *Quarterly Journal of Economics* August: 939–949.

Heckman, James J. (1976). "The Common Structure of Statistical Models of Truncation, Sample Selection, and Limited Dependent Variables and a Simple Estimator for Such Models." *Annals of Economic and Social Measurements* 5:475–492.

———. (1979). "Sample Selection Bias as Specification Error." *Econometrica* 47:153–162.

———. (1993). "What Has Been Learned About Labor Supply in the Past Twenty Years?" *American Economic Review* May: 116–121.

————, and Thomas E. MaCurdy. (1981). "New Methods for Estimating Labor Supply Functions: A Survey." *Research in Labor Economics* 4:65–102.

Hoffman, Saul D., and Laurence S. Seidman. (1990). *The Earned Income Tax Credit: Antipoverty Effectiveness and Labor Market Effects.* Kalamazoo, MI: W. E. Upjohn Institute for Employment Research.

Holtzblatt, Janet, Janet McCubbin, and Robert Gillette. (1994). "Promoting Work Through the EITC." *National Tax Journal* September: 591–607.

Hoynes, Hilary Williamson. (1993). "Welfare Transfers in Two-Parent Families: Labor Supply and Welfare Participation Under AFDC-UP." National Bureau of Economic Research Working Paper no. 4407, July.

Hubbard, R. Glenn, Jonathan Skinner, and Stephen P. Zeldes. (1993). "Precautionary Saving and Social Insurance." Columbia University, University of Virginia, and University of Pennsylvania, October. Mimeo.

Internal Revenue Service. (1993). *Statistics of Income—1990: Individual Income Tax Returns.* Washington, DC: U.S. Government Printing Office.

Johnson, Theodore R., and John H. Pencavel. (1984). "Dynamic Hours of Work Functions for Husbands, Wives, and Single Females." *Econometrica* 52:363–389.

Keane, Michael, and Robert Moffitt. (1991). "A Structural Model of Multiple Welfare Program Participation and Labor Supply." Institute for Research on Poverty, Research Working Group on Problems of the Low-Income Population, Working Paper no. 7, November.

Killingsworth, Mark R., and James J. Heckman. (1986). "Female Labor Supply: A Survey." In *Handbook of Labor Economics,* Vol. 1, Ashenfelter and Layard (eds.), pp. 103–204. Amsterdam: North Holland.

Lyon, Andrew B. (1994). "Individual Marginal Tax Rates Under the U.S. Tax and Transfer System: Effects of the 1986 and 1993 Tax Acts." University of Maryland, July. Mimeo.

MaCurdy, Thomas. (1981). "An Empirical Model of Labor Supply in a Life-Cycle Setting." *Journal of Political Economy* 89:1059–1085.

————, David Green, and Harry Paarsch. (1990). "Assessing Empirical Approaches for Analyzing Taxes and Labor Supply." *Journal of Human Resources* 25:415–490.

————. (1992). "Work Disincentive Effects of Taxes: A Reexamination of Some Evidence." *American Economic Review* May: 243–249.

MacDonald, Maurice. (1977). *Food, Stamps, and Income Maintenance.* New York: Academic Press.

McElroy, Marjorie B. (1990). "The Empirical Content of Nash-Bargained Household Behavior." *Journal of Human Resources* 25:559–583.

Moffitt, Robert. (1983). "An Economic Model of Welfare Stigma." *American Economic Review* December: 1023–1035.

————. (1984). "The Estimation of a Joint Wage-Hours Labor Supply Model." *Journal of Labor Economics* 4:550–566.

————. (1986). "The Econometrics of Piecewise-Linear Budget Constraints: A Survey and Exposition of the Maximum Likelihood Method." *Journal of Business and Economic Statistics* 4:317–327.

————. (1990). "The Econometrics of Kinked Budget Constraints." *Journal of Economics Perspectives* 4:119–139.

————. (1992). "Incentive Effects of the U.S. Welfare System: A Review." *Journal of Economic Literature* March: 1–61.

————, and Barbara Wolfe. (1992). "The Effect of the Medicaid Program on Welfare Participation and Labor Supply." *The Review of Economics and Statistics* 74:615–626.

Mroz, Thomas A. (1987). "The Sensitivity of an Empirical Model of Married Women's Hours of Work to Economic and Statistical Assumptions." *Econometrica* 55:765–799.

Peat, Robert. *New York Times* (1994). "Auditors Say Cutoff for Poverty Should Rise in High-Cost Areas." August 5, A1.

Pencavel, John. (1986). "Labor Supply of Men: A Survey." In *Handbook of Labor Economics*, Vol. 1, Ashenfelter and Layard (eds.), Amsterdam: North Holland, 3–102.

Robins, Philip K. (1985). "A Comparison of the Labor Supply Findings from the Four Negative Income Tax Experiments." *Journal of Human Resources* 20:567–582.

————, and Richard W. West (1983). *Final Report of the Seattle/Denver Income Maintenance Experiment: Design and Results*, Vol. 1. Washington, DC: U.S. Government Printing Office.

Rosen, Harvey S. (1976). "Taxes in a Labor Supply Model with Joint Wage-Hours Determination." *Econometrica* 44:485–507.

Scholz, John Karl. (1994). "The Earned Income Tax Credit: Participation, Compliance, and Anti-poverty Effectiveness." *National Tax Journal* March: 59–81.

Triest, Robert K. (1990). "The Effect of Income Taxation on Labor Supply in the United States." *Journal of Human Resources* 25:491–516.

————. (1994). "The Efficiency Cost of Increased Progressivity." In *Tax progressivity and income inequality*, Joel Slemrod (ed.) pp. 137–169. Cambridge: Cambridge University Press.

U.S. Bureau of the Census. (1992). *Statistical Abstract of the United States: 1992*, 112th ed. Washington, DC.

U.S. Congress. (1990). Committee on Ways and Means, *Overview of Entitlement Programs: 1990 Green Book*. Washington, DC: U.S. Government Printing Office, June 5.

————. (1993). Committee on Ways and Means, *Overview of Entitlement Programs: 1993 Green Book*, Washington, DC: U.S. Government Printing Office, July 7.

U.S. General Accounting Office. (1992). "Earned Income Tax Credit: Advance Payment Option Is Not Widely Known or Understood by the Public." GAO/GGD-92-26, Washington, DC, February.

————. (1993). "Earned Income Tax Credit: Design and Administration Could Be Improved." GAO/GGD-93-145, Washington, DC, September.

Walker, James R. (1994). "Migration Among Low-Income Households: Helping the Witch Doctors Reach Consensus." SSRI Working Paper no. 9423, University of Wisconsin—Madison, April.

Wiseman, Michael. (1993). "Welfare Reform in the States: The Bush Legacy." *Focus* (newsletter of the Institute for Research on Poverty) 15:18–36.

————. (1994). "State Welfare Initiatives and the Clinton Administration." The La Follette Institution of Public Affairs, University of Wisconsin—Madison. Mimeo.

Yin, George K., John Karl Scholz, Jonathan Barry Forman, and Mark J. Mazur. (1994). "Improving the Delivery of Benefits to the Working Poor: Proposals to Reform the Earned Income Tax Credit Program." *American Journal of Tax Policy* 11:225–298.

CIGARETTE TAXATION AND THE SOCIAL CONSEQUENCES OF SMOKING

W. Kip Viscusi
Duke University

EXECUTIVE SUMMARY

This paper assesses the appropriate cigarette tax needed to address potential market failures. There is no evidence of inadequate risk decisions by smokers regarding their own welfare. Detailed calculations of the financial externalities of smoking indicate that the financial savings from premature mortality in terms of lower nursing home costs and retirement pensions exceed the higher medical care and life insurance costs generated. The costs of environmental tobacco smoke are highly uncertain, but of potentially substantial magnitude. Even with recognition of these costs, current cigarette taxes exceed the magnitude of the estimated net externalities.

1. INTRODUCTION

Cigarette smoking has long been the object of social controversy and policy interventions. However, in recent years this scrutiny has become

This paper was prepared for the 1994 National Bureau of Economic Research Conference on Tax Policy and the Economy, Washington D.C., November 1, 1994. Robert Scharff provided superb research assistance. The editor, members of the Duke Public Finance Workshop, and participants in the NBER Tax Policy Conference provided helpful comments.

greater. Within 1994 alone there was an unusually large flurry of anti-smoking activity. The chairman of the Food and Drug Administration speculated that cigarettes should be regulated by that agency because, in his view, nicotine is addictive. The Occupational Safety and Health Administration proposed a ban on smoking in the workplace, except in situations in which firms provide designated, ventilated smoking areas (see *Federal Register,* April 5, 1994, pp. 15968–16039). Similarly, Congress, with the support of the U.S. Environmental Protection Agency, began considering legislation that would lead to a ban on public smoking (see the U.S. Environmental Protection Agency, 1994).

Within the context of this antismoking fervor, legislators have also turned to cigarette taxes as a mechanism for raising revenues to partially finance the proposed health care reforms. Although Federal cigarette taxes are currently 24 cents per pack, the proposed legislation would increase these taxes further. The mid-1994 version of the Clinton plan would impose a tax of 99 cents per pack, the health care proposal by Senate majority leader George Mitchell would impose a tax of 69 cents per pack, and one draft health care bill from the House Education and Labor Committee would impose a tax of $2 per pack.

The legislators who proposed these taxes may overestimate the ultimate tax revenues if they fail to recognize the demand response. Not only is the demand for smoking quite elastic and similar to that of many other goods, but the long-run elasticity is even greater than in the short run. As a result, economists such as Becker, Grossman, and Murphy (1994) have estimated that the long-run revenue effects of the cigarette taxes will be less dramatic than the short-run revenue gains.

There are many reasons why, from a political standpoint, taxes might be imposed. One possible explanation is political expediency. Cigarette smokers now constitute a minority of the population. Moreover, given the social controversy pertaining to smoking, they are a vulnerable minority for which there will be lower political costs associated with taxation than, for example, a more broadly based tax.

There may also be legitimate economic rationales for taxing cigarettes, wholly apart from the desire to raise revenues. Cigarette taxes and alcohol taxes are among the most widely used forms of "sin taxes." The economic rationale for such taxes is that imposing taxes discourages behavior that may be associated with inefficient decisions. The inadequacies in behavior may pertain to the choices by smokers with respect to their own well-being or that of their families. Taxes could be imposed to align these decisions with what would prevail if individual choices were rational from a self-interest standpoint. A second impetus for taxation would arise if there were net external costs imposed on the rest of society by cigarette smoking. In that case, cigarette taxes would function much like a Pigouvian tax to lead smokers to internalize the external costs of their actions.

Although the potential rationales for cigarette taxation are clear, whether or not there should be taxation of any kind from the standpoint of promoting efficient decisions is not theoretically obvious. Smokers may ignore the externality to their future selves and their families and make inadequate self-protective decisions. However, there may also be distortions of the opposite type in which smokers overestimate the risk and place too great a weight on the losses involved. The efficient risk is not necessarily zero but rather one that reflects the competing benefits and costs associated with smoking activity.

The externality aspects of smoking likewise involve competing effects. Cigarette smokers have no private incentive to internalize all of the effects of smoking on others, but these effects are not necessarily adverse on balance. To the extent that cigarette smoking leads to adverse health consequences, there will be higher health insurance costs associated with these illnesses as well as other social externalities, such as life insurance costs. However, there may also be offsetting cost savings from earlier mortality through reduced costs of pensions, Social Security, Medicare, and health expenditures later in life. In tallying these externalities, one should also take into account any adverse health effects of environmental tobacco smoke to the extent that these can be reliably estimated. It is not clear a priori whether the cost savings to society are exceeded by the costs imposed on society. Resolving these issues requires a detailed empirical assessment of the competing influences.

In this paper I will provide a careful examination of the social consequences of smoking both for the smoker and society at large. Past analyses directed at ascertaining the net cost of smoking and the appropriate taxation of smoking have focused only on one of the two components, either the individual effects or the societal insurance effects. This paper will be the first to incorporate both dimensions into the analysis. In addition, the assessment of the social consequences of smoking will include extensions that have not appeared in previous assessments. This analysis incorporates recognition of the possible costs associated with environmental tobacco smoke.[1] In addition, all the risk assessments will recognize the changing character of cigarettes and, in particular, the dramatic reduction in the tar levels of cigarettes over the past several decades. In contrast, past risk assessments and evaluations of cigarettes have all utilized risk

---

[1] Gravelle and Zimmerman (1994) provide a much briefer assessment of the role of environmental tobacco smoke because they do not believe the risk estimates are credible.

estimates that pertain to an era of cigarette smoking in which the product had quite different characteristics from those marketed today.

After reviewing the rationale for setting cigarette taxes in Section 2, I will provide a profile of current cigarette taxes in Section 3. Cigarette tax revenues are quite substantial, but these taxes are also regressive in character, which is an unattractive feature. Section 4 details the shift in the tar characteristics in cigarettes and the implications of this shift for cigarette risk assessments. In Section 5, I assess the externalities of cigarette smoking to the smoker's future self and to the smoker's family. Section 6 assesses the insurance-related externalities associated with smoking, including effects on health insurance, Social Security, pensions, life insurance, and related programs. Section 7 broadens the discussion to include the public health risk consequences of environmental tobacco smoke. As the concluding Section 8 indicates, on balance the net social consequences of smoking do not appear to be adverse. From the standpoint of an optimal sin tax, no additional taxation appears warranted. The current level of taxes already exceeds what is required to reflect the estimated adverse social consequences of smoking.

2. SETTING THE EFFICIENT TAX LEVEL

To determine the optimal sin tax in the case of cigarette smoking, one should assess how this tax should be adjusted to reflect both the potential welfare losses to smokers as well as the losses to society that are not accounted for in private smoking decisions. For the purpose of this discussion, I will hypothesize that individuals potentially underestimate the risks of smoking and that there are net societal costs imposed by smoking. If there are such market failures, how then could the tax system serve a constructive role in rectifying these errors in decisions? Frameworks such as these follow a logic that is natural for economists, but policy makers considering smoking taxes seldom frame these taxes in terms of deterring smoking in an efficient manner. In effect, the potential efficiency properties of the risky decisions are neglected, and there is typically exclusive emphasis on the potential errors in these decisions.

The framework here will focus on an individual decision maker. If this person does not smoke cigarettes, then the consumer will derive a welfare level $W(Y)$ from an income level Y. The consumer has the opportunity to purchase cigarettes at a price P, and doing so will lead to two possible health state outcomes, good health in which the individual derives a utility $U(Y - P)$ and ill health in which the utility level is $V(Y - P)$. The ill health state potentially could be death, in which case V will serve as the bequest function. Assume that there is a true health risk π

posed by cigarettes, where this probability is not necessarily known to the decision maker. There is also a social loss L that does not enter the decision maker's calculus of the attractiveness of smoking, where the probability that the loss will be inflicted is π.

From the standpoint of social desirability of smoking, the individual is making a rational choice if the expected utility derived by the smoker from smoking exceeds the expected cost imposed on society plus the utility derived from not smoking, or

$$(1 - \pi)U(Y - P) + \pi V(Y - P) > W(Y) + \pi L. \tag{1}$$

This formulation ignores the role of taxes, which will be introduced subsequently as a mechanism for eliminating potential errors in decisions.

There are two principal ways in which decisions might be flawed. First, individuals may not have accurate perceptions of the risk π, and second they will have no private incentive to recognize the net externality costs imposed by others. In particular, the private decision in the case in which there is not taxation will be based on the individual's assessed probability of ill health q, which may differ from π, leading to a private choice criterion of

$$(1 - q)U(Y - P) + qV(Y - P) > W(Y). \tag{2}$$

The private decision differs from the optimal social decision in that it neglects the expected externality cost and does not account for the possible discrepancy between π and q. In effect, smokers could fail in two ways—by harming their future selves and by imposing net externality costs on society.

Even if smokers do not accurately perceive the risks, it does not necessarily follow that their decisions are in error. Consider the case in which individuals underassess the risks associated with smoking. It may be that even with an underassessment, the decision to smoke would not be altered if the consumer's risk perception were replaced by the true probability π. Thus, the pertinent issue from the standpoint of efficient decision making with respect to risk information is whether risky decisions would be the same in the presence of better risk information or whether they would change.

Suppose that S is the amount that an individual needs to be compensated in order to be made indifferent between smoking and nonsmoking. In the case of people who prefer to smoke, the value of S is positive, whereas in the case of people who choose not to smoke, the value of S is negative so that they would be willing to pay some non-zero amount to avoid smoking. Suppose that evaluated at the true risk π, people would choose to smoke. Then S is positive and satisfies the following condition:

$$(1 - \pi)U(Y + S - P) + \pi V(Y + S - P) = W(Y). \tag{3}$$

If individuals underestimate the risk initially (i.e., $q < \pi$) but still would have a positive value of S when evaluated at the true probabilities as in equation (3), then cigarette smoking is still rational from the individual's standpoint.

If, however, q is sufficiently below π, then the situation may arise in which, based on the true risk of smoking, it would not be rational to smoke. The value of S evaluated at the time risk π consequently will be negative.

This bias in consumer perceptions can potentially be reduced or eliminated through information provision. The government can convey information about the hazards of smoking so that individuals revise their subjective probability assessments q for the smoking risks and increase them to a more appropriate level π. Nevertheless, even with accurate risk perceptions, the expected societal loss term on the right side of equation (1) will not be incorporated in individual actions. What is needed from an economic standpoint is some mechanism to discourage smoking so individuals will, in effect, have the appropriate disincentive for smoking given the societal costs. This class of problems is the well-known Pigouvian externality situation in which an appropriate tax can lead individual economic actors to incorporate the external effects of their decisions in their behavior. In addition, this tax may also serve the function of discouraging smoking in much the same way as would higher risk perceptions. Thus, a tax can both reflect the societal externality as well as the discrepancy between q and π in situations in which individuals underassess the smoking risk.

The individual will choose to smoke in the presence of a tax T if this tax satisfies

$$(1 - q)U(Y - P - T) + qV(Y - P - T) > W(Y). \tag{4}$$

This tax will lead to the same pattern of individual decisions as in the socially optimal situation characterized by inequality (1) if it is set appropriately.

The focus of the subsequent sections will be twofold. First, I will examine possible discrepancies between q and π and how these influence individuals' propensity to smoke. Second, I will address the wide range of externalities associated with smoking to ascertain their magnitude, direction, and relationship to an appropriate tax level.

3. PROFILE OF THE CIGARETTE TAX

Cigarettes are the most heavily taxed major category of consumer purchases. Relative to the purchase amount, tobacco products are subject to a higher tax rate than alcohol, three times the tax rate of gasoline, and over 10 times the tax rate imposed on items such as utilities and automobiles.[2]

Since roughly one-fourth of American adults continue to smoke, the potential tax revenues associated with the cigarette tax are substantial (see Centers for Disease Control, 1994). For the fiscal year ending June 30, 1993, the total of federal, state, and municipal taxes on cigarettes was $12 billion.[3] This tax share is roughly equally divided between the federal government and the states. The total federal tobacco tax was $5.5 billion in 1993, or an average of 24 cents a pack. The state tax total was $6.2 billion, or 28.6 cents per pack. Overall, the federal and state taxes totaled 31.4 percent of the retail price of cigarettes. Municipal taxes added an additional $187 million. Since almost all of the tobacco taxes are accounted for by cigarettes—98.7 percent in 1993—I will use the cigarette tax and tobacco tax label interchangeably.[4]

Although the absolute magnitude of cigarette taxes has never been higher than at its current level, these taxes have been higher as a percentage of the retail price. These taxes reached a peak of 51.4 percent of the total price of cigarettes in 1965, immediately after the initial government report on lung cancer and smoking. The percentage taxation varies over time because the tax is set in absolute amounts and is varied periodically. Over the past 50 years, federal cigarette taxes have held only five different levels, 7.0 cents per pack beginning in 1942, 8.0 cents per pack in 1951, 16.0 cents per pack in 1983, 20.0 cents per pack in 1991, and 24.0 cents per pack in 1993. The absolute level of the tax and the periodic nature of the tax revision has as a consequence resulted in swings in the cigarette tax percentage relative to retail price.

[2] These assessments are based on the calculations presented by Fullerton and Rogers (1993, p. 74). Their measure of the severity of taxation is the ratio of taxes paid to the value of gross purchases minus taxes paid. Based on this statistic, the implied tax rate in 1984 for tobacco is 0.79, for alcohol it is 0.73, for gasoline it is 0.26, for utilities it is 0.04, and for automobiles it is 0.06.

[3] These and other tax statistics reported in this paragraph are drawn from the Tobacco Institute (1993, p. vii).

[4] This percentage of the cigarette tax share is drawn from p. 5 of the Tobacco Institute (1993).

To assess the regressivity of cigarette taxes, Table 1 provides information on the distribution of taxes by income group. An introductory caveat is that one should be cautious in interpreting the incidence statistics for cigarette taxes, since the income levels are based on reported income at a point in time. Income levels for lower income groups appear to be poorly measured, and these figures substantially understate the lifetime income levels for these groups. As shown in Poterba (1989), the lifetime incidence patterns of taxes tend to be more egalitarian than the cross-sectional statistics would suggest. An additional caveat is that these statistics simply examine the average taxes paid per smoker without using a more detailed model of the nature of the ultimate tax incidence.

Even taking these cautionary observations into account, the patterns in Table 1 appear to be particularly stark. Column 2 of Table 1 indicates the percentage of the different income groups who smoke. This percentage is a high 31.6 percent for those who make less than $10,000 and has a low value of 19.3 percent for those who make $50,000 or more. In terms of the overall share of the smoking population, which is given in column 3, both the smoking prevalence and the income group's share in the population are pertinent. For the income groups shown, the most frequently represented smoking group is the middle income range at $20,000–34,999, but this is also the group with the largest fraction of the population.

A more pertinent statistic is the smoking fraction of the different income group relative to the fraction of the population represented by that income group. This ratio, which appears in column 4 of Table 1, indicates that the smoker ratio is highest for the poorer income groups and lowest for the upper income groups. This ratio ranges from 1.24 for those who make less than $10,000 to 0.75 for those who make $50,000 or more. For the three lowest of the five income groups shown in Table 1, the relative smoking fraction of the group exceeds the population fraction, which is striking evidence of the income status correlation of smoking.

The average taxes paid for each person in the income group range from $49 for those who make $50,000 or more to $81 for those who make less than $10,000. The cigarette tax per person is consequently over one and one-half times as great for the poorest segment of the population when compared with the most affluent group. These absolute differences lead to even starker percentage differences, as is indicated in column 6. As a percentage of individual income, cigarette taxes are negligible for those who make $50,000 or more, as these taxes constitute under one-tenth of 1 percent of this group's income. In contrast, for those who make less than $10,000, the cigarette tax amount averages 1.62 percent.

TABLE 1.
Income Profile of Cigarette Tax Incidence
(data for 1990)

	(1) Fraction of total population	(2) Smoking prevalence (percentage)	(3) Fraction of current smokers	(4) Current smokers' fraction/population fraction	(5) Average taxes paid per person	(6) Cigarette taxes as a percentage of median income	(7) Cigarette taxes as a percentage of smokers' median income
Income							
Less than $10,000	0.1018	31.6	0.1257	1.2352	$80.95	1.62	5.1237
$10,000–$19,999	0.1678	29.8	0.1955	1.1649	$76.32	0.51	1.7074
$20,000–$34,999	0.2216	26.9	0.2330	1.0515	$68.89	0.25	0.9313
$35,000–$49,999	0.1642	23.4	0.1502	0.9147	$59.94	0.14	0.6027
$50,000 or more	0.1995	19.3	0.1505	0.7544	$49.44	0.08	0.3941
Education							
Less than 12 years	0.2115	31.8	0.2638	1.2474	$81.76		
12 years	0.3825	29.6	0.4441	1.1611	$76.08		
More than 12 years	0.4037	18.3	0.2898	0.7178	$47.04		
Race							
White	0.8559	25.6	0.8536	0.9973	$65.35		
Black	0.1116	26.2	0.1139	1.0207	$66.89		

Columns 1 and 2 are from U.S. Department of Commerce, Statistical Abstract of the United States (Washington: U.S. Government Printing Office, 1993) p. 139, table 213.

Population statistics pertain to those age 18 and over.

Column (3) = ((1)*(2)*Sum(1)/Sum ((1)*(2))/100.

Column (4) = (3)/(1).

Column (5) = (4)*1890/(pop. in income group—from U.S. Department of Commerce, Statistical Abstract of the United States [Washington: U.S. Government Printing Office, 1993], p. 459). The average tax paid per smoker is $256. Column 5 is calculated per person in the income group. The figures assume $11.89 billion in taxes are collected. This figure from the Tobacco Institute, The Tax Burden on Tobacco (Washington: Tobacco Institute, 1993) Volume 28, p. vii.

Column (6) = (5)/(7). The assumed median income levels are $5,000, $15,000, $27,500, $42,500, and $65,000.

Column (7) = (6)/(2)*100.

Note: The table is adjusted for population proportions not adding to one.

Note: The analysis assumes uniform smoking patterns in terms of cigarettes smoked per smoker among those who smoke.

These calculations, however, understate the ultimate effect of cigarette taxes on those who pay them, since they average the tax amount over the entire population in the income group, not simply smokers. If one focuses on column 7 in Table 1, one finds that the cigarette tax percentage of the median income of smokers ranges from 0.4 percent for those who make $50,000 or more to a percentage amount that is almost 13 times as great—5.1 percent for those who make less than $10,000. Cigarette taxes are strikingly regressive.

Because of the strong correlation of income and educational levels, the educational breakdown of tax incidence shown in Table 1 follows a pattern similar to what one would expect based on the income breakdowns. The average taxes paid per person decline steadily with educational level, since these amounts exhibit a high value of $82 per person for those with less than a high-school education, and a low of $47 per person with at least some college. The racial differences shown in Table 1 appear to be relatively minor, since blacks pay an average tax per person almost identical to that of whites. The percentage share of the tax in the income of blacks will, of course, be higher.

The starkest distinction shown in Table 1 is the strong linkage of cigarette taxes to individual income levels. An undesirable feature of cigarette taxes is their regressivity. Since cigarette consumption is a decreasing function of income, even the total amount of cigarette taxes paid by the lower income groups is greater than that in upper income groups. Cigarette taxes are consequently regressive in absolute terms, not simply in proportional terms.

4. THE CHANGING CIGARETTE

The increased public concern with the risks of smoking has led to two major changes in the characteristics of cigarette smoking. First, cigarette smoking is much less prevalent now than it was in the past. Second, the kinds of cigarettes people smoke are quite different from those smoked decades earlier. In particular, the "tar" level, which is the most frequently used composite measure of the chemical residues linked to cancer risks of smoking, has declined as smokers have switched to lighter cigarettes. Many assessments of cigarette smoking have taken into account the changing frequency of smoking, but none of these studies has incorporated the shift in tar levels in these risk assessments.

This omission is quite fundamental, as it has broad ramifications for the assessed risks of smoking, the rationality of smoking decisions, and the magnitude of societal externalities. Lower tar levels imply that the risk levels associated with smoking will be less than those that have been estimated. This discrepancy is not a minor nuance. The pertinent smoking era currently used for many risk assessments may be as much as a half a century out of date.

Two lags arise. First, the studies that are used in formulating the risk assessments often are not current, but instead have been undertaken a decade or more ago. Second, the smoking exposures that gave rise to the risks identified in these studies preceded the publication dates for these studies because of the substantial lag involved between exposure to carcinogens and incidence of the disease. If, for example, there is a three-decade lag between cigarette smoking and the onset of lung cancer, and if the study estimating such a linkage is a decade old, then in effect there is a 40-year lag in the pertinence of the evidence.

In this section I will review the changing history of the tar levels of cigarettes and the implications of this shift for the potential riskiness of cigarette smoking. The adjustments that I will make will be linear, since reductions in tar will be weighted proportionally.[5] These adjustments are likely to be overly conservative to the extent that there is a no-risk threshold for carcinogenic exposures, which is consistent with much of the evidence on the causation of cancer.[6]

Figure 1 illustrates the shifting level of tar in cigarettes.[7] The bottom trend, indicated as the "raw" data, pertain to the average level of tar in cigarettes observed in that year. These levels were estimated to be 46.1 milligrams of tar per cigarette in 1944, which dropped to 12 milligrams of tar by 1994.

Figure 1 also illustrates the 20-year and 30-year average of these tar levels, where these averages are for the 20- and 30-year period preceding the date indicated. These moving averages indicate higher average tar levels of cigarettes and smoother declines. Examination of these 20- and 30-year averages is potentially more pertinent to the extent that it is a weighted average of exposure amounts over a long period of time that generates the risk rather than point estimates of the risk level. All of the results in Figure

---

[5] Evidence in support of the linearity of the dose–response relationship appears in the International Agency for Research on Cancer (1985).

[6] For discussion of the zero or minimal risks posed by low levels of carcinogens, see Ames and Gold (1993), especially pp. 154–157. Also see Cothern (1992).

[7] The tar data for 1954 and for 1968–1983 are from the Centers for Disease Control (1989), p. 21. Data for 1955–1967 are from the U.S. Department of Health and Human Services (1981), p. 207. Data for 1984–1993 are derived by running a regression of average tar levels on the percent of cigarettes with less than 15 mg of tar (1967–1983) and using the resulting coefficient to estimate tar levels. Data for 1923–1953 are derived by running a regression of average tar levels on year and using the resulting coefficient to estimate tar levels. The data on percent of cigarettes with less than 15 mg of tar are taken from the U.S. Federal Trade Commission (1992), pp. 28–30.

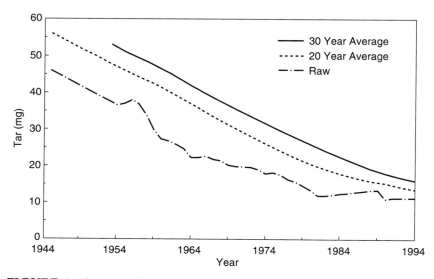

FIGURE 1. *Average Tar Level per Cigarette*

1 pertain to risk levels at a period of time, taking into account only those lags explicitly indicated. If the lag structure is somewhat different, as for example would be the case if risk exposures in the past decade did not affect one's probability of cancer but those in the two previous decades did, then one would want to utilize a different weighting process.

The raw average tar levels of cigarettes display a slight increase in the 1980s in Figure 1. This trend is attributable at least in part to the rising market share of generic cigarettes. Generic cigarettes have a higher average tar level than premium brands, contributing to the observed pattern.

Figure 2 indicates the implications of these tar adjustments for the potential riskiness of cigarette consumption. Those figures represent smoking levels per capita, where the base is the entire adult (age 18 and above) U.S. population, not simply the smoking population. The unadjusted data appear at the top of Figure 2, since the number of cigarettes consumed per capita rose until 1964, which is the year in which the U.S. Department of Health, Education and Welfare issued its landmark report on lung cancer and smoking (see the U.S. Department of Health, Education and Welfare, 1964). Cigarette consumption continued to decline at a moderate pace until around 1983, after which consumption of cigarettes has decreased more starkly.

The bottom pattern of cigarette consumption in Figure 2 makes a tar adjustment, relative to the tar levels in cigarettes in 1944. Whereas unadjusted cigarette consumption was rising for the next two decades, the

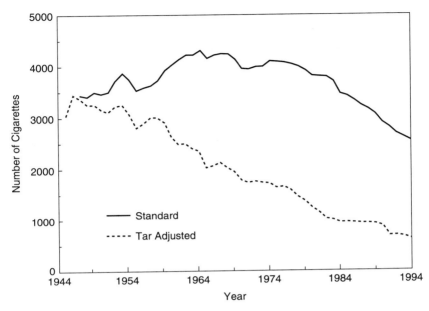

FIGURE 2. *Per Capita Cigarette Consumption*

tar-adjusted cigarette consumption levels were on the decline. This decrease occurred long before the advent of on-product cigarette warnings, television and radio ad bans, and the concern over environmental tobacco smoke. Indeed, the pattern of tar-adjusted smoking exhibits a fairly steady decline over the 1944–1984 period.

One of the steepest periods of decline in the tar-adjusted cigarette consumption and in the average tar levels per cigarette shown in Figures 1 and 2 was 1957 to 1960. This was the era of the "Great Tar Derby" in which the cigarette companies undertook an advertising war to highlight the tar and nicotine levels of their cigarettes. (For further discussion of the Great Tar Derby, see Viscusi [1992b] and Calfee [1986].) This market-based competition led to advertising claims, such as "Today's Marlboro—22 percent less tar, 34 percent less nicotine." The ban on tar and nicotine advertising enacted by the Federal Trade Commission in 1960 halted the dramatic decline in tar-adjusted levels of cigarettes, leading to the flattening of the decline shown in Figures 1 and 2.

The main implication of Figure 2 is that the tar-weighted cigarette consumption has followed a quite different pattern from overall per capita cigarette consumption and should lead to a quite different interpretation of smoking trends. The decline in the risk-weighted cigarette consumption is not as recent a phenomenon as the raw per capita cigarette consumption figures would suggest. Tar-adjusted per capita cigarette consumption has been on the decline for almost the entire past half century. Moreover, because of the linkage of cigarette risk estimates to tar levels, these estimates must be revised to reflect the tar content in order to be pertinent to the changing character of cigarettes.

Figure 3a–c indicates the smoker's lifetime tar-weighted cigarette risks if one assumes various different lags between cigarette consumption and the generation of the risk. Whereas Figure 2 presented data per capita for the entire population, the data in Figure 3a are per capita, where the baseline population consists of smokers only. These figures account for changes in the number of cigarettes smoked as the tar level changes but not whether each particular cigarette was smoked more intensively. Figure 3a is based on risks being contemporaneous; Figure 3b incorporates a 20-year latency where there is a fixed lag of exactly 20 years, not a distributed lag over a 20-year period; and Figure 3c incorporates a 30-year latency period. For example, the risks in Figure 3b for 1994 arose from smoking in 1964. In each case, the trends are indexed so that the relative exposure amount is 100 in 1944.

There is a wide discrepancy between the adjusted and unadjusted lifetime exposure levels for cigarettes in 1994. However, the spread between the adjusted and unadjusted trends is starkest at an earlier date in the case of the unadjusted figures, as recognition of a 20-year latency

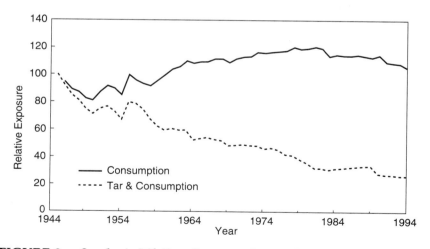

FIGURE 3a. *Smoker's Lifetime Exposure (tar and consumption adjusted). Based on no lag.*

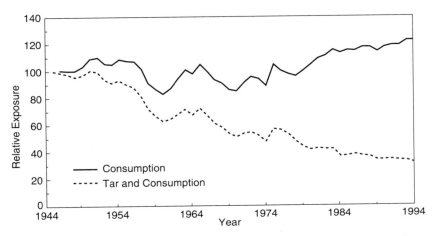

FIGURE 3b. *Smoker's Lifetime Exposure (tar and consumption adjusted). Based on 20-Year Latency Period.*

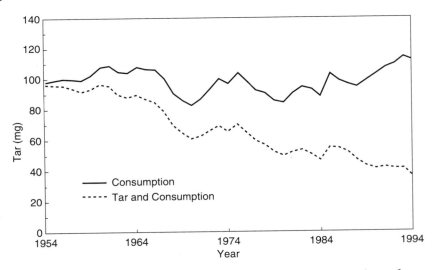

FIGURE 3c. *Smoker's Lifetime Exposure (tar and consumption adjusted). Based on 30-Year Latency Period.*

period narrows the gap between the adjusted and unadjusted figures, particularly through the first three decades, and there is a further narrowing of these early trends in the case of the 30-year latency period. The extent to which the lifetime risk is consequently going to be affected by taking into account the tar and consumption levels will consequently depend both on the era in which the risk assessments are made as well as the lag assumption that is made.

5. EXTERNALITIES TO ONE'S FUTURE SELF

If smoking decisions do not satisfy the efficiency properties outlined in Section 2 from the standpoint of individual rationality, then there will be a market failure. If, for example, smokers underestimate the risk and smoke in situations in which they would not do so if fully informed, then the resulting risk level will be inefficient. Schelling (1984) refers to these errors as externalities to one's future self because there is a time lag before the adverse effects of smoking will become apparent. What Schelling suggests is that one's future self may make different decisions than one would make if fully apprised of the long-term consequences of smoking.

There are several ways in which decisions might err. For example, some observers have hypothesized that even if people understand the risk of smoking, they may not appropriately value the health consequences of smoking or may be addicted to smoking and unable to alter their behavior. I explore these issues in detail elsewhere (1992a), but it is worthwhile to summarize some of the principal empirical results that suggest that smoking behavior follows patterns similar to that of other types of consumption goods. The price elasticity and income elasticity estimates for the demand for cigarettes are similar to those for other products. These elasticity values, which have been documented in dozens of studies for several countries, range from a negative price elasticity from -0.4 to a price elasticity for teenagers of -1.4. (A comprehensive review of this literature appears in Viscusi [1992b].) Becker, Grossman, and Murphy (1994) also find that the long-run elasticity is greater than the short-run elasticity, which is consistent with their model of rational addiction.

The character of the tradeoffs that smokers make in other contexts is also consistent with risk-taking decisions in the smoking domain. In situations involving job hazards, smokers require compensation per expected job injury of $26,100, whereas the average worker receives compensation of $47,900 per statistical injury (see Hersch and Viscusi, 1990, and, more generally, Viscusi, 1992a). The group most averse to risks, nonsmoking individuals who also wear seatbelts, receive compensation per expected injury of $83,200. The sorting of workers in the labor market and the matching up of individuals to jobs of different risk with their corresponding levels of compensation consequently follows the patterns one would expect. Smokers tend to be at the lower end of the range in terms of their implicit value of job injuries. This relative standing is also corroborated by the results in Ippolito and Ippolito (1984), who found that the implicit value of life reflected in smoking behavior was in the range of $300,000 to $600,000 in 1980, which is similar to the implicit values of life displayed by workers who have matched themselves to relatively high-risk jobs. (For a survey of the value of life literature, see Viscusi [1992a, 1993].)

The smoking propensity response to higher-risk perceptions is also consistent with rational decision making. Higher assessed smoking risk probabilities decrease the probability that an individual will smoke. Estimates in Viscusi (1992b) of this linkage indicate that if current average lung cancer risk perceptions were decreased from their level of 0.43 to a value in the estimated risk range based on earlier scientific evidence of 0.05–0.10, then societal smoking rates would rise from 6.5 percent to 7.5 percent.

There is also evidence of responsiveness in terms of the kinds of cigarettes selected (see Viscusi, 1992b). Individuals who express concerns about the health consequences of smoking are much more likely to smoke low-tar cigarettes (less than or equal to three milligrams tar per cigarette), since 87.1 percent of those who smoke low-tar cigarettes indicate such health concerns. In contrast, individuals who smoke high-tar cigarettes (greater than or equal to 21 milligrams tar per cigarette) are much less likely to express concern with the health risks of smoking, since only 54.8 percent of this group indicates concern.

The primary focal point of my discussion will be on whether smokers accurately perceive the risks of smoking. The two sets of survey data I will use pertain to the years 1985 and 1991. The key issue is whether smokers' risk beliefs in those years were as high as would be warranted based on the scientific evidence at that time.

In assessing the accuracy of the risk perceptions, one must first establish the scientific reference point that will be used to ascertain the true estimated risks of smoking. The surveys focus on both lung cancer risks and total mortality risks, so that estimates are needed for each of these risk groups. In addition, I make adjustments for the changing per smoker consumption of cigarettes, since individuals may, for example, smoke more cigarettes if they have switched to lower tar cigarettes. Table 2 summarizes the sensitivity of the mortality estimates to the changing level of tar in cigarettes. The three pairs of columns pertain to the lung cancer risks, the overall mortality risk after making a tar adjustment for lung cancer, and the overall mortality risk making tar adjustments for all risks. Results appear for both 1985 and 1988. The scientific reference point that will be adopted utilizes the adverse health effect estimates presented in the annual reports by the U.S. Surgeon General.[8]

[8] Further details explaining the nature of my calculations using these data appear in Viscusi (1992b). In my earlier treatment I only considered the unadjusted figures, ignoring changes in tar levels. All of the adjusted estimates are new.

TABLE 2.

Mortality Estimate Sensitivity to Tar and Consumption Levels

	Tar and consumption adjustment factor	Smokers' lung cancer mortality		Total smoker mortality lung cancer tar adjustment only		Total smoker mortality all risks tar-adjusted	
		Low	High	Low	High	Low	High
1985 Unadjusted	1.0000	0.0500	0.1000	0.1600	0.3200	0.1600	0.3200
No lag	1.1404	0.0438	0.0877	0.1477	0.2954	0.1403	0.2806
20-Year moving average	1.5836	0.0316	0.0631	0.1351	0.2702	0.1010	0.2021
30-Year moving average	1.8411	0.0272	0.0543	0.1355	0.2710	0.0869	0.1738
20-Year lag point estimate	1.8883	0.0265	0.0530	0.1357	0.2714	0.0847	0.1695
30-Year lag point estimate	2.8181	0.0177	0.0355	0.1381	0.2762	0.0568	0.1136
1988 Unadjusted	1.0000	0.0600	0.1300	0.1800	0.3600	0.1800	0.3600
No lag	1.1029	0.0544	0.1179	0.1684	0.3364	0.1632	0.3264
20-Year moving average	1.4627	0.0410	0.0889	0.1533	0.3040	0.1231	0.2461
30-Year moving average	1.6670	0.0360	0.0780	0.1522	0.3007	0.1080	0.2160
20-Year lag point estimate	1.8500	0.0324	0.0703	0.1492	0.2940	0.0973	0.1946
30-Year lag point estimate	2.3780	0.0252	0.0547	0.1682	0.3287	0.0757	0.1514

The first row of risk estimates pertains to the risk estimated using scientific data available at the time of each of the survey years. These data are not adjusted for changes in tar levels. Both low and high estimates of the risk range appear in each instance. The most recent data available for the survey year 1991 are based on 1988 studies. In the case of lung cancer, the estimated lifetime incremental risk due to smoking ranged from 0.05 to 0.10 in 1985 and from 0.06 to 0.13 based on 1988 evidence. The total smoking mortality amount is roughly triple the lung cancer risk, since it ranges from 0.16 to 0.32 in 1985 and from 0.18 to 0.36 in 1988.

Three sets of mortality estimates appear in Table 2. The first set pertains to lung cancer and the adjusted lung cancer mortality rates. The second set of estimates addresses total smoking mortality, with tar adjustments for only the lung cancer component of total mortality, thus understating the potential role of tar adjustments. The final pair of columns in Table 2 makes tar adjustments for all mortality components, which will tend to overstate the effect of shifts in tar levels.

The effect of the tar adjustments is substantial. In the case of lung cancer, the change in the risk levels based on point estimates of the risk, ignoring lags in the generation of the risk would be to decrease the risk range to 0.04–0.09 in 1985 and from 0.05 to 0.12 in 1988. If, however, lung cancer risks are generated by a moving average or by a lag, then the risk levels that have been estimated by the Surgeon General will have been generated by exposures to much higher levels of tar than are present in the cigarettes today. Making the adjustments for the 20-year moving average or a 30-year moving average decrease the estimated lung cancer risk by 0.02 so that the risk is approximately cut in half by the 30-year moving average. If the risk is generated by the point estimate of the exposure 20 or 30 years before the Surgeon General study, then the lower end of the 1985 risk range is reduced to 0.03 in the 20-year case and 0.02 in the 30-year case. In effect, one can eliminate up to two-thirds of the lung cancer risk level by making an appropriate adjustment for the tar levels of cigarettes.

The adjustments in the case of total smoking mortality are less in relative terms when only the lung cancer component is adjusted. Even in the 30-year lag point estimate case, the 1985 risk range drops only from 0.16–0.32 to a range of 0.14–0.28, which is a very modest decline. If, however, all mortality components are adjusted for changing tar levels, the corresponding 1985 risk range becomes 0.06–0.11 in the 30-year lag point estimate case. The shifts for the 1991 risk estimates follow similar patterns.

The reported risk levels are considerably higher than any of these estimates of the risk. The results reported in Table 3 are based on a

TABLE 3.
Summary of Smokers' Risk Perceptions

Risk perception	Full sample	Smokers
Lung cancer risk (1985)	0.43	0.37
Lung cancer fatality risk (1991)	0.38	0.31
Total smoking mortality risk (1991)	0.54	0.47

Source: Viscusi (1992b, pp. 69, 77).

national survey of lung cancer risk perceptions in 1985 and a North Carolina survey that I undertook in 1991, each of which is reported in Viscusi (1992b). The national smoking survey asked respondents how many out of 100 smokers would get lung cancer because they smoked; these responses have been converted to a fraction for the purposes of reporting in Table 3. My 1991 survey questions alter this wording somewhat, asking about the lung cancer fatality risk level rather than the lung cancer incidence level and asking respondents about the total smoking mortality risk.

In each case, the risk perceptions are substantial. Smokers estimate the lung cancer risk as being 0.37 and the lung cancer fatality risk as 0.31, where each of these estimates is roughly 5 to 10 times larger than the various adjusted lung cancer mortality risk estimates shown in Table 3. Similarly, the overall smoking mortality estimate of 0.47 indicates that smokers believe the risk of death from smoking is almost a 50–50 proposition, unfavorable odds that are considerably more adverse than any of the risk estimates shown in the final columns in Table 2.

One particularly controversial group in society is that of younger smokers, since many smoking critics believe that these individuals will begin smoking at a young age and be discouraged by the transactions costs of changing smoking from altering their behavior. Whereas the popular belief is that the young underassess the risk of smoking, in fact the opposite is the case. Indeed, younger smokers overestimate the risks by more than do their senior counterparts. In the case of the 1985 national survey, respondents aged 16–21 assessed the average lung cancer risk as being 0.49, or a value that is 0.06 greater than that for society as a whole. Smokers in this younger age group assess the lung cancer risks as being 0.45, which is 0.08 greater than that of the entire smoking population. These results are not entirely surprising, since they reflect the different mix of smoking information and the different social context of smoking in recent years. Indeed, even preteens are extremely sensitive to the potential risks of smoking since they believe almost unanimously that smoking is a cause of cancer.[9]

The final rationality issue to be explored is whether smokers understand the extent of the life that will be lost should they die because of their smoking behavior. My 1991 estimates of the life expectancy loss indicate that the overall societal assessment of the expected loss in life expectancy due to smoking is 11.5 years, with smokers assessing the expected life expectancy loss at 9.0 years. Based on the original 1988 estimates of the mortalities shown in Figure 2, one calculates a contemporaneous scientific reference point of an expected life expectancy loss of 10.9 years for smoking females and 6.9 years for smoking males.[10] These figures are below the subjectively assessed life expectancy loss amounts. Adjustments for tar and cigarette consumption levels by making the same proportional adjustments to the mortality loss as for total smoking mortality in Table 2 would reduce the scientifically estimated life expectancy loss further and increase the extent of the overestimation of the life expectancy loss.

Overall, there is little evidence that individuals confer an adverse externality on their future selves through their smoking behavior. All the available empirical evidence suggests that decisions are made in a rational and consistent manner. Although this evidence is not conclusive, the diverse array of information that we have on a wide variety of aspects of smoking decisions, risk perceptions, and smokers' behavior in other contexts conveys a quite consistent picture of smoking behavior.

Such behavior may have broader implications for other kinds of externalities as well, not simply those to the smokers' future selves. Theories of the household typically assume that the household heads make decisions on behalf not only of themselves but also on behalf of other family members. Thus, the husband or wife would take into account his or her own welfare when making the smoking decision as well as the implications that the smoking behavior would have for the well-being of other family members.[11] If individuals do in fact internalize these intrafamily externalities, then they will be already reflected in the individual deci-

---

[9] Indeed, 99 percent or more of all age groups ranging from 7 to 14 believe in the smoking–lung cancer causal link. See Viscusi (1992b) for additional discussion.

[10] These life expectancy loss estimates are derived in Viscusi (1992b). These are higher than those that would be generated using recent data. More recent 1993 estimates of the life expectancy loss, given that a death is smoking-related, imply that 12.1 years of life are lost conditional on a smoking-related death. This figure in turn must be multiplied by the probability of a smoking-related death from Table 2. These new data are discussed further below.

[11] See Becker (1991). Manning et al. (1991) adopt this assumption as well in their smoking externality analysis.

sions. Rational individual decisions consequently will imply that household externalities are internalized as well and need not be considered. As a result, the discussion below will indicate the value of the household externalities in the case of environmental tobacco smoke, but it will not treat these as societal externalities, since rational smokers will internalize these costs in making their smoking decisions. Since the cost of these externalities will be explicitly assessed, those who wish to undertake sensitivity analyses by classifying these costs in a different manner can readily do so.

6. INSURANCE EXTERNALITIES OF SMOKING

A particularly controversial class of externalities linked to smoking consists of the insurance cost effects arising from the estimated health consequences of smoking. States such as Mississippi and Florida are initiating lawsuits in an attempt to recoup state Medicare payments. Hillary Clinton and the Clinton administration more generally have used the argument that cigarette smoking leads to higher health insurance costs as a rationale for a higher cigarette tax. There has also begun to develop a growing sense in the media that smokers are not paying their own way.

This perception contrasts with the results of economic studies of externalities. Assessments by Shoven, Sundberg, and Bunker (1989), Manning et al. (1989, 1991), and Gravelle and Zimmerman (1994) all suggest that consideration of the insurance-related externalities is more complex than many public observers have noted. In particular, if smoking indeed leads to premature death, then there will be competing influences. Higher health care costs may be imposed in the short run, but these deaths may save society additional resources later in life, since these smokers will not be able to collect Social Security and pension benefits for the same amount of time. Which effect is larger is an empirical issue. Moreover, when one is assessing these externalities, it is certainly not appropriate to tally only the potential adverse consequences of smoking, such as the effects on Medicare or health insurance costs, and to neglect systematically the estimated cost savings to society. Proper assessment requires that all legitimate effects be considered.

The most comprehensive study to date is that by Manning et al. (1991), which also forms the basis for much of the analysis in Gravelle and Zimmerman (1994). The approach here will be to take the study by Manning et al. (1991) as the baseline and to update it in a variety of ways. These revisions will include much more than recognition of price changes through shifts in the consumer price index. Rather, using their study as a baseline, the estimates were completely reworked to reflect the changing cost of health insurance as well as our increased understanding of the role of smoking. Because these changes are so extensive and do not involve any conceptual controversies, discussion of the procedure is relegated to the Appendix.

Table 4 reports the external insurance costs per pack of cigarettes for two different cases, one in which there is no adjustment for changes in tar level of cigarettes and a second in which the tar and per capita consumption adjustment is made. The situation in which there is no tar adjustment closely parallels the Manning et al. (1991) analysis in that there is no consideration of the changing character of cigarettes, but there is adjustment for all the different cost factors that have changed since the original Manning et al. (1991) study.[12] These adjustments are nontrivial. In the zero discount rate case, simply updating the Manning, et al. (1991) findings based on the shift in the consumer price index would lead the external insurance cost per pack of cigarettes to be −$1.19, whereas after making all the various adjustments shown in the Appendix, the 1993 cost estimate at the 0-percent discount rate it is −$1.63. The cost savings that smokers provide to society are consequently higher with my estimates than with the simple update of the Manning et al. (1991) estimate. If one were to use a discount rate of 5 percent, there are net costs imposed on society, and these would be higher under my formulation. With a tar adjustment, these costs per pack are $0.32, whereas an update of the Manning study would have made these costs per pack equal to $0.27.

Estimates appear in Table 4 for three different discount rates, where the most reasonable rate corresponding to the long-run real rate of return in the U.S. economy is around 3 percent. The discount rates above and below that amount are intended to indicate the sensitivity of the results to the discounting assumption. The use of any discounting distinguishes these estimates from some that have appeared in the literature.[13] For concreteness, let us focus on the results for the 3-

---

[12] The baseline results from Manning et al. (1991), Table 4.16, pertain to lifetime costs of smokers minus lifetime costs of nonsmoking smokers.

[13] The estimates reported by the Centers for Disease Control and Prevention (1994b) indicate medical costs of $18.5 billion and long-term care costs of $3.4 billion. These estimates represent retrospective costs of smoking an earlier era of cigarettes with a much larger relative smoking population. The nursing home costs were not estimated directly but instead were computed by multiplying the medical costs by a factor of proportionality. None of the cost estimates were discounted. My estimates yielded medical costs of $9.6–13.2 billion and nursing home cost swings of $4.1–5.3 billion. These estimates are specific to these health care components, and pertain to discounted prospective risks for the current smoking population.

TABLE 4.
External Insurance Costs per Pack of Cigarettes

	1993 cost estimate Discount rate			1993 cost estimate with tar adjustment Discount rate		
	0%	3%	5%	0%	3%	5%
Costs						
Medical care <65	0.288	0.326	0.357	0.330	0.373	0.410
Medical care >=65	0.375	0.172	0.093	0.384	0.177	0.096
Total medical care	0.663	0.498	0.451	0.715	0.550	0.505
Sick leave	0.003	0.012	0.019	0.000	0.013	0.020
Group life insurance	0.222	0.126	0.084	0.241	0.136	0.091
Nursing home care	−0.584	−0.221	−0.074	−0.599	−0.226	−0.076
Retirement pension	−2.660	−1.099	−0.337	−2.886	−1.193	−0.365
Fires	0.014	0.016	0.018	0.014	0.016	0.018
Taxes on earnings	0.771	0.351	0.107	0.883	0.402	0.122
Total net costs	−1.571	−0.317	0.268	−1.633	−0.302	0.315

Note: Table 4 is an updated version of the results presented in *The Costs of Poor Health Habits* (Manning, Keeler, Newhouse, Sloss, and Wasserman, 1991). The results from their Table 4.16 are updated for inflation, real cost increases, and other trends (such as the increased proportion of elderly persons in nursing homes). In addition, estimates using a 3-percent discount rate are included. The different cases also adjust for changing tar levels (with varying assumptions regarding the timing and extent of tar's impact). A complete accounting of the adjustments that are made is found in the Appendix.

percent discount rate after making the tar adjustment. Estimates without a tar adjustment also appear in Table 4, and below I will present estimates that take into account the lag time between cigarette smoking and insurance costs. The findings in Table 4 are particularly instructive in indicating which of the externalities are most consequential. The added cost that smokers generate in terms of medical care costs under the age of 65 are $0.37 per pack, and there is an additional cost of $0.18 per pack after age 65, so that the total added medical care cost is $0.55 per pack. Sick leave costs are negligible, since these are under 1 cent per pack. Group life insurance also reflects a higher cost amount, since smokers die sooner than their nonsmoking counterparts, so that this value is $0.14 per pack. Smoking also leads to an additional cost of fires of just under $0.02 per pack.

The main areas of cost savings are nursing home care and retirement pensions. Since smokers die sooner, they will spend less time in nursing homes, leading to a cost savings of $0.23 per pack. In addition, they will be collecting their pensions and Social Security benefits for a shorter period, leading to a cost savings of $1.19 per pack. Since smokers die sooner, society loses the taxes it could have reaped on their earnings. The health and Social Security tax losses from these effects average −$0.40 per pack. The total net costs of smokers to society are −$0.30 per pack. The fire costs in Table 4 reflect only the insurance costs, which adjusted Manning et al.'s (1991) estimates to account for current estimates of fire-related damage. Subsequently, fire-related mortality costs outside the home will be added as well, which is another new feature of this study.

Table 5 extends these analyses to consider various time lags. In the case of the 30-year lag point estimates, one obtains very similar results to what was found above. Including lost taxes on earnings as an externality as well as the other insurance-related costs, one has a total net cost of smokers to society of −$0.23. If taxes on earnings are excluded from consideration, the net externality cost at a 3-percent interest rate is −$0.53. In effect, smokers are already paying their own way in the sense that there is a net externality cost savings to society from their smoking because of the cost savings arising from their premature deaths. These figures exclude from consideration the cigarette taxes already paid by smokers. Thus, there is a net cost savings from the externalities as well as an additional infusion of tax revenues from smokers. Taken at face value, these estimates indicate that, if one were to set the Pigouvian tax amount based in the 3-percent discount rate results, cigarette smoking should be subsidized rather than taxed.

TABLE 5.
External Insurance Costs per Pack of Cigarettes with Tar Adjustments

	20-year moving average 1993 cost estimate Discount rate			20-year point estimate 1993 cost estimate Discount rate		
	0%	3%	5%	0%	3%	5%
Costs						
Medical care <65	0.267	0.302	0.331	0.250	0.283	0.310
Medical care >=65	0.334	0.153	0.083	0.313	0.144	0.078
Total medical care	0.601	0.455	0.414	0.563	0.426	0.388
Sick leave	0.003	0.011	0.017	0.003	0.012	0.016
Group life insurance	0.202	0.114	0.077	0.189	0.107	0.072
Nursing home care	−0.520	−0.197	−0.066	−0.487	−0.184	−0.062
Retirement pension	−2.419	−1.000	−0.306	−2.261	−0.935	−0.286
Fires	0.014	0.016	0.018	0.014	0.016	0.018
Taxes on earnings	0.715	0.326	0.099	0.669	0.305	0.092
Total net costs	−1.405	−0.274	0.253	−1.312	−0.254	0.238

	30-year moving average 1993 cost estimate Discount rate			30-year point estimate 1993 cost estimate Discount rate		
	0%	3%	5%	0%	3%	5%
Costs						
Medical care <65	0.258	0.292	0.320	0.242	0.274	0.301
Medical care >=65	0.317	0.146	0.079	0.290	0.133	0.072
Total medical care	0.576	0.438	0.399	0.533	0.407	0.373
Sick leave	0.003	0.011	0.016	0.002	0.010	0.015
Group life insurance	0.194	0.110	0.074	0.179	0.102	0.068
Nursing home care	−0.495	−0.187	−0.063	−0.453	−0.171	−0.057
Retirement pension	−2.321	−0.960	−0.294	−2.150	−0.889	−0.272
Fires	0.014	0.016	0.018	0.014	0.016	0.018
Taxes on earnings	0.691	0.315	0.096	0.649	0.296	0.090
Total net costs	−1.338	−0.257	0.246	−1.226	−0.230	0.234

Note: See procedures discussed for Table 4.

7. ENVIRONMENTAL TOBACCO SMOKE

Perhaps the most controversial class of external effects pertaining to smoking is environmental tobacco smoke. Long regarded as a nuisance by many nonsmokers, environmental tobacco smoke health risks have now become an object of considerable social controversy. Both the U.S. Occupational Safety and Health Administration and members of the U.S. Congress, with the support of a report by the U.S. Environmental Protection Agency, have proposed taking initiatives against environmental tobacco smoke. In each case, these agencies have suggested that there is a causal link between environmental tobacco smoke and adverse health outcomes, such as lung cancer and heart disease.

In contrast, previous assessments of the external costs of smoking have not included environmental tobacco smoke. The studies by Manning et al. (1989, 1991), did not include environmental tobacco smoke because the evidence at the time of their study was too fragmentary to make a reliable judgment. Since the time of their study, both OSHA and EPA have issued reports with environmental tobacco smoke risk estimates based on this literature. Notwithstanding these agencies' willingness to issue such judgments, other critics continue to suggest that the linkages are not sufficiently strong or well documented to warrant the same kind of treatment as, for example, the risks to the smokers themselves. The recent assessment of environmental tobacco smoke risks by Gravelle and Zimmerman (1994) in their Congressional Research Service study concluded, for example, that evidence was still too inconclusive to warrant calculation of external costs associated with environmental tobacco smoke exposures, particularly in the case of heart disease.

Having made these caveats, I will present estimates of the costs imposed by environmental tobacco smoke based on the EPA and OSHA studies. I will then adjust these estimates to account for factors such as the change in the tar level of cigarettes that were ignored in these government studies. Calculating these estimates in no way implies acceptance of their validity. As a consequence, I will review some of the most salient limitations of these studies in the course of presenting them. Readers who wish to make alternative judgments, such as setting these risks equal to zero, can utilize the results presented here to undertake the appropriate sensitivity tests.

There are two broad classes of environmental tobacco smoke (ETS) risks—lung cancer and heart disease. Most of the debate in the literature has been over the validity of the lung cancer risk estimates. Of the two classes of risk effects, these are the better established. However, as will be indicated below, even the lung cancer estimates are the object of substantial, legitimate controversy. The heart disease estimates have been regarded as being highly speculative by the authors of the heart disease studies as well as by the agencies employing these results. Because all parties have given less credence to the heart disease estimate, these estimates have not been the object of as much public discussion. However, since the heart disease mortality rates are considerably larger than those of lung cancer, it is important both to recognize their potential implications as well as the limitations associated with their estimation.

7.1 Lung Cancer Risks

The first class of ETS risks to be considered is that associated with lung cancer. The scientific evidence that led to the lung cancer risk assessments by EPA consisted of 11 studies of family members exposed to ETS. Eight indicated that ETS led to a higher relative risk, and three indicated that ETS led to a lower relative risk. Of these studies, only one showed statistically significant effects at the 10-percent confidence level, which is a less demanding statistical test than EPA traditionally applies. "Significant" results such as this may occur on a random basis. Despite the fact that only one of the studies yielded relationships that were statistically significant, and the substantial lack of comparability among the 11 studies, which were undertaken with data adjusted in different ways and collected from the 1960s through 1988, EPA pooled the estimates to make an overall ETS risk assessment. Even based on EPA's risk estimates, the ETS risks are at least two orders of magnitude smaller than the risks to smokers themselves.

These estimates neglected a variety of fundamental aspects of the risk. They did not, for example, account for the change in the tar content or per smoker consumption of cigarettes over time. These adjustments will be made below, using the same weighting system of the studies adopted by EPA. Another principal drawback of the ETS studies is that they pertain to risks to other household members. Those exposed to public ETS will typically be exposed to lower concentrations of ETS as well as shorter durations of exposures than the family members of a smoker. To the extent that there is a no-risk threshold, low levels of exposure to ETS may cause no risk whatsoever to the exposed population.

The character of the studies also is quite different from what economists might envision. There were, for example, no detailed multivariate controls to capture differences in demographic characteristics or location, though some studies did make a few primitive demographic adjustments.[14] If smokers choose to live in highly polluted areas, and if they and their families get lung cancer because of their broader environmental exposures, this type of relationship would be captured in these studies and incorrectly attributed to ETS. Similarly, smokers will be more likely to be married to other smokers. Higher mortality rates from ETS may reflect smoking behavior of other family members rather than ETS. Intrafamily correlations in exposure to risks and risk-taking propensities will tend to produce spurious correlations.

The nature of the research results is also difficult to interpret. One recent study "found no adverse effect of exposure to environmental tobacco smoke during adulthood, including exposure to a spouse who smoked" (see Janerich et al., 1990). Whether the apparent ETS risk to children arises from exposure during pregnancy to a smoking mother or ETS exposure after birth is unclear.

In some instances, inconsistent research results have been treated in a way that reflects advocacy of an ETS-cancer link rather than a scientific assessment of causality. One 1992 study found that spouses of low and moderate smokers had a 30-percent lower probability of lung cancer, whereas spouses of heavier smokers had a 30-percent higher probability of lung cancer.[15] Although the authors stress the latter finding, taken at face value their results imply an implausibly shaped dose–response relationship between ETS and cancer that is initially negative and then positive.

In making its estimate of the number of people exposed to ETS, EPA also understates the extent to which workers have already been prevented from being exposed to ETS, thus overstating the potential risk. Many workplaces have installed special smoking lounges and banned workplace smoking. EPA may underestimate the number of workers covered by bans since larger establishments are most likely to have bans or designated smoking areas (74 percent of firms with 750 or more employees versus 55 percent with 50–99 employees) (see U.S. EPA, 1994, Exhibit 7-1). EPA, however, did not adjust for workplace size. The EPA estimates recognize only the efficacy of the 20 percent of the smoking lounges that meet the strict standards proposed in recent legislation (HR3434). However, if the other lounges have some partial efficacy, then one would want to take this influence into account. As a result, I will also explore the sensitivity of the results to

[14] Rather than employ multivariate controls, each study did, however, attempt to have a control group or utilize a cohort study approach.

[15] This example is drawn from Robert J. Barro, "Send Regulations Up in Smoke," *Wall Street Journal*, June 3, 1994.

the assumption one makes about the prevalence of bans and effective smoking lounges.

A final caveat that will be noted before a consideration of the risk estimates is that there is an inconsistency between the EPA and OSHA risk estimates.[16] EPA estimates that each year 2,200 people die from lung cancer due to ETS exposures. When analyzing deaths in the workplace, OSHA estimates that 140–722 deaths per year arise from workplace exposures. In this case, OSHA did not follow EPA's procedure of pooling the results of the risk studies irrespective of their statistical significance. These numbers can be linked, since EPA estimates that 82 percent of nonhome exposures occur at work. If one were to apply this workplace exposure estimate to the OSHA mortality estimate, one obtains an OSHA-based risk estimate of 171–880 lung cancer deaths from nonhome exposures. Thus, there is considerable inconsistency within the federal government in the assessment of the lung cancer risk levels.

To obtain the estimate of the value of statistical lives, I utilize the $5 million value per statistical life from Viscusi (1992a, 1993). This value is the midpoint estimate of the estimated value of life range based on wage-risk tradeoffs. This value of life is pertinent for a worker with an average life expectancy of 36.5 years that will be lost because of an injury. In contrast, an individual who contracts lung cancer because of ETS exposures will incur much less of a loss in life expectancy than would a worker suffering an acute injury. The average life expectancy loss for a victim of a smoking-related disease is 12.1 years (see Centers for Disease Control and Prevention, 1993). For concreteness, I have used the discounted estimated life expectancy loss for smokers in making the calculation. Thus, the pertinent value of life is $5 million, multiplied by the ratio of the discounted expected life years lost from smoking divided by the discounted expected number of life years lost by a worker. One should also, however, adjust this lost value for the fact that it is deferred. People exposed to environmental tobacco smoke are not killed instantaneously, so that there must be appropriate recognition of the time lags involved in making these assessments.

Table 6 provides three sets of estimates. Panel 1 in the table provides estimates based on EPA risk assessments, and the bottom panel provides estimates derived by extrapolating the OSHA ETS risk estimates for the workplace. Within panel 1, the bottom two sections adjust for the discrepancy between EPA's estimate of the number of people at risk and

---

[16] The EPA estimates appear on p. 12 of U.S. EPA (1994), and the OSHA estimates appear on p. 16011 of the *Federal Register*, April 5, 1994. The OSHA figures pertain to the average number of lung cancers over the next 45 years, whereas the EPA estimates pertain to the current risk estimates.

TABLE 6.
Lung Cancer Deaths Caused by ETS Outside the Home.

Panel 1	No lag	20-Year moving average	20-Year point estimate	30-Year moving average	30-Year point estimate
		Tar level assumption linking risk to exposures			
EPA-based estimates					
Number of deaths	1,694	1,694	1,694	1,694	1,694
Cost ($ billions)	$2.80	$1.53	$0.83	$1.05	$0.45
With 50% tar adjustment:					
Number of deaths	1,389	1,285	1,279	1,247	1,220
Cost ($ billions)	$2.29	$1.16	$0.63	$0.77	$0.32
With 100% tar adjustment:					
Number of deaths	1,171	864	696	748	525
Cost ($ Billions)	$1.19	$0.78	$0.34	$0.46	$0.14
OSHA-based estimate—lower bound					
With 50% tar adjustment:					
Number of deaths	444	501	409	399	390
Cost ($ billions)	$0.74	$0.44	$0.20	$0.24	$0.10
With 100% tar adjustment:					
Number of deaths	374	338	223	239	168
Cost ($ Billions)	$0.62	$0.31	$0.11	$0.15	$0.04
OSHA-based estimate—upper bound					
With 50% tar adjustment:					
Number of deaths	1,150	1,296	1,059	1,032	1,010
Cost ($ billions)	$1.89	$1.17	$0.52	$0.64	$0.27
With 100% tar adjustment:					
Number of deaths	970	872	577	620	434
Cost ($ Billions)	$1.60	$0.79	$0.28	$0.39	$0.12

Note: EPA number at risk = 69.1 million (EPA 92); EPA number at risk with 23-percent restrictions = 53.2 million; OSHA number at risk = 14.0 to 36.1 million (OSHA 94-p.16007).

Estimates of workplace risk based on OSHA estimates

Panel 2	No lag	20-Year moving average	20-Year point estimate	30-Year moving average	30-Year point estimate
		Tar level assumption linking risk to exposures			
Lower bound					
Number of deaths	171	171	171	171	171
Cost ($ billions)	$0.28	$0.15	$0.08	$0.11	$0.05
Upper bound					
Number of deaths	880	880	880	880	880
Cost ($ billions)	$1.46	$0.79	$0.43	$0.55	$0.23

Note: EPA (1994, p. 12) says 18 percent of ETS exposure occurs at the worksite and another 4 percent occurs at other covered locations outside the home. This implies that 82 percent of nonhome exposure occurs at the worksite. These data are used to extrapolate the OSHA workplace risk estimates to the entire population. For reference purposes, the lung cancer estimates embodied in the OSHA estimates appear above. See the Appendix for how tar adjustment factors are derived for the differing assumptions regarding latency periods.

the estimated number of people at risk derived from the OSHA study. All risk assessments in panel 1 are based on EPA estimates. In contrast, panel 2 in Table 6 utilizes both the OSHA risk estimates and estimates of the population at risk based on OSHA's assessment. For each of these estimates, the columns indicate the differing assumptions that have been made with respect to the tar level of cigarettes. The first column pertains to that in which the ETS studies correctly capture the tar levels. The next two columns reflect the estimates for which there is a 20-year moving average that determines the risk level and for which it is the 20-year lagged point estimate that determines the risk. The final two columns present estimates for the 30-year moving average and 30-year lag case.

The first two rows in Table 6 indicate the total number of lung cancer deaths and the associated costs attributable to ETS using the EPA assumptions in which there is no tar adjustment. The mortality estimate is a constant value of 1,694 in all cases, but the monetized value of the lives lost differs because the time frame affects the discounted value of the these losses, where a discount rate of 3 percent is used throughout. The next set of rows indicates the mortality costs if one makes an adjustment for half of the reduction in tar levels and 100 percent of the reduction. If nonsmokers benefit to the same extent as do smokers from the decreased tar levels, then the 100-percent estimates are pertinent. If, however, they benefited from only 50 percent of the reduction in tar, only half the change in tar levels is relevant. To the extent that the improvements in tar are achieved through devices such as filters rather than changes in the composition of cigarettes, there would tend to be less than a 100-percent effect.

For purposes of illustration, consider the middle 20-year point estimate set of results. The original EPA estimate of 1,694 deaths is reduced to 1,279 if half of the change in tar levels is accounted for and 696 if the entirety of the tar change is recognized. The value of the mortality costs changes similarly, since it decreases from $0.83 billion in the base EPA case to $0.63 billion in the 50-percent reduction case, and $0.34 billion in the 100-percent reduction case.

If instead one utilizes the EPA risk estimates in conjunction with the OSHA number at risk, one obtains considerably lower estimates of the mortality cost. For the 100-percent tar adjustment case, estimates based on the low end of the OSHA risk assessment are 223 deaths and a monetary cost of $0.11 billion, with the high estimate being 577 deaths and $0.28 billion.

Table 7 adjusts the outside the home ETS lung cancer estimates by assuming that current smoking restrictions are 50 percent effective

TABLE 7.
Lung Cancer Deaths Caused by ETS Outside the Home
With an Assumption of 50% Effectiveness of Current Restrictions

	No lag	20-Year moving average	20-Year point estimate	30-Year moving average	30-Year point estimate
		Number of deaths and discounted cost of deaths (billions of dollars)			
EPA estimate (based on EPA 94 estimate of 1,694 deaths)					
With 50% tar adjustment:					
Number of deaths	902	834	831	810	792
Cost ($ billions)	$1.50	$0.75	$0.40	$0.51	$0.21
With 100% tar adjustment:					
Number of deaths	760	561	452	486	341
Cost ($ billions)	$1.25	$0.51	$0.23	$0.31	$0.09
OSHA-based estimate—lower bound					
With 50% tar adjustment:					
Number of deaths	236	267	218	212	208
Cost ($ billions)	$0.40	$0.24	$0.10	$0.13	$0.06
With 100% tar adjustment:					
Number of deaths	199	180	119	127	90
Cost ($ billions)	$0.33	$0.17	$0.06	$0.07	$0.02
OSHA-based estimate—upper bound					
With 50% tar adjustment:					
Number of deaths	612	690	564	549	538
Cost ($ billions)	$1.01	$0.62	$0.27	$0.34	$0.14
With 100% tar adjustment:					
Number of deaths	516	464	307	330	231
Cost ($ billions)	$0.86	$0.42	$0.15	$0.20	$0.06

See the Appendix for how tar adjustment factors are derived for the differing assumptions regarding latency periods.

Note: The first two panels of Table 6 assumed that 23 percent of worksites (EPA, 1994) are currently subject to restrictions comparable with those proposed by the EPA. Table 7 incorporates evidence that the EPA underestimated the number of persons subject to these restrictions and assumes that 50 percent of workplaces are currently covered. The reasoning for this is as follows:

First, the EPA data suggest that 59 percent of worksites with more than 50 employees are subject to smoking bans or have effective smoking lounges. This is used as evidence that 59 percent of persons working at these sites are subject to these restrictions. This conclusion is not valid, however, because there is a direct correlation between worksite size and smoking restrictions (with 74 percent restrictions for the largest worksites). Since there are more persons working at these larger worksites (and, thus, subject to the greater restriction), one would expect that more than 59 percent of the persons in this category would be subject to restrictions.

Second, the EPA assumes that 10 percent of all worksites with fewer than 50 persons are subject to similar restrictions. This estimate appears to be arbitrary given that there is no available data for these firms. A reasonable extrapolation of rates from worksites with greater than 50 persons would lead to a much higher estimate.

Third, the EPA only includes smoking lounges that would meet the standards of their proposed rule. This is only 20 percent of all smoking lounges. The other 80 percent also afford nonsmokers some protection, which is not recognized by EPA.

Finally, the data used is from 1992, but the policy would not be implemented until 1995 at the earliest. Normally this discrepancy would be considered insignificant. In this case, however, there is already a strong trend toward private (and local public) restriction. Restrictive smoking policies increased from 27 percent in 1985 to 59 percent in 1992.

Given the magnitude of the errors in the EPA analysis, 50 percent restrictions may be a conservative estimate.

rather than EPA's assumption that restrictions are 23 percent effective (U.S. Environmental Protection Agency, 1994, p. 28; also see notes to Table 4). If these adjustments are made, then one obtains estimates in Table 7 that are roughly two-thirds the size of those in the top panel 1 of Table 6.[17] The OSHA-based estimates in Table 7 reflect the population adjustment, not OSHA's risk value adjustment. If additional restrictions on smoking in the workplace are enacted, as would be the case if OSHA enacts its proposed regulation banning workplace smoking except in designated areas, then these estimates of course would be dramatically reduced even further.

In much the same manner, one can calculate the lung cancer deaths caused by ETS inside the home. Table 8 provides these estimates. There are no OSHA-based estimates for Table 8, since OSHA did not address risks within the home. For the EPA-based risk estimates there will be 800 deaths per year within the home. Making the 50-percent tar adjustment reduces these estimates by an average of about one-fourth, and making the 100-percent tar adjustment reduces the estimates by an average of about one-half. It should be emphasized that including any lung cancer death risk estimate inside the home within an externality assessment is problematic, since these costs may be internalized by the smoker who takes into account the well-being of family members in making the smoking decision.

7.2 Heart Disease

The overall mortality costs associated with the ETS-heart disease linkage are even greater. EPA estimates that from 8,760 to 17,520 deaths per year from heart disease are due to ETS exposures outside the home.

Although these estimates are higher than those for lung cancer, they are based on much weaker scientific evidence. Indeed, the recent study by Steenland (1992) that provides the scientific basis for EPA's estimates includes a myriad of caveats and cautionary notes that should make one reluctant to attach much precision to these estimates.[18] To deal with

---

[17] Panel 2 in Table 6 is not adjusted, since OSHA did not indicate its smoking restriction for the underlying risk estimates.

[18] In particular, Steenland (1992) makes the following observations: "While the lung cancer risk among never-smokers exposed to ETS is well established, a possible risk of heart disease due to ETS is more controversial (p. 94). . . . Environmental tobacco smoke is difficult to measure directly (p. 94). . . . The relative contribution of ETS exposure at work to total exposure is not well known (p. 94). . . . The principal weaknesses in the epidemiologic evidence to date have been the indirect methods of assessing exposure (via spousal smoking) and the lack of data on exposures to ETS outside the home (p. 95). . . . Also, there are many risk factors for heart disease, and it is difficult to control well for all of them. Another problem with the epidemiologic data is the seemingly large effect that ETS has on

TABLE 8.
Lung Cancer Deaths Caused by ETS Inside the Home

	No lag	20-Year moving average	20-Year point estimate	30-Year moving average	30-Year point estimate
		Number of deaths and discounted cost of deaths (billions of dollars)			
EPA-based estimate					
Number of deaths	800	800	800	800	800
Cost ($ billions)	$1.32	$0.72	$0.39	$0.50	$0.21
With 50% tar adjustment					
Number of deaths	656	607	604	589	576
Cost ($ billions)	$1.08	$0.55	$0.30	$0.36	$0.15
With 100% tar adjustment					
Number of deaths	553	408	329	353	248
Cost ($ billions)	$0.91	$0.37	$0.16	$0.22	$0.06

The base figure is from the U.S. EPA (1994).

See the Appendix for how tar adjustment factors are derived for the differing assumptions regarding latency periods.

what the author termed "considerable uncertainty" regarding the results, EPA simply scaled down the mortality estimates. It should also be noted that, although EPA adopted the Steenland (1992) findings, it did not adopt Steenland's result that 55 percent of heart disease deaths are due to nonhouse exposures, but instead adopted a 73-percent assumption, which would lead to a higher estimated public externality.

The EPA estimates of heart disease also suffer from the same classes of deficiencies as did the lung cancer risk estimates. In particular, they did not take into account the lag time between exposure and the onset of disease, and they abstracted from changes in the tar level and composition of cigarettes.

Table 9 summarizes the heart disease mortality estimates that will occur outside the home. In each case, low and high estimates based on

---

heart disease compared with the effect of mainstream smoking (p. 95). . . . They showed no excess of lung cancer, and cross-sectional smoking data revealed smoking habits similar to the U.S. referent population. Hence, increased cigarette smoking was unlikely to explain the excess heart disease risk (p. 96). . . . A number of assumptions are involved in estimating the heart disease mortality due to ETS, adding an unfortunate level of uncertainty. The most important assumption is that the relative risks for ETS and heart disease, derived from the epidemiologic evidence, are reasonably accurate. The epidemiologic results may be questioned, given the inherent uncertainties of any epidemiologic study (p. 98). . . . Considerable uncertainty is involved in extrapolating from the epidemiologic data, which consider the relative risks for never-smokers living with smokers, to estimating relative risks for those exposed to ETS (anywhere) vs. those truly not exposed (anywhere)" (p. 98).

the EPA assumptions are presented, and Table 9 also includes low and high estimates based on OSHA's estimates of the mortality costs of ETS. The annual death count in every instance is much higher than the lung cancer mortality rate. If one uses the nonhome exposure amount advocated by Steenland (1992) of 55 percent rather than the 73-percent estimate utilized by EPA, one reduces the mortality estimate and associated costs. Both cases appear in Table 9.

The discounted cost associated with these deaths has a value ranging from $4.3 billion to $8.6 billion in the 20-year point estimate case where these estimates are based on the assumption that the extent of life lost due to heart disease from ETS exposures is the same as the life expectancy loss attributable to smoking overall. If one adopts a 100-percent tar adjustment, these estimates decline to $2.4–$4.8 billion. The other columns in Table 9 represent other tar lag situations, ranging from no lag between EPA studies and tar levels, to the case in which there is a 30-year lag time. The importance of these lags is apparent, since the 30-year point estimates of the costs are considerably below the values in the situation in which there is no lag.

Table 10 presents analogous findings for heart disease deaths caused by ETS inside the home. Results appear assuming 27 percent of exposures are inside the home (EPA's assumption and 45 percent [Steenland estimate]). These mortality amounts are also substantial, since the death count range even in the lowest scenario presented is 3,240 annual deaths. Even with a 30-year lag before these deaths occur, the mortality costs are $1.25 billion if one makes no tar adjustment. As with the public ETS risks, tar adjustments substantially decrease these values.

Table 11 summarizes the passive smoking costs evaluated at a 3-percent discount rate. These are the ETS values that will be used in calculating the total externality costs of cigarettes. Three categories of costs are considered: insurance externalities, ETS mortality costs, and fire-related mortality. The insurance externalities from ETS are the first estimates of this kind and reflect the analog of the insurance externalities from smokers themselves. The inside-the-home heart disease death estimates are excluded for two reasons. First, deaths inside the home may well be internalized by the smoker and consequently are not externalities. Second, as in the case of the other heart disease estimates, the underlying scientific basis for these estimates is extremely fragile and highly speculative. The low and high estimates are quite disparate, so the assumptions one adopts are consequential. For the median estimates and a 20-year point estimate for the tar adjustment, the net ETS cost is 27 cents per pack, virtually all of which is due to heart disease costs.

Table 11 also adds the costs of nonresidential fire-related mortality,

TABLE 9.
Mortality Costs Outside the Home Due to Heart Disease

	No lag	Number of deaths and discounted cost of deaths (billions of dollars)					
		10-Year moving average	10-Year point	20-Year moving average	20-Year point	30-Year moving average	30-Year point
EPA (1994)							
With 73% nonhome exposures							
Low	8,760	8,760	8,760	8,760	8,760	8,760	8,760
	$14.45	$10.41	$7.88	$7.88	$4.28	$5.43	$2.32
50% tar	8,560	8,285	7,645	7,581	6,813	7,094	5,926
	$14.12	$9.85	$6.88	$6.82	$3.33	$4.40	$1.57
100% tar	8,360	7,810	6,529	6,402	4,867	5,427	3,092
	$13.80	$9.28	$5.87	$5.76	$2.38	$3.36	$0.82
High	17,520	17,520	17,520	17,520	17,520	17,520	17,520
	$28.91	$20.83	$15.76	$15.76	$8.58	$10.85	$4.63
50% tar	17,120	16,570	15,289	15,162	13,627	14,187	11,852
	$28.25	$19.70	$13.75	$13.64	$6.67	$8.78	$3.13
100% tar	16,721	15,621	13,058	12,804	9,733	10,854	6,184
	$27.59	$18.57	$11.75	$11.52	$4.77	$6.72	$1.64
With 55% nonhome exposures							
Low	6,600	6,600	6,600	6,600	6,600	6,600	6,600
	$10.90	$7.85	$5.93	$5.93	$3.23	$4.09	$1.75
50% tar	6,449	6,242	5,760	5,712	5,133	5,344	4,465
	$10.65	$7.42	$5.18	$5.14	$2.52	$3.31	$1.18
100% tar	6,299	5,884	4,919	4,824	3,667	4,089	2,329
	$10.40	$7.00	$4.42	$4.34	$1.80	$2.54	$0.62

High	13,200 $21.78	13,200 $15.69	13,200 $11.87	13,200 $11.88	13,200 $8.17	13,200 $3.49
50% tar	12,899 $21.28	12,484 $14.84	11,519 $10.36	11,424 $10.28	10,689 $6.62	8,929 $2.36
100% tar	12,598 $20.78	11,769 $13.99	9,838 $8.85	9,647 $8.68	8,178 $5.06	4,659 $1.23
OSHA (1994)						
Low	2,554 $4.21	2,554 $3.03	2,554 $2.30	2,554 $2.30	2,554 $1.58	2,554 $0.67
50% tar	2,554 $4.21	2,514 $2.99	2,450 $2.21	2,375 $2.14	2,221 $1.37	1,958 $0.52
100% tar	2,554 $4.21	2,475 $2.94	2,347 $2.11	2,196 $1.98	1,889 $1.17	1,362 $0.36
High	15,855 $26.16	15,855 $18.84	15,855 $14.26	15,855 $14.27	15,855 $9.82	15,855 $4.19
50% tar	15,855 $26.16	15,611 $18.55	15,213 $13.68	14,744 $13.27	13,790 $8.54	12,155 $3.22
100% tar	15,855 $26.16	15,368 $18.26	14,571 $13.10	13,634 $12.27	11,726 $7.26	8,456 $2.24

Note: The OSHA estimates are based on a 45-year average. OSHA figures from p. 16011, *Federal Register*, April 5, 1994. The OSHA estimates were adjusted to account for EPA's assumption that 82% of all exposures are at the worksites. See discussion of Table 6 for further details. The EPA tar adjustment is limited to base year of 1988, which is the year of the heart disease study by Wells (1988) used by EPA. The OSHA tar adjustments are based on 1994 tar levels with an assumption that OSHA risk levels are contemporaneous. See the Appendix for how tar adjustment factors are derived for differing assumptions regarding latency periods.

The no tar, 50-percent tar, and 100-percent tar figures are derived by dividing the base number of deaths (and the cost of deaths) by the modified tar adjustment figures. The modification for no tar and 50-percent tar are best illustrated through an example. A 100-percent tar adjustment figure of 1.5 would only be 1.25 under the 50-percent assumption and 1 under a no tar assumption.

The 73-percent nonhome exposure case is taken from EPA 1994. The 55-percent exposure case is from Steenland (1992).

TABLE 10.
Mortality Costs Inside the Home Due to Heart Disease

	Annual deaths	Discounted cost of deaths ($ billion)						
		No lag	10-Year moving average	10-Year point	20-Year moving average	20-Year point	30-Year moving average	30-Year point
EPA-Based Estimates								
With 27% home exposures								
Low	3,240	$3.11	$2.64	$2.29	$2.29	$1.69	$1.91	$1.25
50% tar		$3.11	$2.60	$2.20	$2.13	$1.40	$1.66	$0.96
100% tar		$3.11	$2.56	$2.11	$1.97	$1.10	$1.41	$0.66
High	6,480	$6.22	$5.28	$4.59	$4.59	$3.38	$3.81	$2.49
50% tar		$6.22	$5.20	$4.40	$4.27	$2.80	$3.32	$1.91
100% tar		$6.22	$5.12	$4.21	$3.94	$2.21	$2.82	$1.33
With 45% home exposures								
Low	5,400	$5.19	$4.40	$3.82	$3.82	$2.82	$3.18	$2.08
50% tar		$5.19	$4.33	$3.67	$3.55	$2.33	$2.77	$1.59
100% tar		$5.19	$4.27	$3.51	$3.29	$1.84	$2.35	$1.11
High	10,800	$10.37	$8.80	$7.64	$7.65	$5.64	$6.36	$4.16
50% tar		$10.37	$8.67	$7.33	$7.11	$4.66	$5.53	$3.19
100% tar		$10.37	$8.53	$7.02	$6.58	$3.68	$4.70	$2.22

Note: EPA figures from Exhibit 2-4, U.S. EPA (1994). The 45-percent figure is from Kyle Steenland (1992), "Passive Smoking and the Risk of Heart Disease," *Journal of the American Medical Association*, 267(1), pp. 98–99. See the Appendix for how tar adjustment factors are derived for the differing assumptions regarding latency periods.

The no-tar, 50-percent tar and 100-percent tar figures are derived by dividing the base number of deaths (and the cost of deaths) by the modified tar adjustment figures. The modification for no-tar and 50-percent tar are best explained through an example. A 100-percent tar adjustment figure of 1.5 would only be 1.25 under the 50-percent tar assumption and 1 under a no-tar assumption.

The 73-percent nonhome exposure case is taken from the U.S. EPA 1994. The 55-percent nonhome exposure case is from Steenland (1992).

TABLE 11.

Total Annual Social Costs: Insurance Externalities ($ billions),
assuming 3% discount rate

	No lag	20-Year moving average	20-Year point	30-Year moving average	30-Year point
No tar adjustment					
Smoker's insurance externalities	($7.43)	($7.43)	($7.43)	($7.43)	($7.43)
ETS externalities insurance					
Low	($0.25)	($0.25)	($0.25)	($0.25)	($0.25)
Median	($0.36)	($0.36)	($0.36)	($0.36)	($0.36)
High	($0.46)	($0.46)	($0.46)	($0.46)	($0.46)
Tar adjusted					
Smoker's insurance externalities	($7.79)	($6.74)	($6.26)	($6.32)	($5.65)
ETS externalities insurance					
Low	($0.26)	($0.23)	($0.21)	($0.21)	($0.19)
Median	($0.37)	($0.32)	($0.30)	($0.30)	($0.27)
High	($0.48)	($0.42)	($0.39)	($0.39)	($0.35)
ETS mortality smoking costs					
Lung cancer (nonhome)					
Low	$0.28	$0.15	$0.06	$0.11	$0.02
Median	$1.25	$0.62	$0.27	$0.34	$0.12
High	$2.80	$1.53	$0.83	$1.05	$0.45
Heart disease (nonhome)					
Low	$4.21	$1.98	$0.81	$1.17	$0.36
Median	$12.10	$5.88	$3.20	$4.05	$1.73
High	$27.59	$15.76	$8.58	$10.85	$4.63

	No lag	20-Year moving average	20-Year point	30-Year moving average	30-Year point
Fire deaths (Nonresidential)	$0.03	$0.03	$0.03	$0.03	$0.03

Note: Smoker's insurance externalities are taken from Tables 4 and 5, and are multiplied by the number of packs consumed in the U.S. (The Tobacco Institute, 1993).

ETS insurance externalities are found by dividing ETS deaths by total smoker's deaths due to smoking (CDC 1993) and multiplying this fraction with smoker's insurance externalities.

Costs of ETS deaths from lung cancer are the low, median and high figures from Tables 6 and 7. Costs of heart disease are the low, median, and high numbers from Table 9. The low, median, and high numbers for each category (no lag, 20-year MA, etc.) are found by visual inspection except where the median is an average of the two closest figures. For example, the no-lag, heart disease numbers from Table 9 would be: low = $4.21, median = $17.62 ((14.45 + 20.78)/2), and high = $28.91.

Nonresidential fire deaths are for 1990 (FEMA, 1993) and are valued at $5 million dollars per death.

which are the first such estimates in the literature. These calculations assumed a value of life of $5 million.

8. CONCLUSION: THE NET EXTERNALITY COSTS OF SMOKING

Smokers now pay an average of $0.53 per pack in cigarette taxes. If our objective is to set an appropriate tax level to reflect the externalities generated by cigarettes, the question then becomes whether this tax is sufficient to address the externality costs imposed.

These costs consist of several potential elements. The first of these—the externalities to the smoker's future self—appear to be unimportant. Very few smokers underestimate the hazards associated with smoking, and, indeed, overall smokers over assess the risks of smoking. To the extent that smokers also internalize the ETS risks to household members, this effect would be captured as well in these private decisions.

The focal point of the externality cost debate has not been losses to the smokers' future selves but on the health insurance and related costs associated with smoking. A comprehensive assessment of these costs suggests that on balance, smokers do not cost society resources because of their smoking activities, but rather save society money. Evidence presented in Section 6 indicates that at reasonable rates of discount, the cost savings that result because of the premature deaths of smokers through their lower Social Security and pension costs will more than compensate for the added costs imposed by smokers, chiefly through higher health insurance costs. Thus, not only is there not a rationale for imposing a tax due to these insurance-related externalities, but rather on balance there is a net cost savings to society even excluding consideration of the current cigarette taxes paid by smokers.

The principal externality cost component that might provide the impetus for a cigarette tax consists of ETS costs. Environmental tobacco smoke, however, is now the target of a wide range of explicit regulatory proposals that would limit public exposures to ETS. Legislation before Congress would ban smoking in public places. The Occupational Safety and Health Administration has proposed a regulation that would ban smoking in the workplace except in situations where a designated smoking area meeting stringent ventilation conditions was provided. If these measures are enacted, it would not be appropriate to consider the current levels of external cost of ETS in setting the appropriate tax level because the public externalities would have been addressed by an alternative policy tool, direct regulation.

However, if we proceed under the assumption that these measures will not be enacted, then the costs associated with ETS are potentially very large, if one accepts the very imprecise and conservative risk judgments of EPA and OSHA. If one takes these types of estimates at face value and incorporates them in a net tally of the combined externalities associated with smoking, including the cost of ETS as well as all the insurance-related costs, one obtains the net cost figures indicated in Table 12.[19] The top panel of Table 12 indicates the cost with no tar adjustments, and the bottom panel indicates the tar-adjusted cost. Based on the 30-year point estimates and the median risk assumptions, without a tar adjustment smokers on balance save society $0.18 per pack even including ETS costs. In the tar-adjusted case, smoking is a break-even proposition. Even the worst case scenario shown in Table 12 in which there is a twenty-year moving average link between saving and the observed effects yields as a high estimate in the tar adjustment case a value of $0.41 per pack, which is an amount below current cigarette tax levels. As a consequence, cigarette taxes already exceed the level of the estimated externalities.

It should be emphasized that these calculations were extremely conservative in that they included the very highly speculative ETS estimates. The high end of the range in effect takes the EPA estimates of the ETS risks at face value. Indeed, all the estimates presented here recognized a substantial ETS component, even though one might have reasonably set these costs equal to zero, as in all previous smoking externality studies. These risks are highly debated and uncertain in the case of the lung cancer–ETS risk, and the evidence for the heart disease–ETS risk is at such a preliminary stage that the risk estimates border on being conjecture. If one were to exclude the costs of ETS, the analysis could reduce to the results in Tables 4 and 5 in which smokers saved society $0.23–$0.32 per pack. However, even if we were to accept the highly uncertain risk estimates that have been put forth, the overall conclusion with respect to need for a higher cigarette tax is not affected. Although consideration of the ETS effects leads to a substantial shift in the externality cost estimates from all previous studies of this issue, overall cigarette taxes exceed the associated externalities.

[19] The figures in Table 12 are calculated as the sum of insurance externalities, passive smoking costs, passive smoking insurance externalities, and nonresidential fire deaths. Insurance externalities are computed as the estimates from Table 5 times the number of packs sold in 1993 (The Tobacco Institute, 1993, p. 6). Passive smoking costs are assessed as the low, median, and high numbers from Tables 6, 7 (lung cancer), and 9 (heart disease). Passive smoking insurance externalities are estimated as the insurance externalities figure times the number of deaths due to passive smoking divided by the total number of smoking attributable deaths (CDC, 1994a). The value of nonresidential fire deaths is calculated as the number of nonresidential fire deaths in 1990 (Federal Emergency Management Agency, 1993) times the unadjusted value of life figure.

TABLE 12.
Summary of External Costs of Smoking

	Total net smoking costs (billions of dollars)					External cost per pack				
	No lag	20-Year moving average	20-Year point	30-Year moving average	30-Year point	No lag	20-Year moving average	20-Year point	30-Year moving average	30-Year point
No tar adjustment										
Low	($3.16)	($5.52)	($6.78)	($5.56)	($6.82)	($0.13)	($0.22)	($0.28)	($0.23)	($0.28)
Median	$5.60	($1.25)	($4.28)	($1.53)	($4.43)	$0.23	($0.05)	($0.17)	($0.06)	($0.18)
High	$22.53	$9.43	$1.55	$8.95	$1.17	$0.92	$0.38	$0.06	$0.36	$.05
Tar adjusted										
Low	($3.53)	($4.80)	($5.57)	($4.41)	($4.98)	($0.14)	($0.20)	($0.23)	($0.18)	($0.20)
Median	$5.22	($0.53)	($3.06)	($0.37)	($2.57)	$0.21	($0.02)	($0.12)	($0.01)	($0.10)
High	$22.15	$10.17	$2.80	$10.13	$3.06	$0.90	$0.41	$0.11	$0.41	$0.12

This table is derived by summing the costs found in Table 11. The cost per pack is found by dividing total cost by the number of packs sold in the United States (Tobacco Institute, 1993, p. 6).

APPENDIX

The basic building block for the insurance-related externality cost estimates presented in Section 6 consisted of the results reported in Chapter 4 of Manning et al. (1991) (see, in particular, Table 4-15). This study provided a comprehensive assessment of the external cost of smoking by using data from the Health Insurance Experiment (HIE) and the National Health Interview Survey (NHIS). In their study, the authors attempted to avoid contaminating the smoking estimates by purging the data of systematic differences between smokers and nonsmokers other than their smoking status. In doing this they created a "non-smoking smoker" stylized individual for use in their analyses. The procedure to be described here does not alter the fundamental structure of their assessment, but instead undertakes a large number of revisions in their estimates, most of which were price-related but some of which pertain to more fundamental considerations such as the adjustments for tar levels in cigarettes and per capita cigarette consumption. The most important percentage adjustments included the following: group life insurance costs and total coverage, nursing home costs and frequency of utilization, and overall medical care costs. For ease of reference, these amendments of their analysis are distinguished by topic below.

Medical Care

In the case of medical care expenses for those under age 65, the adjustment figure used is the real rate of medical cost increase since the period of their data. For this age range, the Manning et al. (1991) data is taken from the HIE (1975), so the pertinent adjustment factor to bring the costs to 1993 dollars is 1.585 (medical cost index taken from *Statistical Abstract of the United States, 1993* and *World Almanac and Book of Facts, 1994*). For individuals age 65 and over, the data in Manning et al. (1991) is from the NHIS (1983), leading to an adjustment factor calculated similarly to that for those under 65 of 1.3922.

Sick Leave

Manning et al. (1991) computed the sick leave costs using data in NHIE and NHIS. Manning et al. (1991) used HIE for men under 65 years of age, while they used NHIS for men 65 and older. All the data for women was taken from NHIS, where NHIS data was used in conjunction with 1985 CPS data to determine individual wage rates. Manning et al. (1991) assumed that 38 percent of the work loss was covered by sick leave.

Based on the information included in Appendix G of Manning et al. (1991), 97 percent of the earnings for men occur before age 65. As a result, 97 percent of men's earnings levels were updated from 1975, and 3 percent were updated from 1985, while 100 percent of the women's earnings were updated from the year 1985.

To adjust the sick leave figures, the employment cost index, as reported in *Employment Cost Indexes, 1975–1992* (Bureau of Labor Statistics, U.S. Department of Labor, 1993, p. 21) was used. After the estimates for women and men were obtained, data from the *Statistical Abstract of the United States, 1993* (p. 402) were used to obtain updated proportions of women and men in the workforce, which were then used to assess the weighted average of the workforce mix. Manning et al.'s (1991) assumption that 38 percent of the work loss is covered by sick leave was left unchanged.

Group Life Insurance

Group coverage per worker is estimated by Manning et al. (1991) to be $19,300, which in 1992 dollars is $24,195. In 1992 there were 117.598 million workers, and total group life insurance coverage in the United States was estimated to be $4,240,919 (American Council of Life Insurance in *World Almanac and Book of Facts, 1994*).

Nursing Home Care

Manning et al. (1991) states that 4.79 percent of the population over 65 is in nursing homes and that $9,247 ($12,191 in 1993 dollars) is the annual covered cost per patient. In 1990, 5.09 percent of the population over 65 was in nursing homes (U.S. Department of Commerce, *Statistical Abstract of the United States, 1993* and *World Almanac and Book of Facts, 1994*). In addition to adjusting for the changing nursing home population, there is also an adjustment for the cost of nursing home care. In 1990 the covered cost per patient was $21,290 (amount in 1993 dollars following the same procedure as above).

Retirement Pensions

In estimating the costs of pensions, Manning et al. (1991) included Social Security, Supplemental Security Income (SSI), public assistance, veterans' compensation, and pension income (using 1985 data). To address trends in these amounts, estimates were obtained from the U.S. Department of Labor, *Trends in Pensions, 1992*, and U.S. Department of Health and Human Services, *Annual Statistical Supplement of the Social Security Bulletin, 1993*. The updated figures are for 1992.

Trends in the proportion of the population covered by these programs were also taken into account. A weighted average (weights based on gross outlays of these programs) of the percentage change of those over

65 receiving payments was used to derive the adjustment factor. To calculate the cost adjustment factor, the weighted real increase in the value of payments made to recipients was used.

Fires

Manning et al. (1991) estimate that fires caused by smokers lead to $405.14 million in damages (1990 dollars converted from 1986 dollars). According to FEMA (*Fire in the United States: 1983–1990*, National Fire Data Center, FEMA, 1993), in 1990, there were $354.5 million in damages attributable to smokers.

Taxes on Earnings

Manning et al. (1991) used the 1985 CPS to determine earnings received. This figure was updated using information from the employment cost index, which appears in the U.S. Department of Commerce, *Statistical Abstract of the United States, 1993.*

Taxes on earnings were calculated as being the amount that an individual would pay toward the above costs. It was calculated in such a way that taxes collected equal costs. Since Manning et al.'s (1991) analysis, total costs have risen by 40 percent. However, the demographics of smoking have changed so that the nonsmoking smoker is now of a lower socioeconomic class than in 1975 and, thus, is subsidized by society to a greater extent than before. This would tend to shrink taxes proportionally on earnings for both smokers and nonsmoking smokers.

Per Capita Cigarette Consumption

The cost estimates have been adjusted for changes in the per capita consumption of cigarettes. Data for 1923 to 1990 on per capita cigarette consumption is drawn from the National Cancer Institute, U.S. Department of Health and Human Services, *Strategies to Control Tobacco Use in the United States.* Data for 1991 to 1993 are drawn from the U.S. Department of Agriculture, *Tobacco Situation and Outlook Report*, September 1993.

Percentage of Population Smoking (P)

Data (% smoking ≥ 20 years of age) for 1965–1966, 1970, 1974, 1976–1980, 1983, and 1985 are from *Reducing the Health Consequences of Smoking: 25 Years of Progress* (Report of the Surgeon General, U.S. Department of Health and Human Services, 1989, p. 269). Data (% smoking ≥ 18 years of age) for 1987–88 and 1990 are from *Health: United States, 1991* (U.S. Department of Health and Human Services, 1992, p. 203). Data (≥18) for 1949, 1957, 1958, and 1964 are from *Smoking and Health* (a Report of the

Surgeon General, U.S. Department of Health and Human Services, 1979, p. A-9). Data ($\geq$18) for 1985 and 1991 are from Centers for Disease Control via "Smoking Split Decision" *The Courier Journal* (1/9/94, p. 1). All other years are linearly estimated using the two closest years from which data is available.

Tar (T)

Data for 1954 and 1968–1983 are from *Smoking, Tobacco, and Health: A Fact Book* (CDC, DHHS, p. 21). Data for 1955–1967 is from *The Health Consequences of Smoking: The Changing Cigarette* (A Report of the Surgeon General, DHHS, 1981, p. 207). Data for 1984 to 1993 are derived by running a regression of % < 15 mg on tar for 1967 to 1983 and using the resulting coefficient to estimate tar levels. Data for 1923 to 1954 are derived by running a regression of year on tar and using the resulting coefficient to estimate tar levels.

% Less than 15 mg

Data are taken from *Federal Trade Commission Report to Congress for 1990: Pursuant to the Federal Cigarette Labeling and Advertising Act, 1992* (FTC, 1992, pp. 28–30).

Unadjusted Packs per Smoker (S)

$$S = (C/20)/(P/100)$$

Tar-adjusted Per Capita Cigarette Consumption (CA)

$$CA = C^*T/46.1$$

Tar-adjusted Packs per Smoker (SA)

$$SA = (CA/20)/(P/100)$$

Tar Adjustment (TAR)   The example below is for the 20-year moving average case. The value of CONS is also for this case.

$$TAR = SUM(T_{y-20..}T_{y-1})/SUM(T_{1994..}T_{2013}).$$

Consumption Adjustment (CONS):

$$CONS = SUM(S_{y-20..}S_{y-1})/SUM(S_{1994..}T_{2013}).$$

Discount Rates

The Manning 0% and 5% rates were taken from the Manning et al. (1991) study. The Manning 3-percent rate was calculated in the following manner: First, Table A was constructed using data from Appendix G and pp. 36–37 (in Manning et al., 1991). This gives the absolute and proportional values for medical costs. From this calculation it was found that a 3-percent discount rate is equivalent to the 5-percent number plus 16–20 percent of the difference between 0 percent and 5 percent (depending upon whether the cost in question occurs relatively early or late in life).

REFERENCES

Ames, Bruce N., and Lois S. Gold (1993). "Environmental Pollution and Cancer: Some Misconceptions." In *Phantom Risk*, Kenneth R. Foster, David E. Bernstein, and Peter W. Huber (eds.). Cambridge: The MIT Press, pp. 153–181.
Barro, Robert J. (1994). "Send Regulations Up in Smoke." *Wall Street Journal*, June 3, 1994.
Becker, G.S. (1991). *A Treatise on the Family*. Cambridge: Harvard University Press.
———, M. Grossman, and K.M. Murphy (June 1994). "An Empirical Analysis of Cigarette Addiction." *American Economic Review* 84:396–418.
Bureau of Labor Statistics, U.S. Department of Labor. (1993). *Employment Cost Indexes, 1975–1992*. Washington, DC: U.S. Government Printing Office.
Calfee, J.E. (1986). "Cigarette Advertising, Health Information and Regulation." FTC Working Paper.
Centers for Disease Control and Prevention, U.S. Department of Health and Human Services (1989). *Smoking, Tobacco and Health: A fact book.*
——— (August 27, 1993). "Cigarette Smoking—Attributable Mortality and Years of Potential Life Lost—United States, 1990." *Morbidity and Mortality Weekly Report* 42:645–649.
———. (January 9, 1994). "Smoking Split Decision." *The Courier Journal.*
——— (May 20, 1994a). "Cigarette Smoking Among Adults—United States, 1992, and Changes in the Definition of Current Cigarette Smoking." *Morbidity and Mortality Weekly Report*, p. 342.
Cothern, C. Richard (1992). *Comparative Environmental Risk Assessment*. Boca Raton, FL: Lewis Publishers.
Federal Emergency Management Agency. (1993). *Fire in the U.S.* Washington DC: U.S. Government Printing Office.
Federal Register (April 5, 1994). Washington, DC: Office of the Federal Register, National Archives and Records Service, General Services Administration.
Federal Trade Commission (1992). *Federal Trade Commission Report to Congress for 1990: Pursuant to the Federal Cigarette Labeling and Advertising Act, 1992.*
Fullerton, Don, and D.L. Rodgers (1993). *Who Bears the Lifetime Tax Burden?* Washington, DC: Brookings Institution.
Gravelle, J., and D. Zimmerman (1994). "Cigarette Taxes to Fund Health Care

Reform: An Economic Analysis." Washington, DC: Congressional Research Report.

Hersch, Joni, and W. Kip Viscusi (1990). "Cigarette Smoking, Seatbelt Use, and Differences in Wage-Risk Trade-Offs." *Journal of Human Resources* 25:202–227.

International Agency for Research on Cancer (1985). *Tobacco: A Major International Health Hazard.* New York: Oxford University Press.

Ippolito, P.M., and R.A. Ippolito (1984). "Measuring the Value of Life Saving from Consumer Reactions to New Information." *Journal of Public Economics* 25:53–81.

Janerich, D.T., W.D. Thompson, L.R. Varela, P. Greenwald, S. Chorost, C. Tucci, M.B. Zaman, M.R. Melamed, M. Kiely, and M.F. McKneally (1990). "Lung Cancer and Exposure to Tobacco Smoke in the Household." *The New England Journal of Medicine* 323:632–636.

Manning, W.G., E.B. Keeler, J.P. Newhouse, E.M. Sloss, and J. Wasserman (1989). "The Taxes of Sin: Do Smokers and Drinkers Pay Their Way?" *Journal of the American Medical Association* 261:1604–1609.

———, ———, ———, ———, and ——— (1991). *The Costs of Poor Health Habits.* Cambridge: Harvard University Press.

National Fire Data Center, FEMA (1993). *Fire in the United States: 1983–1990.* Washington, DC: Federal Emergency Management Agency.

Poterba, J.M. (1989). "Lifetime Incidence and the Distributional Burden of Excise Taxes." *American Economic Review* 79:325–330.

Schelling, T.C. (1984). *Choice and Consequence.* Cambridge: Harvard University Press.

Shoven, J.B., J.O. Sundberg, and J.P. Bunker (1989). "The Social Security Cost of Smoking." In *The Economics of Aging*, D.A. Wise (ed.). Chicago: University of Chicago Press, pp. 231–251.

Steenland, Kyle (1992). "Passive Smoking and the Risk of Heart Disease." *Journal of the American Medical Association* 267:94–99.

Tobacco Institute (1993). *The Tax Burden on Tobacco: Historical Compilation 1993*, Vol. 28. Washington, DC: Tobacco Institute.

U.S. Department of Agriculture (1993). *Tobacco Situation and Outlook Report.* September 1993. Washington, DC: U.S. Government Printing Office.

U.S. Department of Commerce (1993). *Statistical Abstract of the United States, 1993.* Washington, DC: U.S. Department of Commerce.

U.S. Department of Health, Education, and Welfare (1964). *Smoking and Health: Report of the Advisory Committee to the Surgeon General of the Public Health Service.* Washington, DC: U.S. Department of Health, Education, and Welfare.

U.S. Department of Health and Human Services (1979). *Smoking and Health, A Report of the Surgeon General.* Washington, DC: U.S. Government Printing Office.

——— Human Services (1981). *The Health Consequences of Smoking: The Changing Cigarette, A Report of the Surgeon General.* Washington, DC: U.S. Government Printing Office.

——— (1989). *Reducing the Health Consequences of Smoking: 25 Years of Progress.* Washington, DC: U.S. Government Printing Office.

——— (1992). *Health United States, 1991.* Washington, DC: U.S. Government Printing Office.

——— (1993). *Annual Statistical Supplement of the Social Security Bulletin, 1993.* Washington, DC: U.S. Government Printing Office.

———, National Cancer Institute (1991). *Strategies to Control Tobacco Use in the United States*. Rockville, MD: U.S. Department of Health and Human Services.

U.S. Department of Labor (1992). *Trends in Pensions, 1992*. Washington, DC: U.S. Government Printing Office.

U.S. Environmental Protection Agency (1994). *The Costs and Benefits of Smoking Restrictions: An Assessment of the Smoke-Free Environment Act of 1993 (H.R.3434)* Indoor Air Division, Office of Radiation and Indoor Air. Washington, DC: U.S. Environmental Protection Agency.

Viscusi, W.K. (1992a). *Fatal Tradeoffs: Public and Private Responsibilities for Risk*. New York: Oxford University Press.

——— (1992b). *Smoking: Making the Risky Decision*. New York: Oxford University Press.

——— (1993). "The Value of Risks to Life and Health." *Journal of Economic Literature* XXXI: 1912–1946.

Wells, A.J. (1988). "An Estimate of Adult Mortality in the United States from Passive Smoking." *Environmental International* 14: 249–265.

World Almanac and Book of Facts, 1994 (1994). New York: Press Pub. Co.

A MAJOR RISK APPROACH TO HEALTH INSURANCE REFORM

Martin Feldstein
Harvard University and NBER

Jonathan Gruber
MIT and NBER

EXECUTIVE SUMMARY

This paper examines the implications of a "major-risk" approach to health insurance using data from the National Medical Expenditure Survey. We study the impact of switching from existing coverage to a policy with a 50 percent coinsurance rate and 10 percent of income limit on out-of-pocket expenditures, as well as several alternative combinations of a high-coinsurance rate with a limited out-of-pocket payment. Our analysis is limited to the population under age 65.

Although 80 percent of spending on physicians and hospital care is done by the 20 percent of families who spend over $5,000 in a year, our analysis shows that shifting to a major risk policy could reduce aggre-

Martin Feldstein is Professor of Economics at Harvard University and President of the NBER. Jonathan Gruber is Assistant Professor of Economics at MIT and a Faculty Research Fellow of the NBER. We are very grateful to Jeffrey Geppert and Kate Baicker for their expert manipulation of the National Medical Expenditure Survey, Daniel Feenberg for help with the TAXSIM calculations reported in Section 5, and to Jim Poterba and members of the NBER Health Care Program for comments. The current paper should not be construed as a proposal or as an advocacy for any particular insurance reform but only as an analysis of some of the consequences of alternative major risk insurance plans.

gate health spending by nearly 20 percent. The reductions would be greatest among higher income individuals.

By reducing the excess consumption of health services, the major risk policy increases aggregate economic efficiency. The extent of the increase in efficiency depends on demand elasticities and the extent of risk aversion. With modest values of both demand sensitivity and risk aversion, we find that shifting to a major risk policy would raise aggregate national efficiency by $34 billion a year. Greater demand sensitivity and/ or greater risk sensitivity imply even larger gains.

Government provision of a major risk policy to everyone under the age of 65 could be financed with a premium of about $150 per person because of the increased tax revenue and reduced Medicare outlays that would result from the provision of universal major risk insurance for the population under age 65. Even without government provision, individuals might be induced to select major risk policies by changing existing tax rules to eliminate the advantage of insurance, either by including employer provided insurance in taxable income or by permitting a tax deduction for out-of-pocket medical expenditures.

The purpose of insurance is to protect individuals against unexpected expenses. At the same time, the presence of insurance alters the behavior of the insured in ways that increase the expected magnitude of losses. Therefore, designing the optimal insurance policy involves balancing the gains from protection against the losses that result from the distortion of behavior.[1]

The character of actual health insurance in the United States reflects not only the balancing of protection and distortion but also the special incentives created by the tax law. The U.S. tax law permits employers to deduct their payments for health insurance as a cost of business while excluding those premiums from the taxable income of employees. This rule substantially lowers the individual's cost of employer-provided health care through insurance. For an individual with a 30-percent marginal tax rate, a $1 health insurance premium costs only 70 cents of after-tax income. This makes it personally optimal to have much more complete insurance than would otherwise be chosen.[2]

---

[1] On the general problem of the design of optimal insurance, see Borch (1968), Gould (1969), Mossin (1968), Pashigian, Schkade, and Menefee (1966), and Smith (1968); the theory is reviewed in Laffont (1990). Some of the specific problems of designing health insurance are discussed in Arrow (1964) and Zeckhauser (1970).

[2] Feldstein and Allison (1974) discuss the relation between the tax exclusion and insurance coverage. An explicit calculation of the effect of the exclusion on the individually optimal level of insurance is presented in Feldstein and Friedman (1977). More recent research on

This more complete insurance results in higher spending on medical care and an increased welfare loss from insurance. An individual with a 20-percent coinsurance rate increases health care spending until the last dollar of services brings a benefit that the individual values at only 20 cents. Since the cost of providing that dollar of services is a dollar, there is an 80-cent welfare loss on that last dollar of spending. Because the extent of the distortion in the structure of insurance (i.e., in the coinsurance rate) can be very substantial, the welfare loss that results from the excessive health care spending can also be very large.[3]

In an earlier paper, Feldstein (1971a) suggested that an insurance policy that combined a 50-percent coinsurance rate with a maximum out-of-pocket limit of 10 percent of income would cause most individuals to be more sensitive than under existing insurance to the costs of health care while protecting them against the financial hardship that would result from medical expenses that are a very large share of income. The present paper examines the implications of such a "major risk insurance" approach in the context of today's medical marketplace. More specifically, we use newly available data on health care spending collected by the National Medical Expenditure Survey (Agency for Health Care Policy and Research, 1991) to answer four questions:

(1) Given the existing distribution of health care spending, is it possible to limit total out-of-pocket spending to a moderate percent of income while still having a sizeable fraction of health spending done by individuals who are facing a large coinsurance rate on the margin? Although this seemed plausible in the early 1970s, reliable data were not available to answer the question. Moreover, because health care costs have risen much faster than income since 1970, an out-of-pocket spending limit of 10 percent of income and a 50-percent coinsurance rate might leave too many people at the limit to provide a useful overall incentive to reduce excessive health care spending.

(2) How would a major risk insurance structure with a high coinsurance rate and an income related out-of-pocket maximum affect individuals at different income levels?

(3) What are the explicit welfare effects of shifting from existing insurance coverage to major risk insurance? Substituting a major risk insurance policy would reduce the welfare loss that now results from consuming health care services that are worth less than they cost to produce. But the effect on the risk that individuals bear is ambiguous. The higher

the relation between tax rules and health insurance includes that by Gruber and Poterba (1994a,b).

[3] Feldstein (1973) discusses the welfare cost of excess health insurance.

coinsurance rate would increase the amount of out-of-pocket risk for many individuals. For them, the gain in reduced distortion must be balanced against the loss of increased risk bearing. For some individuals, however, the maximum out-of-pocket limit would lower their risk so that the gain from decreased risk bearing would reinforce the gain from reduced distortion. The extent of these gains and losses depends on the distribution of income and spending and on the parameters of demand and of risk aversion that are discussed below.

(4) Could a publicly provided major risk insurance policy be financed by eliminating the current favorable tax treatment of health insurance premiums paid by employers?

1. THE NATIONAL MEDICAL EXPENDITURE SURVEY DATA

The present analysis utilizes a remarkable body of data collected by the Agency for Health Care Policy and Research in 1987. The National Medical Expenditure Survey (NMES) began with a population sample in which individuals were asked about their consumption of health services, and about the identity of their employers and insurance companies (if they purchased insurance on their own). Employers and insurers were then asked for details on the individual's insurance plan. Interviews with providers were used to obtain detailed information on the utilization of insured health services to supplement the information reported by the individuals themselves.[4]

In order to have a distribution of health spending that represents what a well-insured family or individual would spend, we have restricted attention to families in which all members are covered by a private group insurance policy. Our sample is also restricted by eliminating any insurance unit with someone who is over 65 years old (since they would be covered by the federal government's Medicare program). The final sample contains approximately 63% of families with no member over age 65.

The resulting sample has 6,000 insurance units, either individuals or families.[5] We use the NMES weights on these observations to reweight

---

[4] For some categories of spending, such as hospital services, spending from each event reported by the individuals was corroborated with the provider. For other categories, such as physician visits, only a subsample of spending events was corroborated, and the resulting evidence was used to adjust reported spending for the remaining events.

[5] An insurance unit can be an individual or a Census family or any subgroup that has separate insurance coverage. For example, an adult child living at home would be part of the Census family but would generally be a separate insurance group.

our sample by income and demographic group to obtain national totals with the correct income and demographic mix.[6] Since the data were collected for 1987, we adjust the individual amounts of income and health care spending to projected 1995 levels. Income is adjusted from 1987 to 1995 by a factor of 1.583, reflecting the increase in nominal per capita income. Health care spending is adjusted by the growth rate in per capita personal health expenditure on doctors and hospitals as projected to 1995 by the Congressional Budget Office (Congressional Budget Office, 1993).

The weighted mean level of spending in this well-insured group of under-65-year-olds at 1995 levels was $3,985.[7] The distribution of spending is very skewed. While 39 percent of insurance units spend less than $500, their spending constitutes only 1.5 percent of total spending. In contrast, only one-sixth of insurance units spend more than $5,000, but their spending constitutes almost 80 percent of total spending. Table 1 presents the distribution of spending, indicating the fraction of insurance units with spending below that limit and the fraction of total health care dollars spent below that limit.

The existing private group insurance policies require insurance units to pay deductibles and coinsurance payments that together represent an average of 39 percent of gross spending on doctors and hospitals. This number is surprisingly high, given the well-insured group which we observe.[8]

Table 2 shows the distribution of this out-of-pocket spending. The distribution is even more skewed than the total spending distribution, with the top 4 percent of spenders accounting for almost 40 percent of out-of-pocket spending. The fact that 83 percent of the sample has out-of-pocket spending below $1,000 in a year under their existing health insurance plans suggests that there is some scope for demand reduction under an MRI-type plan.

[6] Such a reweighting is important because, for example, our average unweighted sample member is richer than the average population member. We cannot adjust, however, for the possibility of self-selection in either insurance status or in the characteristics of the individual's insurance plan.

[7] We use the term *health care spending* as a shorthand for the spending on physicians and hospitals. We exclude other categories of spending because they may not be covered by these individuals' private insurance plans.

[8] Of course, the marginal copayment rate on the last dollar of spending will be somewhat below this average copayment rate, which confounds the effects of deductibles, copayment rates, and out-of-pocket maxima. To the extent that the marginal copayment rate in the individual's original insurance plan is lower, it will strengthen the expenditure reducing effects of our MRI plan.

TABLE 1.
Distribution of Health Care Spending

Spending group	Mean spending	Percent of insurance units pdf	Percent of insurance units cdf	Percent of total spending pdf	Percent of total spending cdf
Under 500	151	38.9	38.9	1.5	1.5
500–1,000	728	13.4	52.3	2.4	3.9
1,000–1,500	1,235	8.5	60.8	2.6	6.5
1,500–2,000	1,718	5.1	65.9	2.2	8.7
2,000–2,500	2,242	3.5	69.4	2.0	10.7
2,500–3,000	2,738	3.5	72.9	2.4	13.1
3,000–3,500	3,246	2.7	75.6	2.2	15.3
3,500–4,000	3,705	1.8	77.4	1.7	17.0
4,000–4,500	4,249	1.8	79.2	1.9	18.9
4,500–5,000	4,764	1.5	80.7	1.8	20.7
5,000–6,000	5,489	2.7	83.4	3.8	24.5
6,000–7,000	6,439	2.3	85.7	3.7	28.2
7,000–8,000	7,498	1.7	87.4	3.2	31.4
8,000–9,000	8,495	1.8	89.2	3.8	35.2
9,000–10,000	9,495	1.1	90.3	2.6	37.8
10,000–15,000	12,139	4.1	94.4	12.4	50.2
15,000–20,000	17,414	1.8	96.2	7.7	57.9
20,000–25,000	22,569	1.1	97.3	5.6	63.5
Over 25,000	52,804	2.7	100.0	36.1	100.0
Total	3,985	82.5 million		329 billion	

Note: Estimates refer to total spending on physician and hospital services in 1995 by the population under age 65. See text for further description.

2. WOULD A MAJOR RISK INSURANCE POLICY REDUCE EXCESSIVE SPENDING?

The very skewed distribution of health care spending raises the question of whether a limit of 10 percent on the out-of-pocket health spending would leave many dollars of health spending exposed to a substantial copayment rate. For example, a major risk insurance policy with a 50-percent copayment rate and an out-of-pocket limit of 10 percent of income would cause a family with $35,000 of income to be sensitive on spending below $7,000 but then to have a zero marginal price for health spending above $7,000. The distribution in Table 1 shows that 68 percent of spending is incurred by insurance units that spend more than $7,000.

More generally, the combination of a 50-percent coinsurance rate and a 10-percent maximum out-of-pocket limit implies that individuals are

TABLE 2.
Distribution of Out-of-Pocket Health Care Spending

Spending group	Mean spending	Percent of insurance units		Percent of total spending	
		pdf	*cdf*	*pdf*	*cdf*
0	0	20.43	20.43	0	0
1–50	26	6.13	26.56	0.21	0.21
50–100	73	8.47	35.03	0.83	1.04
100–250	169	16.70	51.73	3.77	4.81
250–500	362	15.58	67.31	7.55	12.36
500–750	612	8.36	75.67	6.85	19.21
750–1,000	863	6.89	82.56	7.96	27.17
1,000–1,500	1,209	6.81	89.37	11.02	38.19
1,500–2,000	1,736	3.15	92.52	7.33	45.52
2,000–2,500	2,216	2.09	94.61	6.21	51.73
2,500–3,000	2,757	1.40	96.01	5.18	56.91
3,000–3,500	3,237	0.92	96.93	3.99	60.90
3,500–5,000	4,117	1.33	98.26	7.35	68.25
over 5,000	13,727	1.73	100.00	31.73	100.00
Total	747	82.5 million	62 billion		

Note: Estimates refer to out-of-pocket spending on physician and hospital services in 1995 by the population under age 65. See text for further description.

sensitive if their health spending is less than 20 percent of their income and insensitive if their spending is above that amount. The NMES data imply that only 11 percent of nonaged insurance units spend 20 percent or more of their income on health care but that 64 percent of total spending is spent by that 11 percent. A major risk insurance policy with a 50-percent coinsurance rate and a 10-percent of income maximum out-of-pocket amount can therefore reduce excessive spending by shrinking the spending of the 89 percent of insurance units who collectively spend 36 percent of the total health dollars.

An alternative major risk insurance policy that combines a 50-percent coinsurance rate with a 15-percent of income maximum out-of-pocket limit implies that individuals would be sensitive on incremental spending if they spend less than 30 percent of their income on health care. According to the NMES data, such a major risk insurance policy would be able to shrink the spending of 92 percent of insurance units who spend 45 percent of total health spending.

The effect on health care spending of raising coinsurance rates from current levels to 50 percent depends on the price elasticity of demand for health care. Because there is considerable uncertainty surrounding the value of this elasticity, the analysis in this paper examines the implications of elasticities of 0.33 and 0.50. We believe that these values are likely to be relatively modest as estimates of the long-run response of the health care system to changes in coinsurance rates.[9]

Our analysis assumes that spending in excess of 10 percent of income reverts to the spending under the current insurance coverage. Almost all people with private group insurance are already at a zero coinsurance rate when their gross medical spending reaches 20 percent of income, the level at which the 10-percent maximum out-of-pocket limit in the alternative major risk insurance policy reduces the coinsurance rate to zero. Even though the cash price is then zero, utilization is limited by a combination of provider decisions and patient concerns about the risk, discomfort, and time loss associated with increased utilization of care.[10]

Table 3 shows the effect of alternative major risk insurance policies on health care spending, with that spending decomposed to show the amount paid out-of-pocket and by the insurance company. The first line of the table shows the spending under the existing group insurance coverage as reported in the NMES data.[11] The average spending per insurance unit is $3,985 (at 1995 price levels). Of this, the average out-of-pocket spending is $747, and the remaining $3,238 is paid by the insur-

---

[9] The RAND national health insurance experiment (Manning et al., 1987; Newhouse, 1993) estimated an elasticity of health care spending with respect to the net-of-insurance cost per dollar of care of only 0.2. We believe that the RAND procedure of giving different insurance coverage to a random sample of individuals is likely to underestimate the effect on utilization of a community-wide change in coinsurance rates. Changing the policy of isolated individuals, as the Rand experiment did, may change the willingness of patients to visit a physician but will not alter the character of the care given prescribed by physicians or the sophistication of the services provided by hospitals. Earlier (nonexperimental) literature on the price elasticity of demand for health care is reviewed by Phelps (1992). Estimates of the elasticity of demand for hospital care range from −0.47 (Davis and Russell, 1972) to −0.67 (Feldstein, 1971b), and for doctor care from −0.14 (Phelps and Newhouse, 1972) to −1 (for hospital outpatient visits—Davis and Russell, 1972).

[10] This assumption is subject to two offsetting biases. First, we understate the potential gain from the major risk insurance policy by assuming (in effect) that there is only one "draw" from the distribution of medical spending per year. A more realistic picture for spending is one of a series of smaller spending decisions throughout the year. In this case, spending on the "early" events will be reduced by the 50-percent coinsurance rate under the MRI plan, even if that family eventually exceeds the maximum out-of-pocket amount. On the other hand, for some low-income individuals, the maximum out-of-pocket amount may be below the maximum that the family faced under their ex ante insurance plans. For those persons, we do not account for the fact that we are lowering their price to zero above 20 percent of their income, so that we overstate the gains from a major risk policy.

[11] Recall that we are analyzing only those nonaged individuals and families in the NMES data that have group insurance and that this subsample of the population is then re-weighted to correspond to the national nonaged population. Estimates are presented for national aggregate spending and for spending per "insurance unit." The insurance units are the actual individuals and families that are separately insured in the NMES sample.

TABLE 3.
Expenditure Effects of Alternative Major Risk Insurance Plans

| | | Average | | | Aggregate (billions) | | |
	Elasticity	Out-of-pocket expenditures	Insurance	Total	Out-of-pocket expenditures	Insurance	Total
Original		747	3,238	3,985	61.6	267.2	328.7
Plan 50–10	0	1,127	2,857	3,985	93.0	235.7	328.7
	0.33	873	2,385	3,257	72.0	196.7	268.7
	0.5	768	1,990	2,758	63.3	164.2	227.5
Plan 50–15	0	1,292	2,693	3,985	106.6	222.2	328.7
	0.33	959	2,094	3,052	79.1	172.7	251.8
	0.5	828	1,731	2,559	68.3	142.8	211.1
Plan 100–15	0	2,011	1,974	3,985	165.9	162.8	328.7
	0.33	1,367	1,665	3,032	112.8	137.3	250.1
	0.5	1,100	1,256	2,356	90.8	103.6	194.4

Note: All figures in 1995 dollars. "Average" columns refer to calculations per insurance unit; "Aggregate" columns refer to calculations for the nation as a whole, and they are in billions of dollars. See text for further details.

ers.[12] These amounts per insurance unit correspond to an aggregate spending on physician and hospital services by the nonaged population of $329 billion.

The next three lines show the effect of the basic 50–10 major risk insurance plan that has a 50-percent coinsurance rate on all spending until out-of-pocket spending reaches 10 percent of income. With a zero price elasticity, the only effect of the major risk policy is to shift the burden of the cost from the insurance company to the individuals. Aggregate out-of-pocket payments rise by 51 percent from $61.1 billion to $93.0 billion, but there is no change in the $328.7 billion total cost of care.

With a price elasticity of 0.33, aggregate total spending falls by $60 billion to $268.7 billion, a decline of 18 percent. It is striking that even though the higher coinsurance rate applies to only 36 percent of spending and the elasticity is a modest 0.33, the major risk policy reduces total spending by $60 billion a year or 18 percent of the aggregate baseline spending. Because total spending is reduced, out-of-pocket spending is only 17 percent higher, rising from $747 per insurance unit under the existing policy to $873 per insurance unit under the major risk policy.

[12] It is interesting to note that, despite that fact that the average coinsurance rate under existing private insurance plans in our sample is almost 40 percent, the average out-of-pocket amount is less than 20 percent of the average total spending. This reflects the fact that the distribution of out-of-pocket spending is even more skewed than the distribution of total spending.

A long-run price elasticity of 0.50 implies that, in the long run, a major risk policy would reduce total spending by 31 percent or $101 billion a year. With this elasticity, there is essentially no increase in out-of-pocket spending. The decline in the total spending almost exactly balances the increased share paid out of pocket, causing the out-of-pocket amount per insured to rise from $747 to only $768. The amount paid by the insurers and, therefore, the insurance premium declines by $1,248 per insurance unit or 39 percent.

Thus, even with the very skewed distribution of health spending that we now observe, the major risk structure of a high coinsurance rate and a 10 percent of income limit on out-of-pocket spending can reduce total spending very substantially and leave average out-of-pocket spending unchanged, if the demand elasticity is as high as 0.5.[13]

The next three lines of Table 3 show the effect of increasing the maximum out-of-pocket amount to 15 percent of income while keeping the coinsurance rate at 50 percent. Since this 50-percent increase in the maximum out-of-pocket limit only increases the number of cost-sensitive insurance units from 89 percent of all units to 92 percent and only increases the fraction of spending that is cost-sensitive from 36 percent to 45 percent, the effect on total spending is relatively small. With a price elasticity of 0.5, aggregate total spending is $211 billion or $16 billion less than with a 10 percent of income out-of-pocket limit. Average out-of-pocket spending rises to $828.

One final alternative worth considering is a deductible plan. The last three lines refer to a plan with a deductible (i.e., a 100-percent co-insurance rate) equal to 15 percent of family income. The insured are subject to the same maximum risk as under the 50–15 plan but are sensitive over a much smaller range of costs (up to 15 percent of income instead of 30 percent). Although the sensitivity range is smaller, the 100-percent coinsurance rate makes the individuals more responsive within this range. This greater sensitivity does outweigh the narrower range of sensitivity, causing total spending to be nearly $17 billion lower under the 100–15 plan than under the 50–15 plan. Although this total cost saving is achieved without exposing individuals to a higher maximum out-of-pocket spending than under the 50–15 plan, the use of the deductible rather than the 50-percent coinsurance rate increases the average out-

---

[13] Such a program would also affect the incentive to earn and report income, since higher income implies a higher copayment rate under the MRI plan. For the average person, however, the disincentive is likely to be small; as shown in Table 4, average out-of-pocket expenditures do not rise very steeply with income. This disincentive is largest for the person who will exceed his or her out-of-pocket maximum with certainty; under our 50–10 plan, this would imply a 10-percent marginal tax rate on additional income.

TABLE 4.

Effects of the 50–10 Major Risk Insurance Plan by Income Category

	Elasticity	Average			Aggregate (billions)		
		Out-of-pocket expenditures	Insurance	Total	Out-of-pocket expenditures	Insurance	Total
Below poverty							
Original plan		1,304	4,089	5,392	10.8	33.7	44.5
Plan 50–10	0	421	4,971	5,392	3.5	41.0	44.5
	.33	389	4,905	5,294	3.2	40.5	43.7
	.5	370	4,624	4,995	3.1	38.2	41.2
Between poverty and twice poverty							
Original plan		610	3,469	4,079	9.2	52.1	61.3
Plan 50–10	0	908	3,171	4,079	13.6	47.7	61.3
	.33	768	2,798	3,567	11.5	42.1	53.6
	.5	692	2,321	3,013	10.4	34.9	45.3
Between twice poverty and $75,000							
Original plan		647	2,773	3,421	28.3	121.1	149.5
plan 50–10	0	1,078	2,342	3,421	47.1	102.4	149.5
	.33	844	1,883	2,726	36.9	82.3	119.2
	.5	743	1,540	2,283	32.5	67.3	99.8
Above $75,000							
Original plan		863	3,872	4,735	13.4	60.1	73.5
Plan 50–10	0	1,854	2,881	4,735	28.8	44.7	73.5
	.33	1,312	2,058	3,371	20.4	31.9	52.3
	.5	1,122	1,538	2,659	17.4	23.9	41.3

Note: All figures in 1995 dollars. "Average" columns refer to calculations per insurance unit; "Aggregate" columns refer to calculations for the nation as a whole, and they are in billions of dollars. Each block of the table refers to the effect on insurance units in that income bracket.

of-pocket spending from $828 per insurance unit to $1,100 per insurance unit. This is because the deductible plan increases the out-of-pocket spending in the more likely part of the spending distribution.

Before presenting an explicit welfare analysis that combines the effects of the reduced distortion (i.e., the lower total spending) and the changes in individual risk bearing, we look briefly at the way that the major risk policies affect individuals at different income levels.

3. HOW DOES MAJOR RISK INSURANCE AFFECT DIFFERENT INCOME GROUPS?

Because the maximum out-of-pocket payment is limited to 10 percent of income, the major risk policy pays substantially more for lower-income individuals and families than it does for higher-income groups. In comparison with the existing structure of insurance, the result is a substantial redistribution in favor of lower-income groups. This redistribution is in addition to any redistribution that occurs in extending coverage to those low-income individuals who are currently uninsured.

Table 4 divides the population into four different income groups and shows for each group the patterns of spending under the existing insurance coverage and under the 50–10 major risk plan. Before one examines the effects of the major risk insurance, it is worth noting that the average level of spending under the initial insurance coverage differs substantially among the four income groups. The group of individuals below poverty has by far the highest initial level of spending per insurance unit. This may be a reflection of the way that these data are constructed rather than an accurate picture of the spending of below-poverty groups in the population as a whole. The data presented here are based on the rather unlikely combination of being below poverty but still insured by a private group policy. One way that individuals might find themselves in such a situation is by becoming very ill while working for a firm that provides group insurance, causing them to leave their jobs, but retain their health insurance.[14] This distortion of the baseline spending pattern changes the specific numerical values presented in the current section but does not alter the basic conclusion that major risk policies are particularly favorable to lower-income individuals.[15]

[14] Federal legislation under the Consolidated Omnibus Reconciliation Act of 1986 (CO-BRA) mandated that individuals who left jobs where they were covered by health insurance plans could continue to purchase that insurance at the average group rate. Huth (1991) and Long and Marquis (1992) find that such continuation coverage is in fact taken up by the sickest job leavers.

[15] As a check on the results in this section, we have prepared estimates of the distributional effect of the income-related out-of-pocket maximum for a "synthetic" population that is

Two features stand out in Table 4. First, the average out-of-pocket spending under the major risk plan rises very sharply as income rises, reflecting the fact that the maximum out-of-pocket spending rises in proportion to income. With no behavioral response, the average out-of-pocket spending rises from $421 in the below-poverty group to $908 in the group between poverty and twice poverty and eventually to $1,854 in the highest income group. In the lowest income group, the average out-of-pocket spending under the major risk plan is less than one-third of the baseline level under the ex ante insurance policy, while in the highest income group the average spending under the major risk plan is more than twice the baseline level.

Although the behavioral response to higher coinsurance diminishes the strength of this effect, it remains true even with a price elasticity of 0.5. Out-of-pocket spending goes from less than one-third of the baseline level in the below-poverty group to 30 percent above the baseline level in the highest income group.

The second noticeable feature is that the major risk plan reduces the total consumption of health care much more for high-income individuals than for lower-income individuals. This reflects the fact that the higher coinsurance rate applies to an increasing share of spending as income rises. With a price elasticity of 0.5, the lowest income group sees total aggregate health spending decline by only 7.4 percent (from $44.5 billion to $41.2 billion). Among those with incomes between poverty and twice poverty, health spending declines by 26 percent, and in the highest income group, it declines by 44 percent. Thus, the MRI plan reduces total spending in a way that favors lower-income individuals or families.

4. THE WELFARE ECONOMICS OF MAJOR RISK INSURANCE[16]

Substituting a major risk policy for existing health insurance has two effects on individual welfare. It reduces the deadweight loss that results

---

assumed to have the same random distribution of spending for each demographic group regardless of income, thus purging the data of the problematic correlation between spending and income documented in Table 3. The method of doing this analysis and the results are presented in the Appendix to this paper. Those results confirm the general characteristics described in this section of the paper.

[16] This section follows the approach developed in Feldstein (1973). A major difference is that the current paper uses the actual distribution of gross spending, while Feldstein (1973) used very aggregate data to estimate the probability of hospital admission and the parameters of a gamma distribution that was taken to represent the conditional distribution of spending. In order to make the analysis tractable with the resulting mixed poisson-gamma distribution process, the utility function had to be assumed to be one of constant absolute risk aversion.

from the excessive consumption of health care services induced by the very low marginal cost of care under existing insurance policies. It also alters the risk distribution that the individual faces, increasing the risk of modest spending but limiting the maximum risk. The reduction in the deadweight loss is an unambiguous benefit, while the sign of the welfare effect of the change in the risk distribution is ex ante ambiguous, depending on the distribution of health care spending and on the individual's utility function.[17]

We simplify the welfare calculations by assuming that the two welfare effects can be evaluated separately and added together. We also convert the welfare changes into equivalent income variations and then aggregate by adding those equivalent income variation measures over all insurance units in the population.

4.1 The Reduced Distortion of Health Care Spending

Figure 1 shows our approach to measuring the individual gain from reduced distortion. We measure the unit of health care so that its price in the absence of insurance is 1.[18] The existing insurance policy has a coinsurance rate of P_0, which is the net of insurance price to the consumer. Conditional on the individual's medical condition, the individual consumes E_0 units of care. The deadweight loss caused by the induced increase in health spending is given by the area of the triangle ACD.

The major risk policy raises the coinsurance rate for that individual to P_1 (if the resulting out-of-pocket cost is below the maximum out-of-pocket amount) and reduces the consumption of health care to E_1. This reduces the deadweight loss by the shaded area BCDE, which is equal to $(E_0 - E_1)*(1 - P_1) + 0.5*(P_1 - P_0)*(E_0 - E_1)$.

The reduction in the deadweight loss implied by the simple analysis of Figure 1 varies from individual to individual, depending on the individual's medical condition and, therefore, on the initial level of health care spending, E_0. For each individual, the reduction in the deadweight loss is readily calculated for any major risk coinsurance rate (P_1) on the basis of the available data (E_0 and P_0 as reported in the NMES survey) and the assumed price elasticity of demand since $E_1 = E_0 (P_0/P_1)^\epsilon$ where ϵ is the

---

[17] Even in a world where most households have reached the point of zero copay under their old plans by the time that they hit their MRI out-of-pocket maximum (as assumed earlier), MRI can still lower their risk because it reduces the amount of spending below the max. Consider the example of the person with $20,000 of income and a $2,500 deductible. This person will be sensitive to medical spending for a greater range under the MRI plan (up to $4,000) but will face a lower out-of-pocket risk (the maximum MRI expenditure being $2,000).

[18] Our analysis assumes that health care services are supplied at constant cost so that no change in producers' surplus need be taken into account.

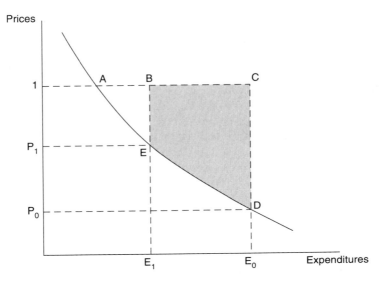

FIGURE 1: *The Deadweight Loss of Excess Insurance*

absolute value of the price elasticity. As noted earlier, if the individual's spending is over the maximum out-of-pocket level, our analysis assumes that the major risk insurance policy has no effect on utilization and, therefore, no effect on the deadweight loss.[19]

Even at our highest elasticity assumptions, there is a further reason why our calculation may understate the gain from reduced spending in the long run. The initial level of spending may exceed what consumers would really want even at the initial price because the physicians who make the detailed health care choices, instead of acting as the agents of their patients, prescribe additional care. Such excessive care could arise because of a concern about medical malpractice, physician preferences for practicing a technically more sophisticated style of medical care, or because it is in the physician's own financial interest to prescribe more extensive care. With increased patient cost sharing, patient sensitivity to the increased costs of care arising from such physician behavior may counteract these supply side tendencies.

---

[19] Once again, our analysis may understate the potential gain from the major risk insurance policy by assuming that there is only one "draw" from the distribution of medical spending per year. A more realistic picture in which spending for the year is the result of a series of spending decisions creates the possibility that total spending will be reduced even though the individual eventually spends enough to exceed the maximum out-of-pocket limit since the "early" spending decisions in the year were influenced by the high coinsurance rate.

4.2 The Change in Risk Bearing

To calculate the effect of the change in the individual's risk bearing, we ask, for each insurance unit in our sample, what that unit would have to be paid to assume the additional risk implied by the increased coinsurance rate (or would pay if the risk-limiting effect of the maximum out-of-pocket limit outweighs the increased risk of the higher coinsurance rate). We then aggregate these amounts over the population as a whole.

More formally, we assume that each individual has utility that is a function of net nonhealth consumption, defined as the difference between that individual's income (Y^i) and the random out-of-pocket expenditure X_0^i: that is, $U(Y^i - X_0^i)$. Thus, the expected utility of the individual is $\mathbf{E}\{U(Y^i - X_0^i)\}$ where the expectation is over the different possible values of X_0^i. The uncertain distribution of out-of-pocket payments can be summarized by the certainty equivalent C_0^i, a fixed amount such that $U(Y^i - C_0^i)\}. = \mathbf{E}\{U(Y^i - X_0^i)\}$.

The shift to the major risk policy replaces each individual's out-of-pocket distribution X_0^i with a new out-of-pocket distribution X_1^i. Since the difference between the mean values of X_0^i and X_1^i is simply a transfer between the insured and the insurer, we calculate the certainty equivalence of the new out-of-pocket risk distribution with an adjustment ($\mu_1^i - \mu_0^i$) to make the mean of the new risk distribution equal to the mean value of the initial distribution (i.e., we evaluate the mean preserving spread in risk). Thus, we define the certainty equivalence payment C_1^i as: $\mathbf{E}\{U(Y^i - X_1^i + \mu_1^i - \mu_0^i)\} = U(Y^i - C_1^i)$.

The difference between the two certainty equivalence values, $C_1^i - C_0^i$, measures the change in the value that the individual attributes to risk bearing. We add these certainty equivalence differences over individuals just as we added the value of the reduced distortion.

To make this approach operational, we need to specify a particular utility function and a method of calculating expected utility. Our analysis uses the constant relative risk aversion utility function $U(Z) = -(1/\rho) Z^{-\rho}$, which implies that the relative risk aversion is $-U''/Z U' = \rho + 1$. A special case of this, the logarithmic utility function $U(Z) = \ln Z$, corresponds to $\rho = 0$. For our numerical calculations, we examine two values of risk aversion: the logarithmic case with constant relative risk aversion of 1 and the more risk averse case with constant relative risk aversion of 3 ($\rho = 2$). These values essentially contain the range of estimated coefficients of relative risk aversion in the macroeconomics literature (Zeldes, 1989).

To calculate expected values, we first create distributions of spending under the existing insurance for each of four demographic types of insurance units in our NMES data: single adults, single adults with children, couples, and couples with children. To create each distribution, we rank all of the observations of that demographic type, divide the rank list into 100 equal intervals, and assign a probability of 0.01 to each interval. To calculate the expected utility for each individual under the initial insurance, $E \, U \, \{Y - X_0\}$, we draw 50 observations from the relevant demographic distribution and calculate the average utility for that insurance unit (given its income). In this way we combine the (reweighted) income distribution of the NMES data and the demographic-specific cumulative frequency distributions of spending.[20] To calculate expected utility for any major risk insurance plan, we repeat the same process with the additional step of transforming the out-of-pocket spending from the initial level to the level corresponding to the major risk coinsurance rate and elasticity of demand.

4.3 Results

The results of the analysis are presented in Table 5 for the three major risk plans and demand elasticity values that we considered in Table 3 and for the two different measures of constant relative risk aversion. Consider first the welfare gain from reducing the insurance-induced distortion of demand. The first row of the table is based on the 50–10 major risk plan with a zero price elasticity of demand and a constant relative risk aversion of 1. Since the zero price elasticity implies that shifting from existing insurance to the major risk plan involves no change in behavior, there is no welfare gain from reduced distortion. With a demand elasticity of 0.33, shown in the next row, there is a reduced distortion. The reduced deadweight loss is equal to $534 per insurance unit, approximately 13 percent of the initial spending level and 73 percent of the reduced spending shown in Table 3. A demand elasticity of 0.5 increases the value of the reduced distortion to $902 per insurance unit.

The major risk plan with a 50-percent coinsurance rate but a wider range of sensitivity corresponding to a maximum out-of-pocket limit of 15 percent of income causes slightly greater reductions in distortion. With an elasticity of 0.5, the value of the reduced distortion is $1,045 per insurance unit (instead of the $902 reported for the 50–10 policy.)

---

[20] Our method assumes that the distribution of spending within each demographic group is independent of the level of income. An alternative procedure of grouping individuals by broad income group as well as demographic group would allow us to relax this assumption, but, by giving us a smaller sample for each group, would make the resulting distribution less reliable. Because of the importance to our analysis of the relatively infrequent large expenditures, we have chosen to use the larger samples to calculate the cumulative distributions for each demographic group rather than recognizing the possible relation between income and spending.

TABLE 5.
Welfare Economics of Alternative Plans

Plan	Elasticity	Per Family Reduced distortion	Per Family Increased risk	Per Family Net gain or loss	Aggregate net gain or loss (billions)
CRRA 1					
50–10	0	0	317	−317	−26.2
	.33	534	118	416	34.3
	.5	902	42	860	71.0
50–15	0	0	534	−534	−44.1
	.33	683	288	395	32.6
	.5	1,045	201	844	69.6
100–15	0	0	1,306	−1,306	−107.7
	.33	426	973	−547	−45.1
	.5	735	504	230	19.0
CRRA 3					
50–10	0	0	−154	154	12.7
	.33	534	−362	896	73.9
	.5	902	−442	1,344	110.9
50–15	0	0	105	−105	−8.7
	.33	683	−158	841	69.4
	.5	1,045	−252	1,297	107.0
100–15	0	0	923	−923	−76.1
	.33	426	570	−144	−11.9
	.5	735	72	663	54.7

Note: All figures in 1995 dollars. CRRA is the level of constant relative risk aversion. Reduced distortion is the reduction in deadweight loss from reduced spending; increased risk is the (potential) increase in the certainty equivalent of the higher risk that individuals bear under the plan. Negative numbers indicate reduced risk in risk column, and a net welfare loss in the net gain or loss column. See text for additional details.

Replacing the 50-percent coinsurance rate with a deductible equal to 15 percent of income (the 100–15 plan) causes lower average levels of spending (as indicated in Table 3) but reduces the average deadweight loss of distortion by less. For example, with an elasticity of 0.5 the 50–15 plan reduces average spending relative to the initial level by $1,426, while the 100–15 plan reduces average spending $1,629. In contrast, the value of the reduced distortion associated with the 50–15 plan is $1,045, while the value of the reduced distortion associated with the 100–15 plan is only $735. The reason that the deductible reduces spending by more but the deadweight loss by less is that deductibles reduce spending within a smaller range. Since some of the spending in that range was valued by the consumer, the reduced DWL per dollar of reduced spending is smaller. That is, it is more efficient to maintain a high price on the marginal dollar of spending than to cut spending deeply over a small range, with a price of zero above that range.

To assess the overall welfare effect of shifting from existing insurance to a major risk plan, these reductions in deadweight loss must be combined with assessments of the change in risk. Consider first the case of the 50–10 major risk plan with logarithmic utility function (CRRA = 1). If the demand elasticity is zero (the first row of Table 5), each individual faces the increased risk associated with a higher coinsurance rate up to the maximum out-of-pocket limit but then may have less risk than under the existing ordinary insurance plan. On average, individuals would be indifferent between the new and riskier distribution and the initial distribution plus a certainty equivalent charge of $317. The net welfare effect of the major risk insurance plan when individuals have a zero demand elasticity, therefore, is an average loss of $317 per insurance unit.

The next row of Table 5 shows that the result is quite different when the individuals have a demand elasticity of 0.33. The reduced distortion of $534 outweighs the increased risk valued at $317, producing a net gain of $217 per insurance unit. This understates the true net welfare gain associated with the elasticity of 0.33 because the behavioral response reduces the amount of out-of-pocket risk relative to what it would be with no behavioral response (as well as reducing the distortion in total spending.) Although the net out-of-pocket risk remains greater with the 50–10 plan than with the existing plan, the combination of the greater coinsurance rate and the reduction in total spending implies that the increased risk has a certainty equivalent change of only $118. This is shown in the second column of Table 5. Subtracting the value of the increased risk from the value of the reduced distortion leaves a net gain of $416 per insurance unit. Since there are 82.5 million insurance units, this implies an aggregate welfare gain of $34.3 billion (shown in the last column of Table 5).

An elasticity of 0.5 implies not only a greater reduction in distortion ($902 per insurance unit) but also a much smaller increase in risk ($42 per insurance unit), implying a net gain from shifting to the 50–10 major risk policy of $860 per insurance unit and an aggregate net gain of $71.0 billion.

Although extending the sensitivity range by increasing the maximum out-of-pocket amount to 15 percent of income (the 50–15 major risk plan) reduces distortion by more than the 50–10 plan, the gain from this source is not enough to outweigh the increased risk bearing when the demand elasticity is 0.5 or less. With an elasticity of 0.5, the reduced distortion is $1,045, and the increased risk bearing is $201, implying a net gain of $844, slightly below the $860 net gain of the 50–10 plan. Comparing the two plans shows that the gap decreases as the demand elasticity increases, from a gap of $217 with no behavioral response to $21 when the demand elasticity is 0.33 and $16 when the demand elasticity is 0.5. The 50–15 plan only produces a greater benefit when the demand elasticity exceeds 0.65.

Substituting a deductible for the 50-percent coinsurance rate is clearly inferior. Not only is the reduced distortion less for each demand elasticity, as noted above, but the value of the increased risk is also greater.

The lower half of the table considers the welfare effects if individuals are substantially more risk averse (a constant relative risk aversion of $\rho + 1 = 3$.) The striking difference between the logarithmic utility function and this case is that there is actually *reduced* risk bearing in the cases of 0.33 and 0.5 elasticity, with both the 50–10 and 50–15 plans. That is, in these cases, the reduced risk associated with the maximum out-of-pocket limit now outweighs the increased risk below that limit.

In fact, even with no behavioral response, the increased protection afforded by the 10 percent of income limit on out-of-pocket expenses outweighs the shift to the 50-percent coinsurance rate under the 50–10 plan and produces a net gain of $154 per insurance unit. With a zero price elasticity, individuals would on average be indifferent between the out-of-pocket risk distribution of the 50–10 major risk policy and the combination of the current insurance policy and paying a fixed lump sum of $154.

An increase in the price elasticity of demand shrinks the amount of risk with the 50–10 plan and therefore makes the risk reduction even greater; with an elasticity of 0.5, the reduced risk of the 50–10 plan is worth $442 per insurance unit. Combined with the distortion reduction worth $902 per insurance unit, the total gain is $1,344 per insurance unit or an aggregate of $110.9 billion.

The greater risk aversion does not alter the relative attractiveness of the three major risk plans. The 50–10 plan still has a greater welfare gain than the 50–15 plan or the 100–15 plan.

Given the plausible range of risk aversion values that we have considered, the analysis of this section implies that the net overall welfare gain of the 50–10 major risk plan is between $34.3 billion (with demand elasticity of 0.33 and relative risk version of 1.0) and $110.9 billion (with a demand elasticity of 0.50 and relative risk aversion of 3.0). The shift to a 50–10 major risk plan would reduce aggregate welfare only with low-risk aversion (which reduces the value of the limit on out-of-pocket spending) and a low elasticity of demand (so that the reduced distortion is small and the distribution of coinsurance payments is not reduced by the major risk plan).

5. ELIMINATING THE TAX EXCLUSION TO FINANCE GOVERNMENT PROVIDED MAJOR RISK INSURANCE

The effects of major risk insurance on health care spending and the welfare gains from substituting a major risk plan for existing insurance would be obtained if the major risk policies are privately selected or if they are provided by the government. Eliminating the current income tax exclusion for employer paid health insurance premiums[21] or providing for tax deductible payments for out-of-pocket expenses[22] might be enough to cause individuals and their employers to choose major risk-type insurance policies. Alternatively, major risk insurance might be provided by the government, as originally suggested in Feldstein (1971a).

This section examines the net cost to the government of financing alternative major risk insurance plans as a function of the elasticity of demand. Table 3 showed that the cost of providing the major risk insurance depends on the design of the insurance and on the elasticity of demand for services. The 50–10 plan with no induced change in demand for health services would have a total cost of $328.7 billion of which $93.0 billion would be paid out of pocket by individuals at the time of care and the remaining $235.7 billion would be paid by the insurer. If, however, the demand elasticity is 0.5, the total cost of a 50–10 plan would be only $227.5 billion of which the insurer would pay $164.2 billion.

If the government were to provide major risk insurance without charge to the entire population, employers would no longer have a reason to provide compensation in the form of health insurance.[23] These

---

[21] Excluding employer paid health insurance from taxable income gives individuals a strong incentive to pay for health care through insurance and, therefore, to have low coinsurance rates. See Congressional Budget Office (1994) or Gruber and Poterba (1994b) for an analysis of recent legislative proposals to eliminate or limit the exclusion of employer-paid health insurance. For earlier discussions of employer payments for health insurance in taxable wage and salary income, see Feldstein (1973), Feldstein and Allison (1974) and Feldstein and Friedman (1977).

[22] Tax deductibility of the out-of-pocket payments could be done directly or through tax-deductible contributions to health savings accounts of the type that have recently been proposed. Either way would eliminate the current incentive to buy all health care through insurance.

[23] Indeed, it would also be necessary to preclude additional insurance by individuals since individuals who insured the coinsurance part of the major risk policies would be increasing the value of those policies and the expected cost of providing them. (On the impact of supplementary insurance on the cost of Medicare, see Pauly [1974].) Alternatively, individuals could be permitted to purchase additional insurance but only by paying a supplementary premium that reflects the additional cost of the major risk insurance. It is for this reason that having a publicly provided MRI policy would require removing the exclusion

premiums would then be converted to wage and salary income and, therefore, would be subject to income tax and FICA payroll tax. Calculations using the NMES data and the NBER's TAXSIM model indicate that this would raise $79.0 billion in federal taxes at 1995 levels.[24] Eliminating as well the deduction for medical expenditures in excess of 7.5% of AGI is estimated to reduce the government's tax expenditures by $4.1 billion in 1995 (Committee on Ways and Means, 1993).

The introduction of major risk insurance would also affect the outlay side of the federal budget in two important ways. First, the major risk policy would replace the existing Medicaid program for those below age 65 and the nondisabled. In 1995, this is a projected $50 billion, or one-third of total federal and state Medicaid spending.[25] Second, the increased cost sensitivity of the nonaged population would alter the cost structure of hospitals and the standards for treating different medical conditions. These standards would presumably spill over to the treatment of the Medicare population, lowering the government costs of that program as well. If one assumes that Medicare costs declined in the same proportion as total "private" health care spending (i.e., the spending by the population covered by major risk insurance), the reduced spending on health care would bring substantial savings in federal outlays. For example, with an elasticity of 0.33 the 50–10 plan reduces total private spending from $328.7 billion under the existing health insurance plan to $268.7 billion, a decline of 18 percent. Applying this same decline to the $174 billion of federal spending on Medicare implies an annual saving of $31.3 billion at 1995 levels.[26] This reduction in spending would not only be a source of financing for the major risk plan but also an improvement in resource allocation since these government insurance

---

from taxable income of medical expenses above 7.5% of AGI; this acts as a form of reinsurance which would undercut the gains from MRI.

[24] Evidence in favor of the substitutability between benefits and cash wages is provided in Gruber (1994) and Gruber and Krueger (1991). The NMES data indicate the dollar amount of the health insurance premiums paid by employers for each health insurance unit in 1987. We have adjusted this to 1995 levels by the actual and projected growth of health care spending per capita. Using the income data in the NMES and the NBER's TAXSIM program, we then calculated the revenue gain that would result from converting these employer-paid health premiums to wage and salary income.

[25] We do not consider MRI's effects on the remainder of the Medicaid program, since most spending on the aged consists of nursing home costs. There may be some effect on the medical treatment of the disabled, leading to an understatement of the federal and state Medicaid savings in our calculations.

[26] We recognize, of course, that any savings in either private spending or government programs would only evolve over a number of years. We state these figures in terms of 1995 dollars even though they would only be fully achieved several years later.

programs induce an excess provision of health services in the same way that private insurance does.

Combining the $83.1 billion increase in tax revenue and the $81.3 billion reduction in government spending provides $164.4 billion toward the $196.7 billion total cost of providing a 50–10 major risk insurance plan with an elasticity of 0.33. Although using the income tax or payroll tax to finance the remaining cost of $32.3 billion a year (see line 2 of Table 6) would involve new sources of deadweight loss, this loss would almost certainly be less than the $34.3 billion aggregate welfare gain associated with the shift to a major risk insurance policy (see line 2 of Table 5). Even this deadweight loss of financing cost could be avoided by using a compulsory fixed-price insurance premium. With 82 million insurance units, the cost of financing the $32.3 billion shortfall would be slightly less than $400 per year.

Although we have not done a formal analysis, we suspect that a major risk policy with a $700 premium would leave almost all taxpayers better off than they are today, a reflection of the substantial overall net welfare gain of $34.3 billion. The tangible form of this benefit would be a large increase in net of tax wages (since employers would no longer be spending an average of about $3,200 a year on insurance premiums) and a possible gain through reduced risk bearing if the individuals are sufficiently risk averse.

A higher price elasticity of demand for health services reduces the government's net financing costs even further. Indeed, row 3 of Table 6 shows that with a demand elasticity of 0.5 the 50–10 major risk plan could be completely financed by a combination of taxing the wages and salaries that result from eliminating private insurance and the savings in federal government outlays that occur from reduced Medicare and Medicaid spending. The higher demand elasticity reduces the insurer's cost to only $164.2 billion, and this is more than offset by the combination of the $83.1 billion in additional revenue and the $102.8 billion in Medicare and Medicaid savings.

6. CONCLUSIONS

The analysis presented in this paper shows that a health insurance plan that has a 50-percent coinsurance rate but limits out-of-pocket spending to 10 percent of income can substantially reduce total medical spending, even though a substantial part of health outlays are incurred by families spending 10 percent or more of family income on health care.

The change in health care spending reduces the deadweight loss that now results because low coinsurance rates induce excessive consump-

TABLE 6.
Eliminating the Tax Exclusion to Finance MRI Plans

($ Billions)

Plan	Elasticity	Insurance cost	Eliminating tax exclusion	Eliminating tax expenditures	Eliminating Medicaid below age 65	Medicare cost reductions	Net cost
50–10	0	235.7	79.0	4.1	50.0	0.0	102.6
	.33	196.7	79.0	4.1	50.0	31.3	32.3
	.5	164.2	79.0	4.1	50.0	52.8	−21.7
50–15	0	222.2	79.0	4.1	50.0	0.0	89.1
	.33	172.7	79.0	4.1	50.0	40.1	−0.5
	.5	142.8	79.0	4.1	50.0	61.4	−51.7
100–15	0	162.8	79.0	4.1	50.0	0.0	29.7
	.33	137.3	79.0	4.1	50.0	41.0	−36.8
	.5	103.6	79.0	4.1	50.0	70.1	−99.6

Note: All figures in 1995 dollars. See text for details.

tion of health care. The combination of this reduction in the deadweight loss of excessive health care spending and the change in the risk of out-of-pocket spending represents a net welfare gain under most plausible assumptions about demand elasticities and risk aversion.

Our estimates of the aggregate welfare gain from shifting to the 50–10 major risk policy (a 50-percent coinsurance rate and a 10 percent of income maximum out of pocket payment) range from $34 billion with a low degree of risk aversion (a logarithmic utility function) and a low price elasticity of demand (0.33) to $110 billion with a higher degree of risk aversion (a constant relative risk aversion of 3) and higher demand elasticity (0.5).

We show that, with a demand elasticity of 0.5, universal government provision of this 50–10 major risk insurance policy could be financed by a combination of the additional tax revenue that would automatically result from the conversion to wage and salary income of the existing employer payments for health insurance and from the reduction in Medicare and Medicaid spending in parallel to the reduction in private health spending.

APPENDIX: "SYNTHETIC" POPULATION ESTIMATES

As noted in the text, a problem with our analysis by income class is that the sample of low income privately insured is not likely to be a representative group. Instead, these are most likely sick individuals whose health has impeded their earnings abilities; this is reflected in their high spending in Table 4.

Therefore, we have replicated our analysis with a "synthetic" sample that is designed to overcome this problem. The basic idea is to replace the individual's own spending with a random amount of spending that is not a function of income but that reflects the demographic-adjusted spending distribution. The method for doing so is similar to that described in Section 4.2. We begin by dividing our sample into four demographic types of insurance units: single adults, single adults with children, couples, and couples with children. We rank each observation within a demographic type by spending, divide the ranked list into 100 equal intervals, and assign a probability of 0.01 to each interval. We then assign each unit in that demographic group a spending level drawn randomly from that distribution. Both here and in Section 4.2, we have expanded the sample so that there are a sufficient number of observations in each demographic group. We do so by replicating our original sample to inflate the size to 20,000 insurance units.

The results of this analysis are presented in Table A1, which parallels the earlier Table 4. The key difference between the tables is that the

TABLE A1.
Effects of the 50–10 Major Risk Insurance Plans by Income Category Using the Pooled Distribution

	Elasticity	Average			Aggregate (Billions)		
		Out-of-pocket expenditures	Insurance	Total	Out-of-pocket expenditures	Insurance	Total
Below poverty							
Original plan		752	2,912	3,663	5.0	26.4	31.4
50–10 plan	0	403	3,260	3,663	3.5	28.0	31.4
	.33	388	3,228	3,617	3.3	27.7	31.0
	.5	378	3,193	3,571	3.2	27.4	30.6
Between poverty and twice poverty							
Original plan		775	3,076	3,851	12.7	56.7	69.4
50–10 plan	0	831	3,021	3,851	15.0	54.4	69.4
	.33	754	2,900	3,655	13.6	52.2	65.8
	.5	710	2,775	3,485	12.8	50.0	62.8
Between twice poverty and $50,000							
Original plan		721	3,150	3,871	30.0	132	161.7
50–10 plan	0	1,230	2,641	3,871	51.4	110.3	161.7
	.33	1,038	2,354	3,392	43.4	98.3	141.7
	.5	935	2,069	3,004	39.1	86.4	125.5
Above $50,000							
Original plan		938	4,489	5,427	14.6	69.7	84.2
50–10 plan	0	2,163	3,264	5,427	33.6	50.6	84.2
	.33	1,675	2,623	4,297	26.0	40.7	66.7
	.5	1,453	2,235	3,688	22.6	34.7	57.2

Note: All figures in 1995 dollars. "Average" columns refer to calculations per insurance unit; "Aggregate" columns refer to calculations for the nation as a whole, and they are in billions of dollars. Each block of the table refers to the effect on insurance units in that income bracket.

ex ante distribution of spending is now flat until the highest income group, and then somewhat higher for that group; this reflects the demographic mix of the highest income group, which is more likely to contain (high spending) married couples with children. This contrasts with the U-shaped pattern seen in Table 4.

The basic findings, however, are quite similar to those discussed in the context of Table 4: There is a substantial rise in out-of-pocket spending with income under the MRI plan, and the reduction in health care spending is much larger for higher-income than for lower-income individuals. Thus, while this approach eradicates the anomalous finding of much higher spending for low-income individuals, the basic income distribution effects of an MRI-type plan are unchanged.

REFERENCES

Agency for Health Care Policy and Research. (1991). *The 1987 National Medical Expenditure Survey.* Rockville, MD: Agency for Health Care Policy Research.

Arrow, K. J. (1963). "Uncertainty and the Welfare Economics of Medical Care." *American Economic Review* 53:941–973.

Committee on Ways and Means. (1993). *1993 Green Book.* Washington, DC: U.S. Government Printing Office.

Congressional Budget Office. (1993). *Projection of National Health Expenditures: 1993 Update.* Washington, DC: CBO.

———. (1994). *The Tax Treatment of Employment-Based Health Insurance.* Washington, DC: CBO.

Gould, J. P. (1969). "The Expected Utility Hypothesis and the Selection of Optimal Deductibles for a Given Insurance Policy." *Journal of Business* 42:143–151.

Borch, K. H. (1968). *The Economics of Uncertainty.* Princeton, NJ: Princeton University Press.

Davis, K., and Russell, L. B. (1972). "The Substitution of Hospital Outpatient Care for Inpatient Care." *Review of Economics and Statistics* 54:109–120.

Feldstein, M. (1971a). "A New Approach to National Health Insurance." *The Public Interest* 23:93–105.

———. (1971b). "Hospital Cost Inflation: A Study of Nonprofit Price Dynamics." *American Economic Review* 61:853–872.

———. (1973). "The Welfare Loss of Excess Health Insurance." *Journal of Political Economy* 81:251–280.

———, and E. Allison. (1974). "Tax Subsidies of Private Health Insurance: Distribution, Revenue Loss, and Effects." In *The Economics of Federal Subsidy Programs,* pt 8, pp. 977–994. Washington, DC: U.S. Government Printing Office.

———, and B. Friedman. (1977). "Tax Subsidies, the Rational Demand for Insurance, and the Health-Care Crisis." *Journal of Public Economics* 7:155–178.

Gruber, J. (1994). "The Incidence of Mandated Maternity Benefits." *American Economic Review* 84:622–641.

———, and A. Krueger. (1991). "The Incidence of Mandated Employer-Provided Insurance: Lessons from Worker's Compensation Insurance." In *Tax Policy and the Economy 5.* David Bradford (ed.), 1991. Cambridge, MA: The MIT Press.

————, and J. Poterba. (1994a). "The Elasticity of Demand for Health Insurance: Evidence from the Self-Employed." *Quarterly Journal of Economics* 109:701–734.

————, and J. Poterba. (1994b). "Tax Subsidies to Health Insurance and Health Care." Mimeo, MIT Department of Economics.

Huth, S. (1991). "COBRA Costs Average 150% of Active Costs." *Employer Benefits Plan Review* 46:14–19.

Laffont, J. J. (1990). *The Economics of Uncertainty and Information.* Cambridge, MA: The MIT Press.

Long, S., and M. S. Marquis. (1992). "COBRA Continuation Coverage: Characteristics of Enrollees and Costs in Three Plans." In U.S. Department of Labor, Pension and Welfare Benefits Administration, *Health Benefits and the Workforce.* Washington, DC: U.S. Government Printing Office.

Manning, W., et al. (1987). "Health Insurance and the Demand for Medical Care: Evidence from a Randomized Experiment." *American Economic Review* 77:251–277.

Mossin, J. (1968). "Aspects of Rational Insurance Purchasing." *Journal of Political Economy* 76:553–568.

Newhouse, J. (1993). *Free For All: Lessons from the RAND Health Insurance Experiment.* Santa Monica, CA: RAND Corporation.

Pashigian, B.P., L.L. Schkade, and G.H. Menefee. (1966). "The Selection of an Optimal Deductible for a Given Insurance Policy." *Journal of Business* 39:35–44.

Pauly, M. (1974). "Overinsurance and the Public Provision of Insurance: The Roles of Moral Hazard and Adverse Selection." *Quarterly Journal of Economics* 88:44–62.

Phelps, C. (1992). *Health Economics.* New York: HarperCollins.

Phelps, C. and J. Newhouse (1972). "Effects of Coinsurance: A Multivariate Analysis," *Social Security Bulletin* 35:20–29.

Smith, V.L. (1968). "Optimal Insurance Coverage." *Journal of Political Economy* 76:68–77.

Zeckhauser, R. (1970). "Medical Insurance: A Case Study of the Trade-off Between Risk Spreading and Appropriate Incentives." *Journal of Economic Theory* 2:10–26.

Zeldes, S. (1989). "Consumption and Liquidity Constraints: An Empirical Investigation." *Journal of Political Economy* 97:305–346.

HAVE TAX REFORMS AFFECTED INVESTMENT?

Jason G. Cummins
Columbia University

Kevin A. Hassett
Board of Governors of the Federal Reserve System

R. Glenn Hubbard
Columbia University and NBER

EXECUTIVE SUMMARY

We improve upon existing approaches used to estimate investment models by exploiting tax reforms as "natural experiments." We find that tax policy has an economically important effect through the user cost of capital on firms' equipment investment following major tax reforms enacted in 1962, 1971, 1981, and 1986. This effect is most pronounced for firms not in tax loss positions and, thus, more likely to face statutory tax rates and investment incentives. We also demonstrate that tax-induced variation in the user cost of capital across equipment asset classes is negatively related to asset-specific investment forecast errors following

We thank David Prince for research assistance, and Kristen Willard and Jim Poterba for helpful comments and suggestions. Cummins thanks the Center for International Business Education, the Center for Law and Economic Studies, and the Chazen Institute for financial support, and the Board of Governors of the Federal Reserve System for their hospitality during an internship. Hubbard acknowledges support from a grant from the John M. Olin Foundation to the Center for the Study of the Economy and the State of the University of Chicago and from the Federal Reserve Bank of New York. The views expressed here are those of the authors and do not necessarily reflect those of the Board of Governors of the Federal Reserve System.

major tax reforms, suggesting that ex ante knowledge of an impending tax reform can improve forecasts of investment.

1. INTRODUCTION

Economists and policy makers have long been interested in the effects of major changes in tax policy on the level and composition of business fixed investment. Indeed, many administrations have relied on investment tax policy as a tool for fiscal stimulus throughout the postwar period. Following in this tradition, President Clinton included an investment tax credit as an important component of his first tax proposal.

An informed policy debate requires estimates of the effectiveness of investment tax incentives. Providing participants in the tax policy process with estimates of the responsiveness of investment to changes in tax parameters is, however, a difficult task for two reasons. First, there is considerable debate over the "right" model of investment, complicating the definition of the theoretical link between tax parameters and the fundamental determinants of investment (e.g., the user cost of capital, tax adjusted q, internal funds, etc.). Second, much of the existing empirical literature is inconclusive (see, e.g., the survey in Chirinko, 1993).

In two papers (Cummins, Hassett, and Hubbard, 1994a,b), we investigate potential econometric problems that might have plagued the past literature. Employing techniques designed to overcome key confounding influences, we find that the familiar neoclassical model of investment—in which investment responds to changes in the net return to investing, subject to convex costs of adjusting the capital stock—describes the responses of business investment to changes in tax policy quite well. The key feature separating our work from much of the literature is that, in the past, researchers have relied upon time-series variation in investment incentives to identify investment models. This approach is appropriate only if that time-series variation in investment incentives is exogenous to aggregate investment patterns. A brief inspection of the historical experience suggests that this is not the case: Policy makers tend to introduce investment incentives when investment is perceived to be low and remove them when investment is perceived to be high (see Cummins, Hassett, and Hubbard, 1994a).

In our earlier work, we improve upon existing approaches for estimating these models by using the cross-sectional implications of *tax reforms* to identify exogenous shocks to firms' investment conditions. Major tax reforms offer "natural experiments" for evaluating the responsiveness of investment to fundamentals affecting the net return to investment because all assets are not equal in the eyes of the tax authority. Therefore, the effects of tax policy on firms depend upon the types of assets they purchase; tax reform will produce different investment incentives for firms purchasing rapidly depreciating machinery and firms investing in slowly depreciating property. We argue that this variation is likely to be exogenous, that is, not depending upon the current level of investment. Applying our approach, we find that tax policy has a significant and large effect on investment. We find very similar effects across many different specifications, over many different tax "experiments," and, in Cummins, Hassett, and Hubbard (1994b), we find that similar large tax effects can be found for many other countries.

In this paper, we focus on investment in producers' durable equipment, and extend our earlier work in several directions. First, we allow for the possibility that firms do not face statutory tax rates and investment incentives by incorporating tax loss carryforwards into our analysis.[1] Our earlier analysis assumed that all firms in our sample had equal access to tax benefits. This is, of course, a simplification. Firms who are carrying forward tax losses may not claim a credit earned today until some point in the future. One might argue that these firms should respond much less to tax incentives than firms that are able to claim credits as they are earned. We believe that identification of this effect is an important additional test of our methods. Second, we explore the usefulness of our estimates for predicting the response of aggregate investment to shifts in tax policy. If our estimates are "structural," the models' implied forecasts should provide a reasonable ex ante prediction of the impact of past tax reforms on investment. We explore this point in several ways; in addition to forecasting aggregate values, we use our parameter estimates to predict out-of-sample compositional effects of reforms across different types of capital goods.

The paper is organized as follows. Section 2 reviews the channels through which changes in tax parameters influence the user cost of capital for fixed investment, and summarizes our technique for estimating these effects. In Section 3, we briefly summarize the tax reforms we intend to study. In Section 4, we present the estimation results obtained in Cummins, Hassett, and Hubbard (1994a). In Section 5, we extend the methodology used in Section 4 to account for additional complications of the tax code, in particular the existence of tax-loss asymmetries. In Section 6, we use the estimates from the previous section to forecast the changes in outlays in categories of investment goods following each of the major U.S. postwar tax reforms. We compare these forecasts to

---

[1] See, e.g., the discussions in Auerbach (1986), Auerbach and Poterba (1987), and Altshuler and Auerbach (1990).

actual investment outcomes in order to construct evidence of the effects of the major policy changes. Section 7 concludes.

2. MODELING THE RESPONSIVENESS OF INVESTMENT TO TAX CHANGES

To summarize effects of tax parameters in investment decisions, we use the familiar user cost of capital model.[2] In this formulation, the firm equates the marginal product of capital and the shadow price of capital, c:

$$C_{i,t} = \frac{p_{i,t}(1 - \Gamma_{i,t})\,(\rho_{i,t} + \delta_{i,t} - \left(\dfrac{\Delta(p_{t+1}(1 - \Gamma_{i,t+1}))}{p_t(1 - \Gamma_{i,t})}\right))}{1 - \tau_t}, \tag{1}$$

where i and t are the firm and time indices, respectively; p is the price of capital goods relative to output; ρ is the firm's real required rate of return; δ is the rate of economic depreciation; Δ is the difference operator; τ is the corporate tax rate; and Γ is the present value of tax savings from depreciation allowances and other investment incentives. For example, with an investment tax credit at rate k:

$$\Gamma_{i,t} \equiv k_{i,t} - \sum_{s=t}^{\infty} (1 + r_s + \pi_s^e)^{-s}\,\tau_s D_{i,s}(s - t), \tag{2}$$

where r is the default risk free real rate of interest, π^e is expected inflation, and $D_{i,s}(a)$ is the depreciation allowance permitted an asset of age a.

The definition of the user cost of capital in Equation (1) makes clear that permanent changes in tax parameters can have a significant effect on the user cost of capital. We now outline an approach to estimate the responsiveness of investment to the user cost of capital. Following our (1994a) paper, we begin by considering the following general model of investment:

$$\frac{I_{i,t}}{K_{i,t-1}} = E_{i,t-1}\,(S_{i,t})\,\gamma + \epsilon_{i,t}. \tag{3}$$

---

[2] The user cost approach follows the seminal contributions of Jorgenson (1963) and Hall and Jorgenson (1967). The setup we use follows a generalization of their work that includes costs of adjustment; see, for example, Auerbach (1989) and Abel (1990).

where I and K denote investment and the capital stock, respectively; S is an underlying structural variable (e.g., the user cost of capital) or set of variables; $E_{i,t-1}$ is the expectations operator conditional on information available at time $t - 1$; and ϵ is a white noise error term reflecting optimization error by firms.

We treat expected S as observable following major tax reforms, so that, in principle, we may rewrite Equation (3) during those periods as:

$$\frac{I_{i,t}}{K_{i,t-1}} = S_{i,t}\gamma + \epsilon_{i,t}. \tag{4}$$

Given Equation (4), the deviation of (I/K) from the value linearly predictable using information available at time $t - 1$ is:

$$\frac{I_{i,t}}{K_{i,t-1}} - P_{i,t-1}\frac{I_{i,t}}{K_{i,t-1}} = (S_{i,t} - P_{i,t-1}S_{i,t})\,\gamma + \epsilon_{i,t}, \tag{5}$$

where P is a projection operator constructed from a nontax subset of the firm's information set.

To construct an estimator, we make the identifying assumption that near a tax reform we can observe expected S, in principle including the nontax elements. To avoid introducing simultaneity bias into the second-stage regression, we assume that the firm's expected value for each nontax component of S equals its value at the beginning of the previous period. For example, for the case of the Tax Reform Act of 1986, we impose the assumption that the expected interest rate in 1987 was the year-end rate for 1985. To avoid confounding timing issues, we sidestep years in which tax changes occurred. Returning to the example of the 1986 Act, we estimate a first-stage projection equation for each firm through 1985, and then construct forecasts for 1987, the first postreform year.

Returning to the model in Equation (3), and incorporating quadratic adjustment costs to the firm's profit function, one can show that current investment depends on current and future expected values of the user cost of capital (see, e.g., Auerbach, 1989). That is, a firm's investment rule is given by:

$$\frac{I_{i,t}}{K_{i,t-1}} = \mu_i + \xi E_{i,t-1}\left[\sum_{s=t}^{\infty} \omega_i^s\, c_{i,s}\right] + \epsilon_{i,t}, \tag{6}$$

where ξ and ω are technology parameters depending on adjustment costs and the long-run average of the user cost term, and c is defined as in equation (1).[3] The subscripts i and s recognize that components of c vary across firms and time.

If we assume, for simplicity that firms believe that a major tax reform is "permanent," then all future values of c are equal, so the expression may be simplified, producing a convenient substitute for S in Equations (3) and (4). It is this version that we investigate below.

3. BUSINESS TAX REFORMS

Our earlier work focused on using periods following tax reforms to estimate the cross-sectional relationship between firm investment and measures of the net return to investing (in particular, tax-adjusted q and the user cost of capital). Our focus is on "major reforms" that changed tax incentives for investment significantly and were expected to be long-lasting.

There were 13 arguably significant changes in the corporate tax code during the period we consider, beginning with the Kennedy tax cut in 1962 and ending with the Tax Reform Act of 1986. Before explaining the details of each change, it is useful to provide an overview of the trend in the corporate tax burden. The statutory corporate tax rate was reduced steadily from 52 percent in 1962 to 34 percent in 1988 except from 1968 to 1971, when a surcharge was imposed. The investment tax credit was first enacted January 1, 1962, and was in effect through the end of 1986, except for two periods from October 10, 1966, to March 9, 1967, and from April 19, 1969, to August 15, 1971. The credit was increased three times, and the number of assets eligible for the credit has expanded. Depreciation allowances became more generous, culminating in the Accelerated Cost Recovery System introduced by the Economic Recovery Tax Act of 1981, but they were subsequently limited by the Tax Equity and Fiscal Responsibility Act of 1982, which introduced the Modified Accelerated Cost Recovery System.

A more complete description of the tax reforms is as follows: The Kennedy tax cut introduced an investment tax credit for most types of equipment. The effective rate was generally 4 percent. The Revenue Act of 1964 lowered the corporate tax rate from 52 percent to 50 percent for 1964, and from 50 percent to 48 percent for 1965. The 1964 Act also modified the investment tax credit so that the credit was no longer deducted from the

---

[3] See the derivations in Auerbach (1989), Auerbach and Hassett (1992), and Cummins, Hassett, and Hubbard (1994a).

cost of the asset before computing depreciation for tax purposes, effectively doubling the benefit of the ITC. The investment tax credit was then suspended in 1966. The Revenue and Expenditure Control Act of 1968 introduced a corporate income tax surcharge of 10 percent. The investment tax credit was reinstated in 1969. In 1970, the surcharge was reduced to 2.5 percent, and the investment tax credit was eliminated. The surcharge was removed for 1971. For 1972, the investment tax credit was reintroduced, and the first major liberalization of depreciation allowances was enacted. Asset lives were shortened through the asset depreciation range (ADR) system. If one takes these changes together, the effective credit rate was generally about 7 percent. The credit was temporarily increased to 10 percent in 1975. In 1979, the corporate tax rate was lowered from 48 percent to 46 percent, and the temporary increase in the investment tax credit was made permanent. The Economic Recovery and Tax Act of 1981 provided the second major liberalization of depreciation allowances. It replaced the numerous asset depreciation classes with three capital recovery classes. Light equipment was written off over three years, other equipment over five years, and structures over 15 years. The reduction was modified one year later by repealing the accelerations in the writeoff that were to occur in 1985 and 1986, and instituted a basis adjustment of 50 percent for the credit. As a result, the effective rate was generally about 8 percent. The Tax Reform Act of 1986 reduced the corporate tax rate to 40 percent in 1987 and to 34 percent in 1988, and eliminated the investment tax credit.

Our specific criteria for identifying "major reforms" were: (1) the value of the tax wedge in the user cost of capital (that is, $(1 - \Gamma)$) must have changed in absolute value by at least 10 percent, (2) no tax shift of that magnitude occurred in either the preceding or succeeding year, and (3) the reforms were unanticipated in the year prior to the reform. Using these criteria, we identified as major tax reforms the set of tax changes occurring in legislation enacted in 1962, 1971, 1981, and 1986.

We illustrate the effects of tax reforms on investment incentives in Figures 1 and 2. The time-series variation in investment incentives is evident in Figure 1, which plots a representative tax wedge, $(1 - \Gamma)$, for equipment over the period from 1953 to 1989.[4] Figure 2 introduces the added dimension of *cross-sectional* variation in the tax wedge across asset classes, plotting $(1 - \Gamma)$ by equipment asset class (using the 22 equipment classes measured by the Commerce Department's Bureau of Economic Analysis, BEA) in each period. As the changing distribution of tax incentives in Figure 2 illustrates, tax reforms are associated not only

---

[4] The tax wedge shown is for special industrial machinery.

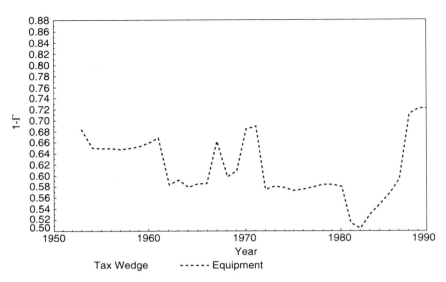

FIGURE 1. *After-Tax Cost of $1 of Investment: Equipment.*

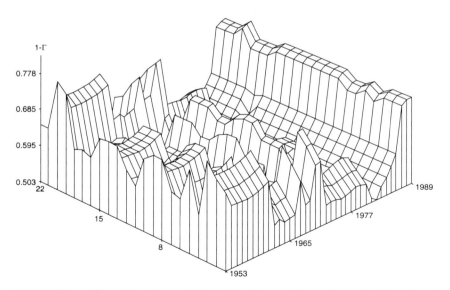

FIGURE 2. *After-Tax Cost of $1 of Equipment Investment: BEA Assets 1–22, 1953–1989.*

with increases or decreases in the *average* level of investment incentives, but also with shifts in the *distribution* of investment incentives across equipment assets. It is this cross-sectional shift in response to tax reforms that we exploit in our empirical work.

4. RESULTS FROM EARLIER WORK

Estimates of the user cost model (Equation [5]) based on firm-level data on equipment investment using firm-level data[5] are presented in Table 1. The first row of Table 1 reports results for the year following the first major tax reform in our sample, 1962.[6] The estimated coefficient on the user cost of capital (-0.605) is negative and statistically significant. Since the mean for the user cost and the ratio of investment to capital are approximately equal in our sample, this estimate implies that a 10-percent decrease in the user cost of capital will increase the equipment investment–capital ratio by about 6 percent. The next three rows report our base-case estimates for the years following subsequent major tax reforms. In each case we find very similar results: The coefficient on the cost of capital is negative and statistically significant, and implies an elasticity of investment with respect to the user cost between -0.6 and -0.75.[7]

5. FIRM TAX STATUS AND THE USER COST

In the previous section, we assumed that the firm choosing the level of investment could claim the tax benefits of investment at the time that the investment is being made. This assumption is clearly inaccurate for firms that carry forward tax losses.[8] For these firms, any tax benefits accrued

---

[5] The dataset and procedures for constructing variables are summarized in the Appendix.

[6] These estimated coefficients do not change qualitatively if lagged cash flow (relative to beginning-of-period capital stock) is added as an explanatory variable.

[7] If one assumes an average value of the user cost coefficient of -0.7 and an average user cost of 0.25, the implied cost of adjustment per dollar of equipment investment is about 30 cents. This estimated adjustment cost is significantly lower than that estimated in many earlier empirical studies (see, e.g., Summers, 1981; Fazzari, Hubbard, and Petersen, 1988).

[8] The potential empirical significance of firms in tax loss positions has been established by Cordes and Sheffrin (1983) and Auerbach and Poterba (1987). Modeling directly the effects of tax-loss carryforwards is difficult, however, as assumptions about the earnings process and effects of firm decisions on carryforward positions are required (see, e.g., Auerbach, 1986; Auerbach and Poterba, 1987). Moreover, accounting measures of tax-loss carryforwards in Compustat do not correspond precisely to measures in federal corporate income tax returns, and the incidence of tax losses in Compustat may not summarize well the incidence of tax losses for firms generally.

TABLE 1.
Estimates of User Cost Model, Major Tax Reform Years

Year	Constant	User cost of capital	$\overline{R}^2$
1963	−0.078	−0.605	0.145
(N = 107)	(2.72)	(4.21)	
1973	0.024	−0.546	0.057
(N = 267)	(1.32)	(4.00)	
1982	−0.047	−0.757	0.032
(N = 469)	(5.06)	(3.89)	
1987	0.013	−0.747	0.022
(N = 549)	(.736)	(3.32)	

Notes: t-statistics are reported in parentheses below the point estimates. The number of firms is reported in parentheses under each year. Estimates are based on the analysis of Compustat data in Cummins, Hassett, and Hubbard (1994a).

today just add to the stock of tax benefits being carried forward. The value of, say, an investment tax credit depends upon how far into the future the firm expects to have to wait before claiming the credit accrued in the current period. Strictly speaking, then, the estimated effect of the user cost of capital on investment—using the technique described earlier and grouping we have used in our earlier work—may be biased downward, since we ignored in previous work the important heterogeneity introduced by differences in tax status. In this section, we extend our previous work, testing for important differences in the responsiveness to investment fundamentals between firms that are in a tax loss position (and currently paying no federal corporate income taxes) and those that are not. We view this exercise as an important additional test of the validity of our results.

Table 2 reports the results of this experiment for each of the major tax reforms described in Section 4 except that for 1962.[9] (We do not report results for this reform, since we had almost no firms in our sample in a tax loss position at that time.) We present the estimated effect of the user cost

---

These concerns, while important, are not serious for the exercise presented here. We are using the tax loss carryforward status only as a signal of a firm's ability to claim tax credits: Sample splitting based upon prior information does not require a "perfect" measure of the existing stock of tax losses. Our split might not be informative if firms enter and exit tax loss status frequently. Studying the period from 1968 through 1984, Auerbach and Poterba (1987) find significant persistence in tax loss status, however. If our measure of tax loss status does not accurately depict the true conditions for the firms in our sample, then we should expect to see little difference between our sets of firms in the responsiveness of investment to the user cost of capital.

[9] As with Table 1, these estimated coefficients are not qualitatively different when lagged cash flow (relative to beginning-of-period capital stock) is added as a regressor.

TABLE 2.
Estimates of User Cost Model By Tax Loss Status, Major Tax Reform Years

	No tax loss carryforwards			Tax loss carryforwards		
Year	Constant	User cost of capital	$\overline{R}^2$	Constant	User cost of capital	$\overline{R}^2$
1973	−0.039	−0.656	0.131	−0.005	−0.266	0.097
	(−3.28)	(−6.21)	(N = 247)	(−0.110)	(−1.43)	(N = 20)
1982	−0.059	−1.02	0.020	−0.118	−0.303	0.010
	(−2.63)	(−2.84)	(N = 440)	(−1.18)	(−0.189)	(N = 29)
1987	0.020	−1.71	0.024	−0.082	0.698	0.005
	(1.04)	(−3.61)	(N = 495)	(−1.60)	(0.529)	(N = 54)

Note: *t*-statistics are reported in parentheses below the point estimates. The number of firms in each category is reported in parentheses in each year. The estimation technique is discussed in the text and is based on Cummins, Hassett, and Hubbard (1994a).

of capital on investment for firms with and without tax loss carryforwards in the year prior to our period of estimation. The pattern of the estimated coefficients presented in Table 2 is intuitively appealing: Within the sub-set of firms that can claim any investment incentives in the current year, the estimated coefficient is larger than in our original sample. (The estimated user cost coefficients are −0.656, −1.021, and −1.70, in the three reforms, respectively.) In addition, we find no evidence that firms with tax loss carryforwards respond to changes in the tax components of the user cost. In particular, the estimated user cost coefficients are −0.266, −0.303, and 0.698, respectively, in the three reforms; none of these estimated coefficients is significantly different from zero. This lack of responsiveness makes sense if firms expect to have to wait many years before they can claim any tax benefits.[10] Three results suggest that, in order to predict the effects of changes in investment tax policy, one will have to control explicitly for the percentage of firms that are expected to be in a tax loss position. Among those firms that are not, we find that the (absolute value of the) elasticity of the investment capital ratio with respect to the user cost of capital may even be larger than unity.[11] In addition, this split

[10] We cannot reject the hypothesis that the coefficients are the same for firms with and without tax loss carryforwards. This is because the standard errors of the estimates for the former group of firms are very large.

[11] An important additional consideration that we do not address here is the alternative minimum tax (AMT). Firms on the AMT face significantly different marginal investment incentives and, thus, may respond differently than firms not on the AMT. This difference may be of increasing importance in the early 1990s. Unfortunately, data limitations make the investigation of this issue impossible in our current study.

provides additional evidence that adjustment costs may be much lower than previous work has suggested. Our largest estimated coefficients are consistent with adjustment costs roughly equal to 15 cents for each dollar of investment.

Finally, it is worth noting that the overall fit of our equations remains low. This suggests that there may be very important omitted variables (e.g., shocks to firms' demand). Our sensitivity analysis suggests that these omitted variables are uncorrelated with the cross-sectional variation in marginal tax rates; if they were not, our results would be sensitive to inclusion of other firm fundamentals. Thus, our estimates of the likely effects of taxes are not invalidated by the low $\bar{R}^2$. On the other hand, investment is a highly volatile variable, and observation of tax effects after tax reforms may be difficult if many other things are changing at the same time. We return to this point in our forecasting discussion below.

6. OTHER AGGREGATE EVIDENCE

In this section, we explore further the plausibility of the substantial effects of tax reforms on investment documented in the previous section. The evidence suggests that forecasts of aggregate investment, adjusted to include tax effects, perform better than forecasts that exclude tax effects. We demonstrate this in an intuitive manner by using vector autoregressions to forecast investment for each of BEA's 22 classes of equipment investment in the year following a tax reform, and then compare the forecast errors for each of the assets to the changes in the user cost for that asset.[12] In Figures 3–6 (one for each major tax reform),[13] we provide plots of these forecast errors constructed from models that exclude taxes against shocks to the user cost of capital for each of the 22 equipment asset classes tracked by the BEA. In addition, we draw a

---

[12] The VAR regressions are run separately for each asset, and, in addition, two autoregressive terms include lags of aggregate output and the six-month Treasury-bill rate. The capital stock data are from the BEA, and are described more fully in Cummins, Hassett, and Hubbard (1994a). For the 1962 experiment, we used only the AR(2) terms because of the very short pre-reform sample period, which reduced the degrees of freedom for the forecasting runs.

[13] There is a difference between the years we report in the "asset experiments" (1962, 1973, 1981, and 1987) and those we report in the "firm" experiments (1963, 1973, 1982, and 1987). This is because the asset data are calculated on a calendar year basis, while the firm data are calculated on a fiscal-year basis. We have chosen the "experiment" year with this difference in the data definitions in mind. As a result, when a tax change occurs relatively early in a year, the asset data will show a response in that year. In contrast, firm data will report much of the change in the next fiscal year. Consider, for example, the Economic Recovery Tax Act of 1981. While the legislation passed on July 31, 1981, the 1982 fiscal year would capture most of the effect for most firms.

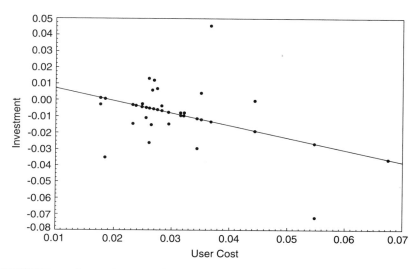

FIGURE 3. *Cross-Sectional Relationship Between Investment and User Cost Forecast Errors: 1987.*

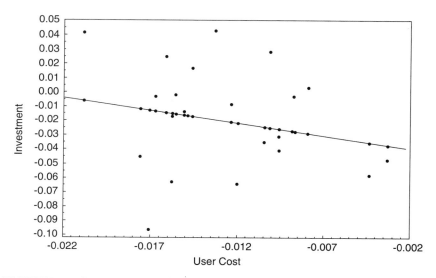

FIGURE 4. *Cross-Sectional Relationship Between Investment and User Cost Forecast Errors: 1981.*

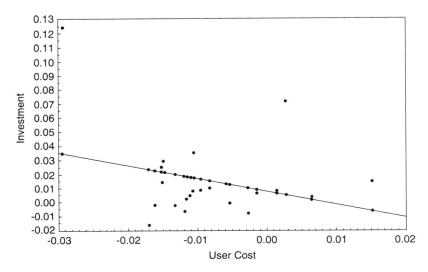

FIGURE 5. *Cross-Sectional Relationship Between Investment and User Cost Forecast Errors: 1973.*

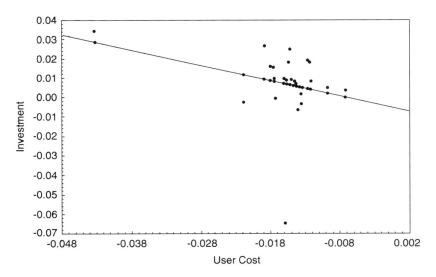

FIGURE 6. *Cross-Sectional Relationship Between Investment and User Cost Forecast Errors: 1962.*

regression line through the scatterplot. The idea is that the forecast errors for investment should be negatively correlated with the forecast errors for the user costs of capital if tax parameters are having the effects suggested by our estimates in Section 3.

These plots suggest a number of points. First, the downward-sloping line in each of the charts indicates a clear negative correlation, although the strength of the correlation varies somewhat across years. In particular, the correlation in 1981—a recession year wherein many other forces were present—appears to be weakest, whereas the correlation in 1987 is the strongest. In all cases, however, the pattern of the two errors suggest that prior knowledge of changes in tax parameters can improve forecasts of asset investment. The second important lesson from the charts is that, while the movements of investment for the individual series are consistent with the predictions of the neoclassical model, a significant amount of the variation across assets is not explained. This should come as no surprise; taxes are not the only thing changing, even in the tax reform years.

Our tax results are to some extent reassuring: A key fundamental variable that alters the marginal tradeoffs for investors is highly correlated with changes in investment. Our forecasting figures suggest, however, that tax parameters are only a piece of the puzzle, and predicting the impact of tax reform on investment remains a formidable task. Consider, for example, the constant terms in our estimated models. These capture the average "year effect" and are an indicator of the total effect on investment of all other changes in fundamentals in a given year. In almost all of our experiments, this year effect is very statistically significant and as important in magnitude as changes in tax policy. For tax reforms occurring during recessions, for example, the year effect may work in the opposite direction of the tax reform, that is, investment is lower than would have been forecast in the prior year, even though an investment tax credit was enacted. This simply reflects the fact that investment is volatile. For our sample period, using our "large"—compared with the past literature—estimated user cost coefficients, the mean absolute predicted effect of a tax reform on the ratio of investment to the capital stock is about 0.01.[14] Over our sample period, the mean of the investment-to-capital ratio is about 0.2, and the standard deviation is 0.04. Thus, the standard error of investment is roughly four times as large as the typical effect of a tax reform. While, all else equal, our estimates provide a clue about the

---

[14] This calculation assumes that tax reforms are unanticipated. The effects of temporary reforms, if anticipated, can be quite large, since they provide incentives to bunch investment in the periods where the best tax benefits are available.

responsiveness of investment to tax-induced changes in the user cost of capital, all else is seldom equal, and analysts should proceed cautiously when attempting to evaluate potential policy actions using our results.

7. CONCLUSIONS

In this paper, we find that tax policy had an economically important effect through the user cost of capital on firms' equipment investment following major tax reforms enacted in 1962, 1971, 1981, and 1986. This effect is most pronounced for firms not in tax loss positions and, thus, more likely to face statutory tax rates and investment incentives. We also demonstrate that tax-induced variation in the user cost of capital across equipment asset classes is negatively related to asset-specific investment forecast errors following major tax reforms. This correlation is consistent with the standard neoclassical model, and suggests that ex ante knowledge of an impending tax reform can improve forecasts of investment.

APPENDIX: FIRM-LEVEL DATA AND ESTIMATION

The data set used to generate the results in Tables 1 and 2 is a 36-year (1953–1988) unbalanced panel of firms from the Compustat Industrial data base. Compustat data are reported in 20-year waves, so the 1989 file is combined with the 1973 file to make a continuous panel. Variable definitions are standard except for our measure of the user cost of capital. We exploit additional firm level information in Compustat to construct more precise estimates of the user cost of capital and to add to the cross-sectional variation in the panels.

The variables used are defined as follows: Gross investment is the sum of the change in the net stock of property, plant and equipment and in depreciation. Gross equipment investment (used in estimating the user cost of capital model) is the change in the net stock of machinery and equipment grossed up by the estimated firm-specific rate of equipment depreciation (estimated as in Cummins, Hassett, and Hubbard, 1994a). The investment variables are divided by the values of their own beginning-of-period capital stocks. Where appropriate, variables are deflated by the implicit price deflator for gross domestic product.

We experimented with including additional macroeconomic variables as first-stage instruments. These included the price of investment goods, oil prices, and various interest rates (available from Citibase). We found that including additional variables had little impact on the results. For the reported results, we use the most parsimonious specification, including only lags of investment, cash flow, and a time trend.

There are several data construction issues that merit attention. The number of firms in the panel decreases in 1971. The Compustat Industrial file reports data only for those firms still in existence at the end of the 20-year reporting period. As a result, in 1971, the year in which the 1989 file begins, there are firms included in the old wave but not in the new wave. We chose to retain those firms to avoid deleting data from our relatively small beginning-of-period panels, excluding those firms that did not significantly affect the results. Additional difficulties arise in using equipment data. Data on the gross stock of equipment capital are first reported in 1969. In order to construct the gross stock of equipment capital before 1969, we multiply the firm's gross stock of property, plant, and equipment by its two-digit SIC code, year-by-year share of equipment in gross capital stock as reported by the BEA. As a result, the number of firms reported in the equipment investment models decreases in 1969, the point we begin using data on gross investment instead of calculating it.

We make two significant improvements in the construction of the user cost of capital. First, we construct firm-specific depreciation rates rather than using the one-digit SIC code depreciation rates constructed with Hulten and Wykoff (1981) depreciation data combined with aggregate capital stock weights (see Cummins, Hassett, and Hubbard, 1994a). Second, for our user cost of capital experiments, we construct a firm-specific required rate of return using Compustat data on firms' interest expense and total long-term and short-term debt.[15] These changes necessarily introduce measurement error. Despite this, we believe that the benefits of better capturing firm-specific investment incentives outweigh the cost of increased measurement error.[16]

Firm data were deleted or modified according to the following rules. If the estimated firm depreciation rate is negative or greater than unity, we set it equal to the mean for firms in the same four-digit SIC code. If the estimated interest rate is above 25 percent, we also set it equal to the mean for firms in the same four-digit SIC code. If the replacement value of the capital stock or inventory is estimated to be negative, we set it equal to book value. If dividend payouts on preferred stock are reported

---

[15] We experimented with using Compustat data on the firms' S&P debt rating and bond rating as measures of the real interest rate firms face. We opted to use the method above because Compustat reports those data items only from 1978 onward. We believe the class of debt and bond rating may provide a better measure of a firm's real interest rate but did not find that using either measure in our sample after 1978 significantly improved our results.

[16] Estimates of models with a fixed real required rate of return of 4 percent produced virtually identical results.

as missing, we set them equal to zero. If no inventory valuation method is specified, we assume the firm used the FIFO system. If multiple variation methods are reported, our calculations assume that the primary method is used.

We delete observations if the ratio of investment to the beginning-of-period capital stock is greater than unity. We also delete observations if the ratio of cash flow (or net income) to the beginning-of-period capital stock is greater than 10, in absolute value. These two rules delete observations that represent especially large mergers, extraordinarily firm shocks, or Compustat coding errors. They delete fewer than 5 percent of the firms used in first-stage estimation. Finally, we delete observations whose forecast errors from the first-stage are more than 20 times higher than the mean forecast error. These large forecast errors typically occur when there are very few observations for the firm so that forecasting is very imprecise. Again, these rules usually delete a very small fraction of the data (for about 1 percent of the firms, and never more than 5 percent). The results are not sensitive to which specific cutoff values are used.

REFERENCES

Abel, Andrew B. (1990). "Consumption and Investment." In B. M. Friedman and F. H. Hahn (eds.). *Handbook of Monetary Economics*, Vol. 2. Amsterdam: North-Holland.

Altshuler, Rosanne, and Alan J. Auerbach. (1990). "The Significance of Tax Law Asymmetries." *Quarterly Journal of Economics* 105:61–86.

Auerbach, Alan J. (1986). "The Dynamic Effect of Tax Law Asymmetries." *Review of Economic Studies* 103:205–225.

———. (1989). "Tax Reform and Adjustment Costs: The Impact on Investment and Market Value." *International Economic Review* 30:939–962.

———, and Kevin A. Hassett (1992). "Tax Policy and Business Fixed Investment in the United States." *Journal of Public Economics* 47:141–170.

———, and James M. Poterba (1987). "Tax Loss Carryforwards and Corporate Tax Incentives." In *The Effects of Taxation on Capital Accumulation*, Martin Feldstein (ed.). Chicago: University of Chicago Press.

Chirinko, Robert S. (1993). "Business Fixed Investment Spending: A Critical Survey of Modeling Strategies, Empirical Results, and Policy Implications." *Journal of Economic Literature* 31:1875–1911.

Cordes, Joseph J., and Steven M. Sheffrin. (1983). "Estimating the Tax Advantage of Corporate Debt." *Journal of Finance* 38:95–105.

Cummins, Jason G., Kevin A. Hassett, and R. Glenn Hubbard. (1994a). "A Reconsideration of Investment Behavior Using Tax Reforms as Natural Experiments." *Brookings Papers on Economic Activity* 2:181–249.

———, ———, and ———. (1994b). "Using Tax Reforms to Study Investment Decisions: An International Study." Columbia University. Mimeograph.

Fazzari, Steven M., R. Glenn Hubbard, and Bruce C. Petersen. (1988). "Financing Constraints and Corporate Investment." *Brookings Papers on Economic Activity* 1:141–195.

Hall, Robert E., and Dale W. Jorgenson. (1967). "Tax Policy and Investment Behavior." *American Economic Review* 57:391–414.

Hulten, Charles R., and Frank Wykoff. (1981). "The Measurement of Economic Depreciation." In *Depreciation, Inflation, and the Taxation of Income from Capital*, Charles R. Hulten (ed.). Washington, DC: The Urban Institute.

Jorgenson, Dale W. (1963). "Capital Theory and Investment Behavior." *American Economic Review* 53:247–259.

Summers, Lawrence H. (1981). "Taxation and Corporate Investment: A q-Theory Approach." *Brookings Papers on Economic Activity* 1:67–127.

TAXATION AND MUTUAL FUNDS: AN INVESTOR PERSPECTIVE

Joel M. Dickson
Board of Governors, Federal Reserve System

John B. Shoven
Stanford University and NBER

EXECUTIVE SUMMARY

Shareholder level taxes are taken into account in determining the performance of growth and growth and income mutual funds over the 1963–1992 period. We rank a sample of funds on a before- and after-tax basis for investors in different income classes facing various investment horizons. The differences between the relative rankings of funds on a before- and after-tax basis are dramatic, especially for middle- and high-income investors. For instance, one fund that ranks in the 19th percentile on a pretax basis ranks in the 63rd percentile for an upper-income, taxable investor. We also present an analysis of the extra taxes that shareholders bear because of the failure of mutual funds to manage their realized capital gains in such a way as to permit a substantial deferral of taxes.

This research was undertaken while Dickson was a doctoral candidate in the Department of Economics at Stanford University. The research presented and opinions expressed are solely those of the authors and do not necessarily reflect those of the Board of Governors, the Federal Reserve Banks, or other members of its staff. The authors would like to thank Victor Fuchs, John Andrew McQuown, James Poterba, Charles Schwab, William Sharpe, Mark Wolfson, and seminar participants at Stanford University, UCSD, and NBER for helpful comments and discussions. Financial support was provided by Charles Schwab & Company.

While it is not possible to determine precisely this magnitude, the extra taxes almost certainly amounted to more than $1 billion in 1993.

1. INTRODUCTION

American households invest vast sums of money in U.S. equity markets through mutual funds. According to the Federal Reserve's *Flow of Funds Accounts*, investors purchased an additional $67.1 billion in corporate equity via mutual funds in 1992 alone. By the end of 1992, individual assets in equity mutual funds totalled $466.4 billion versus $181.7 billion just five years prior. The result has been a huge demand for information about the performance of mutual funds in all types of media. Magazines such as *Consumer Reports, Forbes, Fortune, Business Week,* and *Money Magazine* frequently feature mutual fund performance rankings. Newspapers and public television cover these matters, and a small industry has developed providing newsletters and tabulated data regarding mutual funds.

Are the media and the funds themselves providing the most relevant performance information for most investors? Our answer is "no." This negative response results because tax considerations matter a great deal for most mutual fund investors, while many published performance measures and rankings ignore taxes.[1] As Table 1 suggests, a significant portion of the total assets of growth and growth and income funds are subject to shareholder level taxation. As of December 31, 1992, at least 58.6 percent of the total assets of growth and growth and income funds were subject to shareholder level taxes. In this paper we document that taxes not only affect the level of returns of equity mutual funds for taxable investors, but also that taxes dramatically affect the relative rankings of the funds.

A mutual fund's returns can be described in at least three ways. First, there is the return on the fund's underlying portfolio. Second, the gross-of-tax return is the return on the fund's portfolio after fees, loads, and bid/ask spread losses due to a fund's turnover are taken into account. This gross-of-tax return (usually without load adjustments) is the return reported by the funds themselves and used by academics and the popular press to determine mutual fund rankings. The third measure, and the

---

[1] Prior to 1993, only *Fortune* magazine regularly published after-tax returns. In general, mutual fund returns are ranked over relatively short horizons—one, three, or five years. A fund's sensitivity to the taxes of its shareholders, however, can not be easily determined over such a short horizon, since variations in pretax returns among equity mutual funds may mask the beneficial or detrimental tax management of a fund's advisor. This paper considers much longer investment horizons (10 years at a minimum) when a fund's "tax sensitivity" can be discerned with more confidence.

TABLE 1.

Mutual Fund Asset Composition of Growth and Growth and Income Funds, Year-end 1992 (millions of dollars)

Growth and growth and income funds	
Total net assets	301,496.3
IRA assets	61,729.0
Self-employed retirement plan assets	10,193.1
Other retirement plans (est.)	23,633.3
Other nontaxable institutions (est).	29,398.9
Taxable assets	176,542.0
	(58.6%)

Source: Investment Company Institute (1993).

Fiduciaries, Corporations, Retirement Plans, and Other Institutions are included in the category "Institutional Assets," which is not available by investment objective. At the end of 1992, institutional assets represented 31.73 percent of the total assets of equity, bond, and income funds. The estimate of institutional assets, therefore, is taken to be 31.73 percent of the total net assets within each classification. The estimates for retirement plans and other institutions (assumed to be tax exempt) represent each component's share in the institutional assets category.

one we argue is the relevant statistic for investors subject to shareholder level taxation, is the net-of-tax return. The net-of-tax return equals the gross return minus the amount of taxes that the shareholder must pay on dividend and realized capital gains distributions.

Many people need both pretax and posttax performance information. Consider an equity investor who is accumulating money in a tax-sheltered 401(k) pension plan and also investing after-tax income in an equity mutual fund outside the pension system. It matters a great deal which fund is used in each case, but the published information gives little, if any, guidance as to which funds have been most appropriate under each scenario. This paper provides a substantial amount of information that should be valuable to investors with both taxable and tax deferred mutual fund accounts.

Since the seminal work of Treynor (1965), Sharpe (1966), and Jensen (1968, 1969, 1972), there have been hundreds of academic papers on mutual fund performance and evaluation. One class of these papers (e.g., Kon and Jen, 1978, 1979; Lehmann and Modest, 1987; Grinblatt and Titman, 1993) compares and contrasts the myriad ways to evaluate performance relative to some benchmark. The other class of papers on this topic (e.g., Chang and Lewellen, 1984; Henriksson, 1984; Ippolito, 1989) focuses more on the opportunity cost of mutual fund investing. Topics in the second class include whether mutual funds are able to "outperform" the market through timing and selection ability and whether mutual funds offer superior returns to the market as a whole in order to offset their expenses, fees, and load charges. In the context of academic research, only Horowitz (1965), who focuses on the internal rate of return of alternative mutual fund investments, and Jeffrey and Arnott (1993), who focus on the relationship between turnover and net-of-tax performance, adjust mutual fund returns for the effects of personal taxes.

Instead of focusing solely on the pretax performance of mutual funds prevalent in both academic studies and the popular press, we will consider three different performance measures. The pretax return is relevant for those individual investors who enjoy tax-deferred status on their asset accumulations (e.g., IRA accounts). For individuals subject to shareholder level taxation, we compute posttax returns by adjusting the pretax return for any required tax payments. Posttax returns are calculated for individuals in three different tax brackets. We also calculate liquidation values for each of the three tax rates. The liquidation value is the amount that an individual would receive by selling all of her mutual fund shares and subtracting the required tax payments for previously unrealized capital gains.

The remainder of the paper proceeds as follows: Section 2 describes the data used in our analysis. Section 3 presents our basic methodology. Section 4 demonstrates how startling mutual fund performance changes can be when shareholder taxes are considered. Section 5 discusses risk-adjusting the mutual fund returns. Section 6 looks at the aggregate tax saving that might be possible if mutual funds distributed less realized capital gains and allowed shareholders to defer taxes. Section 7 examines the contention that a fund's turnover rate is related to its posttax performance, while Section 8 concludes and summarizes.

2. DATA

We compiled a data set of mutual funds using the following criteria. As of October 31, 1992, the fund must have been classified as a Growth or Growth and Income fund in the Morningstar Mutual Funds data base. Since the tax effects we wish to consider should compound over a long time horizon, we required the fund to have been in existence for at least 10 years. Each fund meeting these criteria was ranked on total net assets with the largest 150 funds chosen.[2] Our largest fund is Fidelity Magellan

---

[2] There is certainly a selection bias induced by choosing, ex post, the 150 largest funds. Since our focus is how taxes change the relative rankings of mutual funds and not on quantifying the return of a representative fund over a particular horizon, this bias should not affect our basic conclusions.

with $20.55 billion in total assets. The 150th fund, Eaton Vance Stock, had total assets of $86.91 million as of October 31, 1992.[3] As of December 31, 1992, these funds had combined total net assets of $209,104.1 million, or 69.4 percent of the total reported in Table 1.

Investment Company Data Institute (ICDI) maintains a data base of mutual fund disbursements dating back approximately 30 years. For each fund in our sample, we obtained from ICDI month-end net asset values (NAV), dividend and realized capital gains payments per share, "ex" dates for the dividend and capital gains distributions, reinvestment prices for the distributions, and split dates and ratios.[4] NAVs are net of expenses and fees but not adjusted for any load charges. The data cover the entire history of the mutual fund or the 30-year span 1963–1992 for those funds in existence for more than 30 years.[5] Sixty-two of the 147 funds had data for the entire 30-year period, and 126 funds had been operating for at least 20 years.

The data from ICDI combine short-term and long-term realized capital gains distributions in the reported capital gains distribution amounts. Under the United States Tax Code, however, short-term realized capital gains are taxed as ordinary income and do not qualify for the preferential tax treatment historically afforded long-term realized capital gains. The ICDI data, then, overstate the posttax return of those funds that distribute short-term capital gains.

The capital gains distributions reported by ICDI are checked against both Moody's *Annual Dividend Record* and Standard and Poor's *Annual Dividend Record*. Both the Moody and Standard and Poor's publications report the short-term and long-term realized capital gains distributions by mutual funds. If either issue reports short-term capital gains, then the capital gains distribution reported by ICDI is adjusted to reflect the respective short-term and long-term realized capital gains components.[6]

---

[3] Three funds had to be deleted from our original list. In November 1992, the Shearson Appreciation Portfolio Fund was merged into the Shearson Appreciation Fund. Data acquisition problems led to the deletion of the General Electric S&S Program Fund. Finally, Lexington Corporate Leaders is set up as a unit investment trust whose distributions include nontaxable return of capital. Since our data do not break down the taxable and nontaxable portions of their payments to shareholders, we deleted Lexington Corporate Leaders from our list of funds. Our total sample, therefore, consists of 147 growth and growth and income funds.

[4] We are indebted to Bill Crawford, Sr. of ICDI for making this data available to us.

[5] ICDI data for four funds are available only quarterly from January 1963 through September 1967 and are not included in our analysis over that time period.

[6] Prior to the late 1970s, short-term capital gains breakouts in the Moody's and Standard and Poor's publications are more limited, a fact that could result in some short-term gains still being treated as long-term gains in the data.

3. RETURN CALCULATIONS

We define the monthly total return as the percentage change in value at the end of the current month of one mutual fund share purchased at the end of the previous month. Returns are calculated on both a pretax and a posttax basis. Intuitively, the pretax measure reinvests the entire distribution while the posttax measure reinvests only the after-tax payment. In notational terms:

$$R_t = \frac{(shares_t * NAV_t - NAV_{t-1})}{NAV_{t-1}},$$ (1)

where

$$pretax: shares_t = 1 + \sum_{i=1}^{n_{dt}} \frac{Divs_{it}}{PD_{it}} + \sum_{j=1}^{n_{ct}} \frac{KGains_{jt}}{PKG_{jt}}$$

$$posttax: shares_t = 1 + \sum_{i=1}^{n_{dt}} \frac{(1 - \tau_{dt})Divs_{it}}{PD_{it}} + \sum_{j=1}^{n_{ct}} \frac{(1 - \tau_{ct})KGains_{jt}}{PKG_{jt}}.$$

Returns are adjusted for splits as necessary. NAV_t is the fund's net asset value at the end of month t. $Divs$ and $KGains$ are the dividend and realized capital gains payments per share that are reinvested at prices PD and PKG, respectively. There are n_{dt} dividend distributions and n_{ct} capital gains distributions in a given month. Dividends are taxed at the marginal rate on ordinary income, τ_{dt}, and realized capital gains are taxed at τ_{ct}. A provision of the tax code is that long-term realized capital gains distributed by mutual funds are taxable as long-term gains, even though, at the time of the distribution, an individual might not have held her mutual fund shares for the time normally required for an investment to qualify for the preferential long-term rate.

Since our data report "ex"-dates instead of actual payment dates, our methodology assumes that a distribution's "ex"-date and payment date fall within the same month. For the long horizons we consider in this paper such an assumption should not adversely affect accumulations. In addition, the tax code currently states that any distribution announced in October, November, or December is treated as income in that calendar year even if the payment is not disbursed until January of the following calendar year. The tax code, therefore, treats any payment with a December "ex"-date, when many distributions are made, as payable in December.

There are two additional assumptions embedded in equation (1). First, all distributions are taxed immediately. Second, for multiple distributions on different days within the month, we assume that the fund has already gone "ex." In other words, the new shares received from reinvesting one payment have no claim on any further distributions made within the same month.

Posttax returns are computed for investors in three different tax brackets. Using the Internal Revenue Service's *Statistics of Income*, we calculate the median adjusted gross income (AGI) for each year between 1963 and 1989. Median AGI is assumed to grow at the rate of the consumer price index from 1990 to 1992. These calculations lead to a value of $21,314 for median AGI in 1992. We define a "low-tax" individual as having taxable income equal to the median AGI less the standard deduction for married persons and three exemptions. We feel that such an individual probably represents the low end of the mutual fund marketplace. A "middle-tax" and "high-tax" individual are similarly defined using three times median AGI and 10 times median AGI, respectively. Investors are assumed to retain their tax status (low, middle, high) throughout the analysis.[7]

Table 2 presents the annual marginal tax rates for ordinary income and long-term realized capital gains based on the taxable income of each of our three individuals. These rates are compiled from Pechman (1987) and various issues of IRS Publication No. 17. Throughout most of this period, the first $200 of dividend income could be excluded from taxation for married persons filing jointly. We assume that any dividends paid by the mutual funds in our analysis are not subject to the dividend exclusion.

Prior to the 1986 tax reform, an individual was allowed to exclude 60 percent of his realized long-term capital gains (50 percent prior to November 1978) from the ordinary income tax, and the marginal tax rate on gains was limited to a maximum of 25 percent for most investors. During the 1970s, however, gains in excess of $50,000 were subject to an additional tax on the excluded portion of the gain, resulting in a higher marginal rate that varied with the amount of the realized gain (see Minarik, 1981). We assume that realized capital gains for each of our individuals total less than $50,000 annually over this period. Beginning in 1987, realized long-term capital gains are taxed at the maximum of the ordinary income rate or 28 percent.[8]

---

[7] We consider only federal tax rates. Returns can differ even more when state and local taxes are taken into account.

[8] The reader should note that our posttax return calculations discount realized capital gains distributions by the full marginal tax rate on long-term gains. This implicitly assumes that the taxpayer either does not realize capital losses on other assets or uses losses to offset realized gains from investments other than the mutual fund.

TABLE 2.
Marginal Tax Rates for Three Investor Types

Year	Low tax rate		Middle tax rate		High tax rate	
	Income	K Gains	Income	K Gains	Income	K Gains
1963	20	10	26	13	59	25
1964	17.5	8.75	27	13.5	53.5	25
1965	16	8	25	12.5	50	25
1966	17	8.5	25	12.5	50	25
1967	17	8.5	25	12.5	53	25
1968	18.275	9.1375	26.875	13.4375	56.975	25
1969	18.7	9.35	30.8	15.4	58.3	25
1970	19.475	9.7375	28.7	14.35	56.375	25
1971	17	8.5	28	14	55	25
1972	19	9.5	28	14	55	25
1973	19	9.5	28	14	58	25
1974	19	9.5	32	16	58	25
1975	19	9.5	32	16	58	25
1976	19	9.5	32	16	60	25
1977	19	9.5	36	18	60	25
1978	19	a	36	a	62	a

Year					
1979	18	7.2	37	14.8	64	25
1980	18	7.2	43	17.2	64	25
1981	17.775	7.11	42.4625	16.985	63.2	25
1982	16	6.4	39	15.6	50	20
1983	15	6	35	14	50	20
1984	16	6.4	33	13.2	49	19.6
1985	16	6.4	33	13.2	49	19.6
1986	16	6.4	33	13.2	49	19.6
1987	15	15	28	28	38.5	28
1988	15	15	28	28	33	28
1989	15	15	28	28	33	28
1990	15	15	28	28	33	28
1991	15	15	28	28	31	28
1992	15	15	28	28	31	28

Source: Pechman (1987) and Internal Revenue Service, Statistics of Income (*SOI*), various years.

[a] The marginal tax rate on long-term capital gain realizations in 1978 is the lesser of 50 percent of the income rate or 25 percent for realizations made from January through October. For November and December capital gains realizations, the marginal rate is the lesser of 40 percent of the income rate or 25 percent.

Taxable income for the low-tax-rate individual is computed as the median adjusted gross income (AGI) (computed from *SOI*) less the standard deduction for married couples and less three exemptions. Taxable incomes for the middle- and high-tax-rate individuals are comparably calculated using three times median AGI and 10 times median AGI, respectively. Median AGI for 1990–1992 is held constant (in real terms) at the 1989 level.

4. RESULTS

We generate mutual fund returns under three different scenarios. The pretax return is relevant for investors whose assets are in tax deferred accounts (e.g., IRAs and Keoghs). The posttax return is most relevant for those taxable investors with long holding periods or who plan to pass their assets through their estate.[9] The liquidation value is the amount of money an investor would receive if he were to liquidate his mutual fund position at the end of the holding period. This value best describes the opportunities for those investors divesting assets at the end of the period for a specified purpose (e.g., tuition payments, down-payment for a house, purchasing a yacht). The liquidation value for a $1 initial investment is calculated by the following formula:

$$L_T = \prod_{t=1}^{T} (1 + R_t) - \tau_{cT} (\prod_{t=1}^{T} (1 + R_t) - basis_T);$$

$$basis_T = 1 + \frac{1}{NAV_0} \left(\sum_{i=1}^{n_{dl}} (1 - \tau_{dl})Divs_{il} + \sum_{j=1}^{n_{cl}} (1 - \tau_{cl})KGains_{jl} \right) \qquad (2)$$

$$+ \frac{1}{NAV_0} \sum_{t=2}^{T} \left[(\prod_{k=1}^{t-1} shares_k) \left(\sum_{i=1}^{n_{dt}} (1 - \tau_{dt})Divs_{it} + \sum_{j=1}^{n_{ct}} (1 - \tau_{ct})KGains_{jt} \right) \right].$$

R_t and $shares_k$ are the monthly posttax return and shares calculated from equation (1), and NAV_0 is the share price of the fund at the beginning of the holding period. The number of shares are adjusted for splits as necessary. equation (2) shows that the end-of-period liquidation value, L_T, is simply the accumulation of the posttax returns less the amount of taxes that must be paid at the time of sale on previously unrealized capital gains.[10]

Table 3 presents our results for the 30-year period 1963–1992. This table shows the end-of-period value of a $1 investment made at the beginning of the holding period. The top half of the table shows that the median result for the 62 mutual funds with 30-year returns was that $1 in 1963 would have grown to a pretax $21.89 by the end of 1992. Over this period, investing $1 in the S&P 500 index would have resulted in

---

[9] Because of the step-up in basis at the time of death, any unrealized capital gains would not be taxed if an heir were to immediately liquidate a decedent's holdings.

[10] As shown in equation (2), the liquidation value would be greater than the posttax value if the accumulated basis is greater than the posttax value of the mutual fund at the time of liquidation. Implicitly this assumes full loss offsets.

TABLE 3.
Mutual Fund Returns, 1963–1992 (nominal value of $1 investment)

Method	Regime	TBills	Min	Median	Max	Std Dev
			Number of funds = 62 (Pretax S&P 500 = 22.13)			
Pretax	N/A	6.91	8.45	21.89	76.03	12.99
Posttax	Low tax	4.97	7.06	16.51	61.02	10.01
values	Mid tax	3.69	5.97	12.75	50.14	8.05
	High tax	2.53	4.63	9.82	40.26	6.41
Liquidation	Low tax	4.97	6.59	16.04	55.56	9.24
values	Mid tax	3.69	5.29	12.04	41.49	6.77
	High tax	2.53	4.46	8.93	33.17	5.34

Table 3 reports the value of a $1 initial investment at the end of the 30-year period concluding in 1992. TBills is the terminal value of a T-Bill investment, while all of the other columns refer to results obtained with the sample of 62 mutual funds with 30-year returns described in the text. Posttax values are computed for hypothetical investors facing three different sets of tax rates (low, mid, high) and assume that the investment is not sold at the end of 1992. The liquidation values assume that the mutual fund investment is sold at the end of 1992 and any remaining capital gains (or losses) are taxed according to the tax rates at the end of 1992.

$22.13. The numbers for the median posttax numbers are $16.51, $12.75 and $9.82 for the low, middle, and high income investors respectively. The median liquidation values are $16.04, $12.04, and $8.93 for taxable holders in our three different tax circumstances.[11] The differences in actual return over the 30-year period to a taxable investor are immediately evident. The high-tax investor who reinvests only after-tax distributions has an accumulated wealth per dollar invested on the order of 45 percent of the amount published by the funds in their prospectuses and promotional material.

Table 3 also reports the value of a $1 investment in Treasury Bills (T-Bills) (the risk-free investment in our analysis) over the relevant period.[12] Notice that over the 30-year period, even the worst performer in our mutual fund sample did better than T-Bills. For tax-free investors, the last place fund outdistanced T-Bills by 22 percent, the median fund produced 217 percent more, and the best fund resulted in 11 times as much wealth per dollar invested as T-Bills.[13] The return multiples rela-

[11] Table 3 presents results for the median fund within each category. Because of differences in the pretax and posttax rankings, the median fund is not the same mutual fund under each case.

[12] S&P 500 and T-Bill returns are taken from Ibbotson (1993).

[13] Because of the selection bias in our data set, it is quite likely that the worst growth or growth and income mutual fund investment over this period involved an investment in a fund that was not included in our data.

tive to T-Bills are larger for taxable investors since T-Bills are more heavily taxed than equity mutual funds, at least at the federal level. This is because T-Bill interest is taxed at full ordinary rates (as are dividends), while realized capital gains have usually been taxed at lower rates (See Table 2).[14] Even if a high-tax-rate individual had the misfortune of investing in the worst of our funds, she would have 84 percent more money accumulated (77 percent if she were to liquidate her position) between 1963 and 1992 than if she had invested and accumulated with T-Bills. The median and best performing funds generate 3.9 and 15.9 times more wealth (3.5 and 13.1 times as much wealth upon liquidation) for the high-tax investor than T-Bills.

Figure 1 illustrates the degree to which the pre- and posttax rankings of our funds differ (for a high-tax investor) over the 30-year horizon.[15] To facilitate comparisons across different horizons where the number of funds change, we report the rankings in terms of percentiles. The worst fund has a percentile rank of zero, and the best fund ranks at the 100 (1 − 1/n) percentile, where n is the number of funds ranked.[16] Figure 1 plots a fund's after-tax percentile ranking versus its pretax percentile ranking. If tax considerations did not change the relative performance of these mutual funds, then the rankings would be unchanged, and all funds would show up on the 45-degree line shown in Figure 1. One glance at the figure indicates that shareholder level taxes cause considerable changes in the relative ranking of funds. Obviously, funds appearing above the 45-degree line have a higher after-tax ranking than before-tax ranking and vice versa.

Table 4 presents summary statistics on the ranking differences shown in Figure 1. The movement of an average fund in our sample is plus or minus 9.8 percentile points. The maximum change in relative position was Franklin Growth, which improved its rank by an enormous 43.6 points going from the 19.4 percentile on a pretax basis to the 63.0 percen-

---

[14] The monthly post-tax return on T-Bills is $R_t = (1 - \tau_{dt})$ TBill$_t$, where TBill$_t$ is the nominal, pretax T-Bill return in month t.

[15] A previous version of this paper entitled "Ranking Mutual Funds on an After-Tax Basis" (National Bureau of Economic Research Working Paper No. 4393), provides an appendix detailing the individual performance of the funds pictured in Figure 1.

[16] We also considered another performance measure based on a fund's return relative to the median return. Fund X, for example, might have a pretax value 20 percent greater than the median pretax value, while its posttax value might be 10 percent above the median posttax value. We would then say Fund X lost 10 percentage points relative to the median. This median performance measure, unlike the percentile rankings, might be able to distinguish large relative movements if funds' returns are tightly bunched. In the text we report the percentile differences. Results for the median measure are available from the authors upon request.

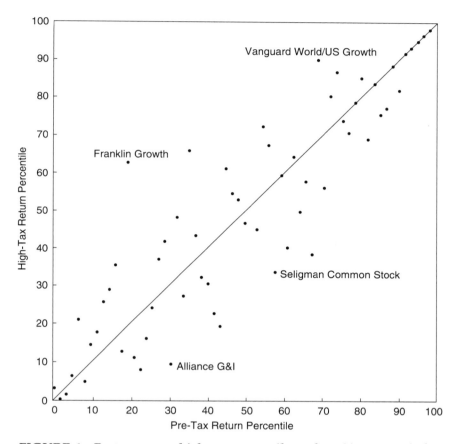

FIGURE 1. *Pretax versus high-tax percentile ranks—30-year period (1963–1992).*

tile for a high-tax investor.[17] For a high-tax investor, Franklin Growth returned an average of 8.27 percent each year over the 1963–1992 period. In contrast, the fund that performed at the 19.4 percentile on a posttax basis (National Stock) yielded its investors a 6.95-percent after-tax annual return. Franklin Growth's percentile ranking movement, therefore, represented an additional return of 132 basis points per year (after tax)

---

[17] Using the median measure discussed in footnote 14, Franklin Growth gained 37.8 percentage points relative to the median over the 1963–1992 period. Franklin Growth performed 27.9% below the median on a pretax basis but 9.9 percent higher than the median for a high-tax investor.

TABLE 4.
Percentile Differences of Rankings over a 30-Year Period (1963–1992)
Number of Funds = 62(absolute deviations)

Comparison	Tax regime	Max(−)	Med	Max(+)	Mean
Posttax	Low	9.7	1.6	12.9	3.1
vs.	Mid	19.4	4.8	25.8	6.2
pretax	High	29.0	8.1	43.6	9.8
Liquidation	Low	8.1	1.6	8.1	2.4
vs.	Mid	12.9	4.8	14.5	4.9
pretax	High	29.0	8.1	25.8	8.6
Liquidation	Low	6.5	1.6	4.8	1.8
vs.	Mid	16.1	1.6	9.7	3.1
posttax	High	17.7	1.6	9.7	2.9

Max(−) reports the percentile point reduction for the fund with the largest relative ranking decrease. Med is the median absolute value difference among the sample of funds. Max(+) gives the percentile point increase for the fund with the largest relative ranking increase. Mean is the average absolute percentile change within the sample.

over the 1963–1992 horizon. Overall, our interpretation of Figure 1 and Table 4 is that the pretax rankings, which are the rankings usually provided to investors, are inappropriate for providing necessary performance information to taxable investors.

As shown in Table 4, the difference between the pretax and the posttax rankings of funds over the 30-year horizon is still considerable for intermediate-tax-rate investors. The average absolute value percentile change between pre- and posttax rankings is 6.2 points for our middle-tax-rate investor, with the maximum change still being Franklin Growth, which gained 25.8 percentiles. The additional return for our midtax investor in this case represented a 111-basis-point increase per year in after-tax return over the amount the investor would have received if Franklin Growth's pretax and midtax percentile ranking remained constant. As one would expect, the difference between the pre- and posttax rankings is not terribly great for our low-tax-rate investor where the average percentile change (in absolute value) drops to 3.1 points.

The liquidation value rankings for the 1963–1992 period are much closer to the posttax rankings than the pretax rankings as shown in Figure 2 for high-tax investors.[18] Figure 2 contains two panels. The left panel plots a fund's liquidation value ranking versus pretax ranking, whereas the right panel plots a fund's liquidation ranking versus posttax ranking. The mean absolute value change between liquidation value and

[18] Previous versions of this paper contain similar graphs for midtax and low-tax individuals.

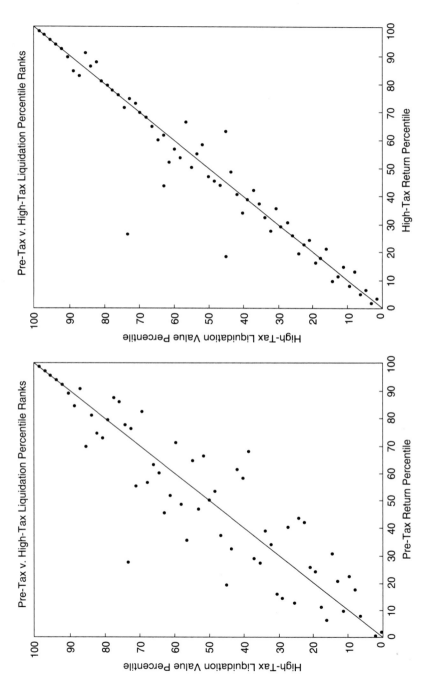

FIGURE 2. *Rank comparisons with high-tax liquidation values—30-year period (1963–1992).*

pretax return rankings reported in Table 4 is 8.6 points for the high-tax investor, 4.9 points for the midtax people, and only 2.4 percentile points for the low-tax investor. The average absolute value change in position between the liquidation ranking and the posttax ranking was roughly three percentiles for both the high- and middle-tax-rate investors but only 1.8 points for the low-tax asset holder.

These results show that the differences between the various after-tax rankings and the published pretax rankings are large over a 30-year horizon, particularly for middle- and high-income investors. A natural question that arises is whether it takes a 30-year period for these tax differences to become important. To provide the answer, we separately calculated mutual fund performance rankings for the three 10-year subperiods within our 30-year data set.

Our conclusion is that the ranking differences are still considerable for 10-year intervals. For example, the average absolute value change in rank for high-tax investors between the posttax and pretax rankings was roughly five percentile points for the first two 10-year periods and 8.7 points (7.1 and 3.7 points for midtax and low-tax investors, respectively) for the most recent 1983–1992 period. The performance rank changes over the most recent decade, in fact, are not that much smaller than for the entire 30-year period. Once again we see that the effect of shareholder taxation is quite important for the midtax investor but much less significant for the low-tax household. Figure 3 plots the posttax return rank for high-tax investors against the pretax return rank for the 1983–1992 period.[19] The largest increase in rank between the two concepts was 35.4 percentile points (Fidelity Value), which moved from the 17.0 percentile (pretax) to the 52.4 percentile (high-tax). Fidelity Value earned 10.94 percent per year for a high-tax investor, whereas if it would have remained in the 17th percentile, the fund would have earned only 9.08 percent annually. The biggest downward movement was Putnam Growth & Income (A), which fell a total of 37.4 percentile points, a movement that represented a 247-basis-point decrease relative to the after-tax return Putnam would have posted had it maintained its pretax return percentile.

The case of Vanguard's Index 500 Fund illustrates how a tax conscious fund could improve its relative performance. The Index 500 Fund follows the passive strategy of investing in the component stocks of the Standard and Poor's 500 (S&P 500) index in the same value-weighted proportions as the index. This fund realizes capital gains for three main

---

[19] A detailed list of the 147 mutual funds with computed pretax and posttax returns is available from the authors.

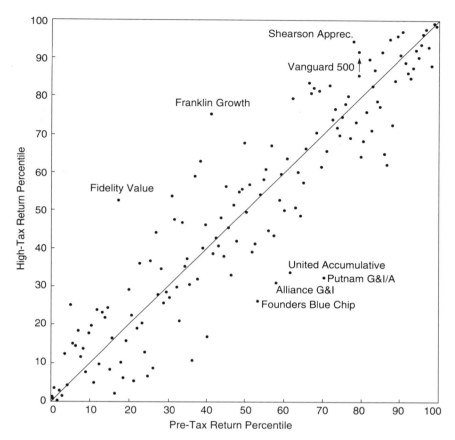

FIGURE 3. *Pretax versus high-tax percentile ranks—10-year subperiod (1983–1992).*

reasons: constituent changes in the S&P 500, share repurchases of the 500 firms, and net redemptions by the fund's shareholders. The relatively passive investment approach of the Index 500 Fund resulted in the posttax return ranking 6.1 percentiles higher than the pretax return (85.0 percentile posttax versus 78.9 percentile pretax) for the high-tax investor over the 1983–1992 period. As depicted in Figure 3, if the Vanguard 500 portfolio could have deferred all of its realized capital gains (without sacrificing any pretax return), it would have ended up at the 91.8 percentile for the high-tax investor. Dickson and Shoven (1994) show that managing such a fund to defer all capital gains realizations is feasible. While Dickson and Shoven (1994) are able to replicate the pretax return of the Index 500 within a few basis points, the after-tax return to high-income investors is increased by as much as 97 basis points per year relative to the Index 500. This result is solely from the deferral of all realized capital gains that Dickson and Shoven (1994) show could be easily attained through the use of simple accounting and trading strategies over the sample period.[20]

Mutual fund rankings change dramatically not only for taxable versus nontaxable investors but also for high-tax versus low-tax investors. Table 5 clearly shows there is a considerable difference in the standings of the various funds in our sample for the two different types of investors. The average absolute movement between low-tax and high-tax percentile ranking is 7.2 points (6.6 points upon liquidation) over the 1963–1992 period. The relative movements are still considerable over each of the three 10-year subperiods. In the 1983–1992 period, for example, the average movement is plus or minus 5.4 points (4.3 points upon liquidation). This table suggests that it is not merely sufficient to choose one tax rate to measure after-tax returns. Individual taxable investors, instead, should be able to determine relative rankings based on their own marginal rates.

5. RISK-ADJUSTED RETURNS

All of the above rankings consider only the average return over the 10- and 30-year horizons and do not take risk into account. We recognize that investors are risk averse and, in general, would be willing to trade some expected return for increased safety. Since our focus is on the relative rankings when shareholder taxation is taken into account, any risk-adjusting measure we use must allow for straightforward comparison on both a pre- and posttax basis.

The usual starting point when one risk adjusts mutual fund returns is the method first employed by Jensen (1968). Jensen uses the capital asset pricing model (CAPM) as a benchmark to determine whether or not a mutual fund manager is able to engage in successful stock selection and market timing activities. The assumptions underlying the CAPM approach are that the investor holds the market portfolio, is only interested in the riskiness of the entire portfolio, and, therefore, needs to ascertain the contribution of each asset to the riskiness of the total portfolio. One problem with this approach is that many mutual fund investors are not

---

[20] As Dickson and Shoven (1994) show, a tax conscious fund that tracks the S&P 500 is not an index fund in the usual sense, since it has to deviate slightly from the true portfolio weights in order to offset realized capital gains with capital losses while adhering to the wash-sale restrictions.

TABLE 5.
High-Tax versus Low-Tax Percentile Differences over a 30-Year Period and 10-Year Subperiods
(absolute deviations)

	30-year horizon (1963–1992) Number of funds = 62			
	Max(−)	Median	Max(+)	Mean
Posttax return	21.0	6.5	30.6	7.2
Liquidation return	24.2	6.5	19.4	6.6

10-year subperiods

	Subperiod 1 (1963–1972) Number of funds = 62				Subperiod 2 (1973–1982) Number of funds = 126				Subperiod 3 (1983–1992) Number of funds = 147			
	Max(−)	Med	Max(+)	Mean	Max(−)	Med	Max(+)	Mean	Max(−)	Med	Max(+)	Mean
Posttax return	12.9	3.2	9.7	3.4	11.1	3.2	11.9	3.7	23.1	4.1	20.4	5.4
Liquidation return	6.5	1.6	8.1	2.2	11.9	2.4	11.9	3.0	26.5	3.4	15.0	4.3

Max(−) reports the percentile point reduction for the fund with the largest relative ranking decrease. Med is the median absolute value difference among the sample of funds. Max(+) gives the percentile point increase for the fund with the largest relative ranking increase. Mean is the average absolute percentile change within the sample.

nearly this diversified. For many mutual fund investors, their entire equity portfolio is a particular diversified mutual fund, and the riskiness of their portfolio is given by the variance (or standard deviation) of that fund's returns.

A second problem for our analysis is that the usual CAPM model of riskiness does not take shareholder level taxation into account. In order to adjust posttax mutual fund returns for risk, we would need to make some statement about the realized capital gains of the market portfolio. This calls for some knowledge of the effective tax rate on accrued gains, and we do not think it is straightforward to make such a calculation.

One possibility might be to use one of our funds, the Vanguard Index 500, as a measure of the before-tax and after-tax market returns. Since the investment strategy of the Index 500 is to track the S&P 500 (the benchmark portfolio in many empirical CAPM studies), its performance is an obvious candidate for a market portfolio. Two potential difficulties, however, come to mind. First, consider a fund that, at all times, holds the same stocks and makes the same trades as the benchmark portfolio. On a pretax basis, the familiar CAPM β will equal unity (and α will equal zero), as expected. On an after-tax basis, though, the estimates of α and β will differ from zero and one respectively if the sole difference between this fund and the benchmark fund is the months in which distributions are made.[21]

Another possible risk-adjusting method would be to use the consumption CAPM (CCAPM). The argument for such an approach is that the riskiness individuals are really concerned about should be the variability of their total wealth including such assets as human capital, Social Security wealth (and other government programs such as welfare and unemployment insurance), and housing. The principal advantages of the CCAPM are that, with this broad definition of wealth, almost everyone is somewhat well diversified, and, consumption, by definition, is an after-income tax concept. As with the market portfolio CAPM, however, the CCAPM does not allow for easy comparisons since the after-tax consumption portfolio would also have to be used as the pretax benchmark in order to consider changes in relative performance. In addition, the CCAPM has not fared well in most empirical tests of the model's implications.

Because of the difficulties noted above, the risk measure we decide to employ is Sharpe's (1966) reward-to-variability measure (a.k.a. Sharpe

---

[21] This result rings true for any mutual fund relative to the benchmark. If the fund under consideration makes taxable distributions in different months than the benchmark fund, then the estimates of α and β will depend on the distribution months in addition to actual differences in stock selection, market timing ability, or "risk" of the fund.

ratio), which is simply the ratio of the average monthly excess return of the mutual fund to the standard deviation of its monthly excess returns. This measure is admittedly crude. Implicitly, it assumes that the mutual fund is the whole portfolio of the investor or, at least, that its riskiness is assessed separately from that of other assets. While this sounds extreme, it may not be further from the truth than the assumptions of the standard CAPM involving the level of diversification in the investor's portfolio. The main advantage of the Sharpe ratio, however, is that it can easily be calculated on a posttax basis as well as on a pretax basis, allowing relative comparisons to be made.

The results of the Sharpe ratio are depicted in Figure 4. The top half of the figure plots pretax average excess return against pretax standard deviation, whereas the bottom half plots both concepts for an upper-income, taxable investor. The importance of adjusting returns for risk can be seen by the considerable horizontal spread in the funds in both panels. (Their monthly standard deviations range from roughly 3.5 percent to 7.5 percent.) We implicitly assume that investors have the opportunity to invest in T-Bills (and also to borrow at that rate).

The optimal fund for all investors is the one with the largest ratio of average excess return to standard deviation. If you consider running a line from each point in Figure 4 to the origin, the highest ranked fund will be the one whose corresponding line has the steepest slope. Every high-tax investor, regardless of their degree of risk aversion, should choose this fund (Mutual Shares) in preference to all others.[22] The line through the fund represents the opportunities that investors have by choosing different combinations of this fund and T-Bills.

Figure 4 shows that our earlier story that taxes dramatically affect relative rankings is still true when the rankings are risk adjusted. The largest improvement in ranking due to tax considerations is Franklin Growth. The top half of the figure shows that roughly 80 percent of the funds offered a better opportunity set (when combined with T-Bills) than does Franklin Growth. However, the bottom half of the figure shows that only about 35 percent of the funds offered a better after-tax opportunity set than Franklin Growth. Tax considerations caused it to "pass" more than half of the funds that ranked higher on a pretax basis.

The amount by which the risk-adjusted rankings vary from tax effects are very similar to the non–risk-adjusted returns. For the 30-year horizon, the average absolute value change in the high-tax, risk-adjusted rankings was 9.2 percentiles compared to 9.8 percentiles shown in Table 4 for the non–risk-adjusted case. In the 10-year subperiod from 1983 to

---

[22] We are, of course, using ex post returns and make no claim about future performance.

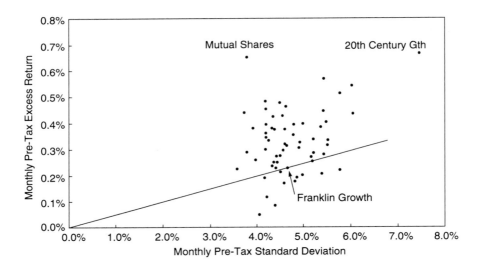

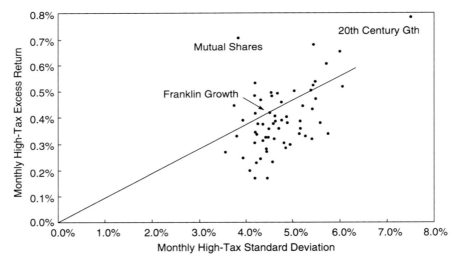

FIGURE 4. *High-tax versus pretax risk adjusted returns—30-year period (1963–1992).*

1992, the average change was 7.7 percentiles for the reward-to-variability ratios versus 8.7 percentiles for the average returns. The differences between midtax and low-tax ranking movements are even smaller between the risk-adjusted and non–risk-adjusted cases.

6. THE POSSIBLE AGGREGATE TAX SAVING

A natural question to ask is how much money could investors save in taxes if mutual funds became more conscious of shareholder level taxes and adopted strategies to defer the net realization of capital gains? Of course, it must be recognized from the outset that the flip side of shareholder tax saving is a loss of revenue to the Treasury Department. Estimating the aggregate amount of the possible tax saving is difficult in the extreme, and we can only hope to arrive at the approximate order of magnitude.

The first step in making the calculation is to examine the amount of capital gains distributed by mutual funds. Table 6 displays the dollar amount of net realized capital gains distributions of equity, bond, and income funds from 1970 to 1993. It should be emphasized that this is a much broader universe of funds than the sample of large growth and growth and income funds discussed in all of the other analyses of this paper. Nonetheless, the vast bulk of the net realized capital gains in the larger set of funds result from net realized appreciation on common stock positions and could conceivably be eliminated or deferred if the managers of the mutual funds were so inclined. The Potential Gross Tax Saving column of Table 6 results from a multiplication of the Net Realized Capital Gains figures by the estimated fraction of equity mutual fund assets held by taxable shareholders (58.6 percent) as of the end of 1992 and then by the marginal personal income tax rates for realized capital gains for our middle-income investors from Table 2. These numbers bound from above the amount of money that investors might save. In fact, the saving would certainly be less for several reasons.

If mutual funds permit their shareholders to defer capital gains by managing the portfolio in such a way that capital gains distributions are not required, then shareholders will have larger realized capital gains when they liquidate or exchange their mutual fund shares. By and large, the shareholders would be postponing taxes, not eliminating them. Table 7 provides some information about how long people remain in a given mutual fund. A survey of those who fully or partially redeemed their shares in 1991–1992 indicated the distribution of tenures with the fund as shown in Table 7.[23] The median person in the sample had been

---

[23] It should be noted that there is a selection bias problem with this data source. The sample is taken from those who sell their shares, whereas we would like to have information about how much longer a person who currently owns a fund (and who is able to defer capital gains because of the policies of the mutual fund manager) will continue to own it. It must be acknowledged that the information in Table 7 is only suggestive, but it is not exactly appropriate to the problem at hand.

TABLE 6.
Distributions to Mutual Fund Shareholders and Gross Potential Tax Saving: Equity, Bond, and Income Funds (millions of dollars)

Year	Dividends	Net realized capital gain	Potential gross tax saving
1970	1,414.1	922.1	77.5
1971	1,330.7	775.5	63.6
1972	1,286.6	1,402.6	115.1
1973	1,300.2	943.3	77.4
1974	1,563.2	484.3	45.4
1975	1,449.1	219.2	20.6
1976	1,580.0	470.9	44.2
1977	1,789.7	634.8	67.0
1978	2,116.0	710.6	75.0
1979	2,451.4	929.0	80.6
1980	2,669.0	1,774.2	178.8
1981	3,143.0	2,697.2	268.5
1982	3,832.9	2,350.1	214.8
1983	4,981.0	4,391.6	360.3
1984	7,238.4	6,019.2	465.6
1985	12,864.2	4,984.6	385.6
1986	22,273.4	17,463.8	1,350.9
1987	31,823.7	22,975.6	3,769.8
1988	31,078.3	6,345.3	1,041.1
1989	34,096.1	14,802.8	2,428.8
1990	32,917.7	8,054.6	1,321.6
1991	35,322.2	14,116.1	2,316.2
1992	59,177.0	22,335.6	3,664.8
1993	73,302.4	36,105.3	5,942.2

Source: First two columns, *1994 Mutual Fund Fact Book*, p. 112; third column, authors' computations.

TABLE 7.
Tenure in Fund From Which Shares Were Redeemed, 1991–1992

Tenure	Full redemptions (percent)	Partial redemptions (percent)
2 Years or less	24	23
3–4 Years	20	18
5–6 Years	23	17
7–9 Years	19	20
10+ Years	14	22

Source: 1993 Mutual Fund Fact Book, p. 85.

with the fund for five years. Fifty-four percent of the sellers were fully liquidating their positions, whereas 46 percent were only selling part of their holdings. It is difficult to know whether people would be significantly less inclined to sell their holdings or switch between funds if that would trigger a large and taxable realization of previously accrued capital gains. Certainly, given the current practice of most funds of realizing gains quickly after they accrue, tax considerations have not been a major consideration in determining the behavior summarized in Table 7. If the turnover of mutual fund shares remained approximately what is shown in Table 7, the Treasury would still collect, at least in present-value terms, taxes on most of the capital gains realized within mutual funds. Five years of deferral would save the investor in present value terms a maximum of 25 percent of the bill, meaning that the investors' gains and the Treasury's loss would only be roughly one-fourth the potential gross magnitudes shown in Table 6. There are even additional complications, of course.

If mutual funds allowed their investors the opportunity to defer capital gains by refraining from annual net realized capital gains distributions, the shareholders would then have some discretion about the tax year in which to realize the gains. A household whose income fluctuated sufficiently would have the opportunity to realize the gain when their marginal tax rate was lower (15 percent rather than 28 percent, e.g.). Some investors would be able to postpone the realization until retirement, which often involves lower marginal tax rates. Finally, due to the step up of cost bases at death, there is some probability that a deferral of capital gains taxes will result in the effective elimination of the taxation of the gains. It is considerations such as these that make impossible a precise estimate of the magnitude of the tax advantage of mutual funds permitting the deferral of capital gains.[24]

Our guess is that investors could gain between one-quarter and one-half of the potential gross tax saving shown in Table 6. These savings would be available annually and in 1993 would have been between $1.5 and $3 billion. This would be the impact of allowing mutual fund shareholders to benefit from the same tax strategies that people who hold stocks directly have employed for decades. No government regulations need to be changed, simply the behavior of the money managers who are, after all, paid handsomely for acting in the best interests of their shareholders.

It is interesting to note that the level of awareness of shareholder level

---

[24] In the analysis of Section 4 we assumed that investors' incomes were relatively constant (i.e., high-income investors always had high incomes, etc.). Widely fluctuating incomes (and therefore widely fluctuating marginal income tax rates) would have complicated the previous analysis of the changes in pre- and posttax percentile rankings as well.

taxes seems to be increasing in the mutual fund industry. Charles Schwab introduced the Schwab 1000, the first fund that we are aware of that explicitly managed realized capital gains in April 1991. The firm now offers three index funds with this feature (the Schwab 1000, the Schwab Small-Cap Index Fund, and the Schwab International Index Fund). Recently, Vanguard has introduced its Tax-Managed Portfolios, which include a growth and income fund, a capital appreciation fund, and a "balanced" portfolio. It will be interesting to see the market receptivity to these tax sensitive offerings.

7. AFTER-TAX RETURNS AND TURNOVER

We have shown that shareholder level taxation can dramatically change the relative rankings of mutual funds. An important issue for taxable investors deciding between the plethora of funds available is whether a fund's future relative posttax performance movements might be inferred from its investment policies. Our basic intuition is that the amount a fund "turns over" its portfolio should be related to the amount of its taxable distributions to shareholders. Many of our funds churn their portfolios significantly over a single year (100 percent is not uncommon), possibly realizing capital gains as they accrue and, thus, subjecting their shareholders to tax liabilities. Those funds that do not turnover their portfolios and more closely adhere to a buy-and-hold strategy, the argument continues, realize less of their accrued gains, allowing their investors to defer capital gains taxes into the future.

The relationship between turnover and mutual fund performance has been discussed by a couple of authors. Ippolito (1989) presents evidence of no relationship between turnover and pretax performance net of fees and expenses. In other words, Ippolito finds that funds with high turnover rates earn sufficiently greater risk-adjusted returns to offset the costs (other than taxes) associated with increased turnover. Jeffrey and Arnott (1993) consider the relationship between turnover and after-tax returns. Assuming a 35-percent marginal tax rate for realized capital gains over the 1982–1991 period, they report a statistically significant correlation coefficient of approximately 0.4 between a fund's average turnover and the amount of taxes due from its capital gains distributions.

Jeffrey and Arnott (1993) conclude that taxable investors should consider funds with relatively passive investment strategies (i.e., low turnover) to avoid large tax liabilities. A conclusion that high turnover funds may be unwise for shareholders subject to taxation, however, does not immediately follow. Consider a mutual fund with a high turnover rate that is successful at stock selection and market timing activities. A higher pretax return (if one assumes a dividend yield commensurate with other funds) implies there are more capital gains to realize. Hence, this fund will most likely impose a larger capital gains tax burden on its shareholders relative to other funds. However, if its pretax return is sufficiently large, taxable investors may still want to invest in this fund even if the shareholders will have to pay large amounts of realized capital gains taxes.

To consider the effect of turnover on after-tax performance, we computed average annual turnover rates for each of our funds over the 10-year period 1983–1992 from Morningstar. Consistent with our intuition, the fund with the lowest average turnover (Franklin Growth—3.2 percent) jumped from the 40.8 pretax percentile to the 75.5 percentile for a high-tax investor over the 1983–1992 period. The fund with the highest average turnover (Fidelity Value—296 percent), however, also dramatically improved its posttax performance, jumping 35.4 percentiles (the largest increase over this period).

Table 8 reports sample correlation coefficients between average turnover rates and the ratio of posttax value (liquidation) to pretax value.[25] The numbers in parentheses are P values under the null hypothesis of zero correlation between after-tax performance and average turnover. The P value represents the minimum level of statistical significance at which we would reject the null hypothesis. We use ratios of posttax to pretax measures instead of rank changes since the best performing funds typically outdistance other funds by large amounts, and their rankings may not change even if their posttax to pretax ratios are lower than those of most other funds. If our intuition is correct, we would expect negative correlations between turnover rates and the posttax to pretax performance ratios. Table 8 shows that the intuition is basically correct. All of the computed correlations are negative, and most correlations are significant at the 5% level. Overall, for high-tax investors over this period, the correlation between average turnover and the ratio of high-tax to pretax value was −0.20 (P value = 0.015).[26] These results suggest that turnover can be an indicator of a fund's relative posttax performance.

Table 8 is certainly not a formal test of the relationship between turn-

---

[25] Because of the problems associated with risk-adjusting after-tax returns discussed in the previous section, we do not consider the relationship between turnover and risk-adjusted performance. This analysis is consistent with Jeffrey and Arnott (1993).

[26] The corresponding table in previous versions of this paper showed that, in general, turnover was not strongly correlated with posttax performance. Those earlier calculations were undertaken before we had broken out the short-term versus long-term capital gains. The fact that the turnover correlations are significant when short-term capital gains are explicitly accounted for strengthens our argument that many managers sacrifice their shareholders' after-tax returns not only by realizing capital gains but also by realizing relatively more tax disadvantaged short-term capital gains instead of long-term capital gains.

TABLE 8.

Turnover Correlations over a 10-Year Subperiod (1983–1992) (p-values in parentheses)

Number of funds Average turnover (%)		Growth 96 84.83	Growth and income 51 65.99	Overall 147 78.29
Posttax value over Pretax value	Low	−0.16 (0.130)	−0.33 (0.018)	−0.17 (0.045)
	Mid	−0.16 (0.110)	−0.34 (0.015)	−0.17 (0.037)
	High	−0.20 (0.057)	−0.39 (0.005)	−0.20 (0.015)
Posttax Liquidation over Pretax Value	Low	−0.25 (0.015)	−0.20 (0.165)	−0.20 (0.013)
	Mid	−0.25 (0.012)	−0.18 (0.194)	−0.20 (0.014)
	High	−0.29 (0.003)	−0.33 (0.019)	−0.25 (0.003)

Average turnover is the annual average of turnover percentages reported by Morningstar. Turnover data for 1992 were not yet available, and a nine-year average was computed for 27 of the funds in our sample.
  The numbers in the table refer to the correlation across the sample of funds between a fund's average turnover and its ratio of posttax value (liquidation) to pretax value over the 10-year sample period. The numbers in parentheses represent P values under the null hypothesis of zero correlation.

over and relative posttax performance. In fact, funds with higher turnover rates may still be good investments for the tax conscious investor. This point is illustrated by the example of Vanguard's Index 500 Fund discussed earlier. If this fund were able to defer all capital gains disbursements to its shareholders, it would have performed even better on an after-tax basis. Deferring capital gains relative to the S&P 500 index, however, necessarily implies that the fund would turn over its portfolio at a greater rate (7 percentage points per year in Dickson and Shoven, 1994).

8. CONCLUSION

Mutual funds seem to pay very little attention to shareholder level taxes. Funds publish long-term performance statistics that ignore taxes, and the financial press ranks them on these pretax measures. Most funds realize large fractions of their accrued capital gains each year. This type of investment policy eliminates an investor's opportunity to defer taxes on accrued capital gains and adversely affects after-tax returns to a fund's shareholders.

We have calculated both pre- and posttax mutual fund returns for individuals in different tax brackets over various investment horizons. While it is not surprising that taxes lower the accumulations that one can achieve with mutual fund investments over all holding periods, our calculations show that the relative rankings of funds on a posttax basis (and on our liquidation basis) differ quite dramatically from the published pretax rankings. That is, taxable investors cannot easily and reliably determine which of two funds would have offered them a better after-tax return with the publicly available information. While we feel that more work is necessary to account satisfactorily for risk, this consideration does not dampen our main conclusion that after-tax performance rankings are very different from pretax performance rankings.

Our analysis of the aggregate impact of the failure of mutual funds to tax manage their portfolios indicates that the consequence is that the present value of investors' tax bills is raised considerably. In 1993, when mutual funds distributed $36 billion in net realized capital gains, taxpayers probably paid more than $1 billion in extra (present value) taxes over and above what would have been required with tax sensitive management of the funds.

REFERENCES

Chang, Eric C., and Wilbur G. Lewellen (1984). "Market Timing and Mutual Fund Investment Performance." *Journal of Business* 57:57–72.

Dickson, Joel M., and John B. Shoven (1994). "A Stock Index Mutual Fund Without Net Capital Gains Realizations." NBER Working Paper no. 4717.

Federal Reserve Board of Governors (1993). *Flow of Fund Accounts,* second quarter. Washington, DC: U.S. Government Printing Office.

Grinblatt, Mark, and Sheridan Titman (1993). "Performance Measurement without Benchmarks: An Examination of Mutual Fund Returns." *Journal of Business* 66:47–68.

Henriksson, Roy D. (1984). "Market Timing and Mutual Fund Performance: An Empirical Investigation." *Journal of Business* 57:73–96.

Horowitz, Ira (1965). "A Model for the Evaluation of Various Mutual Funds as Investment Alternatives." *Industrial Management Review* 6 (Spring):81–92.

Ibbotson and Associates (1993). *Stocks, Bonds, Bills, and Inflation.* Chicago, IL: Ibbotson and Associates.

Internal Revenue Service. *Statistics of Income,* various years.

———. *Publication 17,* various years.

Investment Company Institute (1993). *Mutual Fund Fact Book.* Washington, DC.

——— (1994). *Mutual Fund Fact Book.* Washington, DC.

Ippolito, Richard A. (1989). "Efficiency with Costly Information: A Study of Mutual Fund Performance, 1965–1984." *Quarterly Journal of Economics* 104:1–23.

Jeffrey, Robert H., and Robert D. Arnott (1993). "Is Your Alpha Big Enough to Cover Its Taxes?" *Journal of Portfolio Management* Spring:15–25.

Jensen, Michael C. (1968). "The Performance of Mutual Funds in the Period 1945–1964." *Journal of Finance* 23:389–416.

——— (1969). "Risk, the Pricing of Capital Assets, and the Evaluation of Investment Portfolios." *Journal of Business* 42:167–247.

——— (1972). "Optimal Utilization of Market Forecasts of the Evaluation of Investment Portfolio Performance." *Mathematical Methods in Investment and Finance*, G. P. Szego and Karl Shell (eds.). Amsterdam: North-Holland.

Kon, Stanley J., and Frank C. Jen (1978). "Estimation of Time-Varying Systematic Risk and Performance for Mutual Fund Portfolios: An Application of Switching Regression." *Journal of Finance* 33:457–76.

——— (1979). "The Investment Performance of Mutual Funds: An Empirical Investigation of Timing, Selectivity, and Market Efficiency." *Journal of Business* 52:263–289.

Lehmann, Bruce N., and David M. Modest (1987). "Mutual Fund Performance Evaluation: A Comparison of Benchmarks and Benchmark Comparisons." *Journal of Finance* 42:233–265.

Minarik, Joseph J. (1981). "Capital Gains." In *How Taxes Affect Economic Behavior*, Henry J. Aaron and Joseph A. Pechman (eds.). Washington, DC: Brookings Institution.

Moody Corporation. *Annual Dividend Record*, various years.

Pechman, Joseph A. (1987). *Federal Tax Policy*, 5th ed., Washington, DC: Brookings Institution.

Sharpe, William F. (1966). "Mutual Fund Performance." *Journal of Business* 39 (supplement):119–130.

Standard and Poor's Corporation. *Annual Dividend Record*, various years.

Treynor, Jack L. (1965). "How to Rate Management of Investment Funds." *Harvard Business Review* 43:63–75.